p. 146

44, 47, 95, 129, 132-3

Misc
pt, 13, 108, 165-6, 174-5, (193)
194, 196, 198, 205, 214

215, 222, 228, (230)

CLIMATE
COUP

CLIMATE COUP

GLOBAL WARMING'S INVASION OF OUR GOVERNMENT AND OUR LIVES

EDITED BY

PATRICK J. MICHAELS

CATO INSTITUTE
WASHINGTON, D.C.

Library of Congress Cataloging-in-Publication Data

Michaels, Patrick J.
    Climate coup / Patrick J. Michaels.
        p. cm.
    Includes bibliographical references and index.
    ISBN 978-1-935308-44-7 (hardback: alk. paper)   1. Climatic
changes—Government policy—United States.   2. Environmental
policy—United States.   3. Greenhouse gas mitigation—Government
policy—United States.   I. Title.

    QC903.2.U6M53 2011
    363.738'745610973—dc22   2011003309

Printed in the United States of America.

CATO INSTITUTE
1000 Massachusetts Ave., N.W.
Washington, D.C. 20001
www.cato.org

Contents

Foreword

This volume goes to the printer following two great tectonic shifts in the American electorate: the election of Barack Obama and a filibuster-proof Senate, followed two years later by a remarkable repudiation of what that combination wrought. One factor that contributed to the second earthquake was the passage of cap-and-trade legislation by the House of Representatives on June 26, 2009.

Many members who voted for that—largely unread—bill paid the ultimate political price. Imagine had they known that before the year would end a trove of e-mails hacked from a University of East Anglia server would raise serious questions about the integrity of climate science. Imagine if they knew that the United Nations' Intergovernmental Panel on Climate Change (IPCC) would admit to using advocacy science to influence international politics. Imagine if they knew that *nothing* would come from the UN's December 2009 Copenhagen meeting, trumpeted for years as the point at which the world would agree to dramatic reductions in carbon dioxide emissions.

They would likely have voted against cap-and-trade, and the House leadership may not have changed hands.

But what cost the Democratic Party its majority in the House has done nothing to deter our other institutions from seizing on global warming to fatten their budgets, their reach, and their power. This book documents how far unelected bureaucracies have pushed this issue into our lives. These include the military, the education establishment, and the intellectual elites acting as the gatekeepers of accepted climate knowledge.

Edited volumes are supposed to be boring, uneven, and unread. I don't think this one will garner those labels. It has been a true privilege to work with my contributors, both within and outside of Cato.

With regard to Cato itself, I can't think of a more wonderful place to work. Its reputation for scholarship instead of shrillness, for nonpartisanship instead of polarization, raises its influence to the level held by major universities.

Specifically, I would like to thank Cato's founder and president, Ed Crane, for continuing to put up with me and my brightly colored shoes. How limited the discourse of political economy would be without his influence cannot be calculated. My assistant, Brian Maxwell, and my intern, Joe Trotter, labored through the various versions of the manuscript. My dear friend Rachel Schwartz kept me focused on climate science as an issue of public choice and keeps me from being completely crazy, too.

But this book—my sixth—is dedicated to Paul C. ("Chip") Knappenberger, the best researcher that any scientist could hope to have. He's been my analyst, mathematician, librarian, and general savior for 20 years. No one should have to listen to me rant for so long. Many thanks, Chip. When the history of the global warming mess is written you will come out big.

Patrick J. Michaels
Washington, D.C.

Introduction

Patrick J. Michaels

More than a decade ago, I would begin my global warming class at the University of Virginia with a challenge: Students were to name any subject in the current political discourse, and I would demonstrate how it related to global warming. It was hard to tire of this game, and I could usually occupy half the one-hour lecture period fielding answers.

Little has changed since then.

Global warming's reach has become ubiquitous. While one could speculate in 1995 that the military would use it as a vehicle to enhance its budget, that process has become institutionalized today. Global warming has become a "threat multiplier."[1] In 2003, the Department of Defense published an absurd scenario in which the United Kingdom has the climate of Siberia fewer than nine years from now.[2]

In 1995, the Clinton administration was debating what commitments the United States would agree to at an upcoming meeting of the signatories of a United Nations climate treaty in Kyoto. The commitments were never kept. But today, the Obama administration is directing its Environmental Protection Agency to issue regulations severely restricting our emissions of carbon dioxide. Those regulations will reach into virtually every aspect of our lives. Congress never specifically passed any carbon dioxide emissions restrictions, but they will go forward, administered by the executive branch and enforced in the courts.

Simply expressing any opinion that global warming may not be the end of the world brings charges of being a "denier." Writing a scientific manuscript with any similar implication engages a review process that makes publication next to impossible. Global warming is tainting the very canon of scientific truth, our refereed professional literature.

1

The list goes on. But rather than provide glib answers to insouciant students, I decided to consult some experts on the reach of global warming into our lives.

I started off with Cato's Roger Pilon and Evan Turgeon, our highly regarded experts in constitutional law. I asked them how global warming and the law would interact to affect so much of our lives. Their very disturbing analysis is the first chapter of this volume. They note that the "executive state" that emerged from the Progressive Era is perfectly suited—and perfectly capable—of executing the policy desires of global warming fanatics without any additional legislation whatsoever. Congress need not apply, and, in fact, has purposefully punted global warming regulation from its own purview to the executive branch via the EPA. The president is now perfectly capable of agreeing to an internationally binding commitment to reduce domestic emissions of carbon dioxide and of enforcing that commitment, according to Pilon and Turgeon.

While the House of Representatives passed a draconian "cap-and-trade" bill in 2009, the Senate has not agreed to analogous legislation. The reasons are complex, but the result is that the EPA will do the regulation. Pilon's and Turgeon's model of the executive state is all that we need.

I wrote Chapter 2, detailing in large part why the Senate was reluctant to act. First, they saw the public reaction to the House's vote on June 26, 2009. It was that very week that President Obama's "approval index," as given by Rasmussen Reports, slipped into negative territory. It has been there ever since.

Then the scientific community inadvertently provided remarkable cover for Senate inaction when a large volume of academic e-mails was released from a probable hacking of a server at the University of East Anglia. To date, no one has determined who or from where the job was done. It may even have been an inside job.

It's not coincidental that the "Climategate" e-mails appeared less than a month before an important meeting of the Conference of the Parties to the United Nations' 1992 Framework Convention on Climate Change. This meeting, held in Copenhagen in December 2009, was to provide a new international agreement to limit carbon dioxide emissions, replacing the failed Kyoto Protocol, which has had absolutely no influence on global climate because its emission reduction mandates were so small. And even though they were so small, virtually no one came close to meeting their Kyoto "targets."

On the first day of the Copenhagen conference, the EPA announced that carbon dioxide emissions "endangered" human health and welfare. As a result of the 2007 Supreme Court decision, *Massachusetts v. EPA*, the EPA must consequently issue regulations reducing emissions to the point where there is no longer an endangerment.

The EPA timed its announcement in order to provide President Obama with some bona fides to take to Copenhagen. They weren't sufficient. Major developing nations, such as China and India, proposed no domestic emissions reductions; indeed, they both specifically proposed increases. Instead of providing a follow-on protocol to replace Kyoto, the Copenhagen meeting ended in abject failure, with nations agreeing to provide "plans" for emission reductions early in 2010. Before they were due, the UN waived even this requirement. President Obama rushed home to Washington in order to beat a blizzard descending on the capital; the blizzard won the race.

As a result of the heightened scrutiny of climate science brought on by Climategate, the United Nations' Intergovernmental Panel on Climate Change also came under increasing scrutiny, and several embarrassing scientific irregularities were discovered. Instead of acknowledging errors, the head of the IPCC, Rajenda Pauchari, denounced its critics as practitioners of "voodoo science."

The failure of Copenhagen and the demise of the IPCC provided further ammunition for those in the Senate who opposed cap-and-trade.

Concurrently, several articles appeared in the scientific literature that further deflated the urgency of the climate issue.

The very scary notion that Greenland could suddenly shed the majority of its ice in this century, championed by the National Aeronautic and Space Administration's bomb-throwing James Hansen, lost a lot of its steam as the island's glaciers' march to the sea slowed to a crawl.[3] The notion that global warming is worsening hurricanes was undermined by the fact that both Atlantic and global hurricane energies have descended to their lowest points since measurements began in 1979.[4] Despite Pachauri's repeated statements that storminess is increasing because of global warming,[5] the evidence is against him.[6]

Despite the IPCC's blatant misrepresentations of the state of Antarctic ice, multiple independent analyses show an obvious and statistically significant increase in sea ice coverage in the Southern Hemisphere.

3

I noted earlier that the scientific climate is very inhospitable to manuscripts finding that global warming is likely to be less severe than many have anticipated. In chapter 3, Ross McKitrick describes in considerable detail the problems that are arising with regard to publication in the science literature. McKitrick writes:

> I decided to take this story public because of what it reveals about the journal peer review process in the field of climatology. Whether climatologists like it or not, the general public has taken a large and legitimate interest in how the peer review process for climatology journals works, because it has been told for years that it will have to face lots of new taxes, charges, fees, and regulations because of what has been printed in climatology journals. Because of the policy stakes, a distorted peer review process is no longer a private matter to be sorted out among academic specialists. And to the extent the specialists are unable or unwilling to fix the process, they cannot complain that the public credibility of their discipline suffers.

There's hardly a greater intrusion into our policy process. We are repeatedly told that "the science is settled" on global warming (whatever that means) because of what is in our scientific journals. But if the review process is being compromised, so is science and related policy. At any rate, the irregularities noted by McKitrick are manifold, and they paint a picture of pervasive bias.

Even without blatant reviewer discrimination, there's the notion of "publication bias" that I documented in my 2009 book *Climate of Extremes*. A quantitative analysis of the scientific literature shows a profound bias against publishing results that argue warming or its effects might be less than those published in a previous finding.[7] In a world of unbiased science, the probability of "worse than" or "not as bad as" results should be equal, assuming that background work is itself unbiased.

It's not hard to see how this bias affects policy.

And that includes military policy. In chapter 4, Ivan Eland quotes the May 2010 *National Security Strategy* from the White House:

> The danger from climate change is real, urgent, and severe. The change wrought by a warming planet will lead to new conflicts over refugees and resources; new suffering from drought and famine; catastrophic natural disasters; and degradation of land across the globe.[8]

This is nothing new. In 1996, the *National Security Strategy* stated: "Environmental threats such as climate change, ozone depletion and the transnational movement of dangerous chemicals directly threaten the health of U.S. citizens. . . . Our national security planning is incorporating environmental analyses as never before."[9]

Never mind that ozone depletion is primarily a high-latitude winter phenomenon, when people are exposed very little to the sun, or that international shipment of chemicals has never been on the radar screen with regard to U.S. public health; the point is that environmental issues are simply conflated with security without regard to their actual effect on our day-to-day lives.

Eland notes that the global warming and "national security" concern is a bipartisan issue. Neoconservatives like Frank Gaffney and James Woolsey, the former Clinton-era director of Central Intelligence, have been playing it together as a security issue for nearly a decade. So have more traditional institutions and their representatives.

Conservative think tanks such as the Center for Strategic and International Studies aren't above hyping global warming, concluding that climate change could represent a greater national security problem than terrorism, energy security, and the current international economic disorder.[10] Kurt Campbell of the Brookings Institution (and currently assistant secretary of state for East Asian and Pacific affairs) edited a book called *Climate Cataclysm: The Foreign Policy and National Security Implications of Climate Change*. Academics recognize the utility of hyping global warming as a security issue. For example, University of California professor Oran Young stated: "The only way we're going to make changes of the magnitude required to address this problem is to cast it as a security issue. When you talk about major change in behavior in allocations in the budget, it's easier to accomplish if it's a matter of national security."[11]

According to Eland, the root of the global-warming-as-security issue is the easily falsifiable "conflict over scarce resources" theory. Even the Obama administration's science adviser and global warming alarmist John Holdren has written that resource wars are unlikely because trade is more economically efficient than war.[12] In general, Eland finds that most security threats from global warming are easily debunked as exaggerations.

What is amazing is the persistence of failed theories of international conflict, reemerging with global warming as the vehicle. John

Podesta, head of the Center for American Progress (known in Washington as "Obama's think tank"), even brings back the Vietnam-era "domino theory," writing that "it is therefore critical that policymakers do all they can to prevent the domino of the first major climate change consequence . . . from toppling."[13]

Sallie James's chapter 5, "Climate Change and Trade," takes a slightly different tack from earlier ones in that she examines the consequences of proposals to deal with global warming rather than simply the intrusion of global warming into the policy arena. In other words, she posits that *given* global warming's reach into our trade agreements, there will be consequences unanticipated by their proponents.

Some consequences are not as bad as previously thought. James demonstrates that the concept of substantial "leakage" of carbon emissions—from nations with large mandated reductions to those without—is largely overestimated. Also overestimated are the effects of carbon tariffs, because the energy-intensive goods produced by India and China are largely not traded to the United States.

Furthermore, she finds that existing international agreements, such as the World Trade Organization, may not allow many proposed emission reduction strategies. For example, the House's June 2009 legislation subsidizes hybrid cars produced in the United States, a clearly actionable item for WTO adjudication that causes "adverse impacts" on the manufacturers of such automobiles outside the United States compared with their domestic counterparts. While the WTO allows for environmental exceptions to its trade rules, environmental protection must indeed be demonstrable. But as shown in chapter 2, the effects of the Waxman-Markey cap-and-trade bill, even if adopted by all developed economies, would likely be too small to create any demonstrable environmental benefit.

With regard to carbon tariffs, perhaps because they are in fact not very efficient for emission reductions, the WTO may very well find them in violation of international trade agreements. As James writes, "All of the available WTO jurisprudence to date would caution governments against framing their climate-related policies in terms of fairness to domestic producers that face competition from un[carbon]capped firms abroad."

James finds that threats to take carbon tariffs to the WTO have already materialized. She quotes the Indian environmental minister, Jairam Ramesh:

If they impose such a tax, we will take them to the WTO dispute settlement forum. . . . [W]e will deal [with this] through hard negotiations. Such barriers are not going to be WTO-compatible and we will fight it.[14]

In chapter 6, Indur Goklany attacks the notion that global warming will reduce the quality of life in developing countries, a mantra of the United Nations. Indeed, he finds that the economic development powered by fossil fuels is literally orders of magnitude greater than any putative negative effects from climate change. The ancillary notion that development will be slowed by climate change is found to be equally unsupportable.

Nonetheless, these erroneous notions continue to dominate the discussion of global warming, which has invaded development economics.

In a section called "Reality Check: Empirical Trends versus Global Warming Hype," Goklany shows that claims that global warming reduces crop productivity in the developing world are 180 degrees out of phase with reality. Crop yields and total production continue to increase dramatically in the developing world. Worldwide, the largest increases in total food production are in recent years, contrary to decades of alarmist predictions of an imminent decline in agricultural productivity.

The percentage of people undernourished declined through the early years of the 21st century only to rise at the same time that food production had its greatest increases. The logical explanation is the massive diversion in recent years of food crops to ethanol fuel production. The logic of subsidizing the combustion of the world's food supply will surely elude our descendents.

Life expectancies continue to rise, with the greatest rises in the developing world, where they are now within years of those in the developed world. If global warming is hindering development, where are the bodies?

Global warming nonsense has also invaded the public health sphere, with grim forecasts of the spread of infectious diseases, even as *the ranges of the most critical climate-sensitive diseases have shrunk.* Data from 1900–2008 show that cumulative annual deaths from all extreme weather events—droughts, floods, extreme temperature, and so forth—have declined globally by 93 percent since the 1920s, and the death rate (deaths per million) dropped by an astounding

98 percent. How the United Nations and the environmental community can continue to insist on net increasing weather-related mortality is a sheer mystery.

Even using the IPCC's reference climate-driven scenarios for gross domestic product per capita around the world, it is obvious that statements about global warming's stilting economic development are egregious errors. Using IPCC's numbers and the 95th percentile estimate of Sir Nicholas Stern for warming-related losses, Goklany finds that in 2100, net GDP per capita will be 11 to 65 times higher than today (in constant dollars) in what are now developing countries. Under the warmest IPCC scenario, which prompts so much of the apocalyptic rhetoric about global warming, net GDP per capita of inhabitants of now-developing countries will be twice that in the United States in 2006, in 1990 dollars.

As Goklany writes, after two centuries of global warming, or by 2100, "developing countries will be wealthy by today's standards, and their adaptive capacity should be correspondingly higher." So much for development retarded by climate change. Nonetheless, the United Nations continues to assume that technologies are largely static, with few if any major innovations in this century. Given that the last century saw the rise of the computer, the Internet, nuclear fission and fusion, and trebled agricultural yields, the UN's assumptions are simply fatuous.

Goklany closes with the question, "Which is deadlier—global warming or global warming policies?" In fact, biofuel mandates are already increasing malnutrition in developing countries—in an era when base grain production is increasing faster than ever. Poverty figures give rise to an estimate of nearly 200,000 additional deaths per year in 2010 from biofuel mandates, which is 50,000 greater than the UN's estimate of global warming deaths. But those are based on what Goklany calls "unverified models and scientific shortcuts."[15]

The University of Virginia's Robert Davis examines global warming and human health in additional detail in chapter 7. While dire projections of global warming–related diseases are rife in the scientific literature, Davis shows how they are often based on profoundly unrealistic assumptions.

One archetypical example is that epidemiological studies generally suffer from profoundly naive climatology. He cites a standard study on tick-borne encephalitis that assumes that global warming will increase the spread of this disease because ticks like warm, wet conditions. In fact, the tick can select its own climate simply by changing the depth at which it resides in the duff on the forest floor. The tick's "microclimate," not the human-altered "macroclimate," is what determines where it resides. As Davis says:

> So even if the weather changes are generally consistent with creating a tick-friendly environment that is consistent with [computer] model projections of how weather will change as climate changes from increasing greenhouse gases, we are stuck with the problem that the tick only cares about the conditions in the few millimeters that surrounds its little arachnid body.

Davis is particularly concerned about the infiltration of global warming misinformation into the biomedical sciences. He cites an extensive piece by Emily K. Shuman in the prestigious *New England Journal of Medicine* that is riddled with scientific errors and misstatements,[16] though the *NEJM* is supposed to be rigorously peer reviewed. Its influence is worldwide. What better example of how global warming exaggeration has spread into our lives?

The problem, both in health sciences and in other fields covered in this book, is that nonexperts declare themselves authorities and are nonetheless published with impunity. As Davis states:

> If I, for example, wrote an article about my suggestions for new techniques in spinal surgery, my work wouldn't see the light of day. Nor should it. My training is in atmospheric science with an emphasis in climatology and its impact on health and mortality, so I know nothing about spinal surgery. But the presumption that the nuances of my profession can be well understood by people with no training in it results in the publication of misinformed and/or incorrect random musings masquerading as applied science. The literature of many professions—economics, biology, public policy—is overrun with hundreds of comparable examples with virtually analogous language.

Davis (along with this author) has published extensively on heat-related deaths. Despite highly publicized mortality in the 2003 and 2010 heat waves in Europe and western Russia, a dispassionate analysis reveals that heat wave mortality is *declining* because of adaptation. Cities become warmer with or without global warming, thanks in large part to "nonclimatic" warming caused by bricks, buildings, and pavement (and discussed in chapter 2). Consequently, heat waves become more severe, and some cause considerable mortality, such as the aforementioned two or the great upper midwestern heat wave of July 1995.

Both the 1995 and 2003 heat waves were followed in subsequent years by another of similar magnitude but with *less* mortality than expected; this subject was covered extensively in my last book.[17] Despite voluminous research demonstrating this adaptation, Eric Klinenberg, a sociologist at New York University, let this statement appear in the prestigious University of Chicago Press description of his 2002 book *Heat Wave*, which was about the 1995 event:

> We know that more heat waves are coming. Every major report on global warming—including the recent White House study—warns that an increase in severe heat waves is likely. The only way to prevent another heat disaster is to address the isolation, poverty, and fear that are prevalent in so many American cities today.

In fact, heat wave–related mortality in Chicago has been declining for decades, as Davis's work has shown.

While Davis's chapter shows how warming has infiltrated the health sciences, he also demonstrates how adaptable humans are to environmental hazards. Not only is heat-related mortality declining, so are deaths from tornadoes and hurricanes, the two most intense storms on earth.

Finally, Neal McCluskey tackles global warming and K–12 education. Here the issue cuts both ways.

McCluskey cites Michael Sanera and Jane Shaw's pioneering 1999 review of textbooks, *Facts Not Fear*, showing lurid and inaccurate descriptions of global warming.[18] But the contentious nature of global warming, where both "sides" are often wrong (i.e., "global warming as apocalypse" or "there's no such thing"), could ultimately result in it being removed from the curriculum entirely. McCluskey analogizes controversies over teaching evolution and global warming. In fact, as he notes, in 2010 the *New York Times* reported that opponents of the teaching of evolution have added global warming to their agenda.

Simply ignoring an important subject is what *can* take place at the level of the school district, and it has temporarily occurred at

Figure 1
THE 50-YEAR TREND IN CALIFORNIA TEMPERATURE, 1960–2009

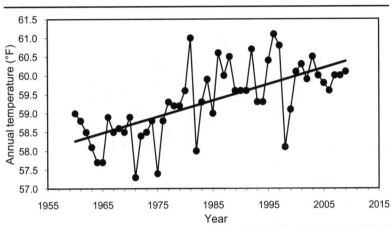

SOURCE: National Climatic Data Center, http://www.ncdc.noaa.gov/oa/climate/research/cag3/ca.html.
NOTE: The 50-year trend in California temperature is indeed 0.43 degrees per decade, as given by the California climate curriculum guide.

the state level. The California Education and Environment Initiative originally included seven topics, *none of which were global warming.* In this case, global warming has so worked itself into the fabric of society that it is *ignored.* Talk about being conspicuously absent!

Obviously, ignoring an issue of this magnitude only provokes an opposite reaction. So the state did undertake production of a climate change curriculum guide, and, of course, it takes the opposite tack: climate change is coming and it is our doom. Pictures as well as words drive home the message.

Here's just one example of how the new California curriculum misleads.

It states that according to data from the U.S. National Climatic Data Center, the 50-year trend in California temperatures is 0.43 degrees Fahrenheit per decade, or 4.3 degrees per century.[19]

Indeed, this is largely true, as shown in Figure 1. But starting in 1960 is highly misleading. All the statewide National Climatic Data Center records begin in 1895. Using the whole record, the trend is

Figure 2
TEMPERATURE TRENDS IN CALIFORNIA, 1895–2009

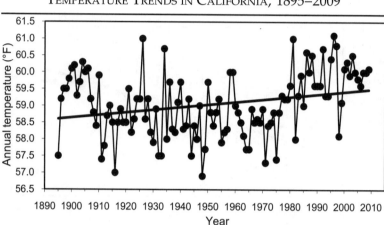

SOURCE: National Climatic Data Center, http://www.ncdc.noaa.gov/oa/climate/research/cag3/ca.html, last accessed August, 2010.

NOTE: The actual trend in all the California data is only 0.08 degrees Fahrenheit per decade, or less than 20 percent of what is given in the state's curriculum guide.

only 0.08 degrees. California's alarmist guide overestimates the overall trend by over 500 percent (see Figure 2). Further, it is rather apparent, even in the 50-year sample, that the warming takes place largely between 1960 and 1980, with no net change in the succeeding 30 years.

Nor is California above threatening students with death from global warming:

> The question is: will we survive the changes of the future? The better we understand the causes and effects of climate change, the better we can predict how Earth will be affected. This understanding is key to our planetary and personal survival as the global climate continues to change.[20]

When students are threatened with death from global warming, when our military raises the threat of war from global warming, when the state has the apparatus to run our lives because of global warming without any additional legislation, when our Congress legislates tariffs that could provoke trade wars because of global warming, when the threats of global warming to the developing world are egregiously exaggerated, when the biomedical community hypes unfounded health and mortality fears, and when the scientific peer-review process becomes skewed against anything moderate, we have witnessed a coup. Global warming has taken over our government and our lives.

1. The Executive State Tackles Global Warming

Roger Pilon and Evan Turgeon

Roger Pilon and Evan Turgeon show how, contrary to the nation's first principles and the Constitution's plan for limited government, the modern "executive state" emerged over the 20th century such that the executive branch today has all the power it needs to implement a far-reaching global warming agenda—quite without any specific authorization from Congress.

Early in the century, Progressives laid the intellectual foundations for the executive state. Then, during the New Deal, Congress and the president brought it into being, aided by a Court that first reinterpreted the Constitution's limits on Congress's powers and then sanctioned Congress's delegation of those powers to the executive and to burgeoning executive branch agencies. In fits and starts, that process has continued to this day, with the Court's 2007 decision in *Massachusetts v. EPA* being the latest example of how the executive state has come to assume all but plenary power—here, through claims about global warming—over almost every area of life.

The result is rule by unelected, largely unaccountable bureaucratic "experts" making decisions that in the end are often value-laden and political. This pattern will not change, Pilon and Turgeon conclude, until Congress reclaims the authority that it alone was granted under the Constitution.

The chapters that follow in this volume will show that in recent years, "global warming," however uncertain its scientific foundations or practical implications, has permeated and often distorted virtually every area of life and public policy in America, from science

15

to business, education, trade—even foreign policy. Law, and American constitutional law, in particular, is no exception. But long before global warming's massive regulatory agenda was upon us, more basic distortions afflicted American law, and those today are fertile ground for turning the global warming agenda into binding public policy.

More precisely, the "executive state" that emerged from the Progressive Era, as institutionalized by the New Deal Supreme Court and expanded through modern administrative law, affords the president today all the power he needs to execute global warming's agenda through his domestic and foreign affairs powers—powers so far-reaching that they would shock the Constitution's Framers, who thought they had checked executive excesses through the separation of powers. James Madison, whose plan for limited government the Constitution reflects, wrote in *Federalist 45* that the powers of the new government would be "few and defined," yet today the executive branch alone, in the name of addressing global warming, is able to regulate virtually every human activity in this nation. Indeed, shortly before President Obama arrived at the December 2009 "Climate Summit" in Copenhagen, the Climate Law Institute's Center for Biological Diversity released a study, the title of which captures today's legal world perfectly: "*Yes, He Can*: President Obama's Power to Make an International Climate Commitment without Waiting for Congress."[1]

This chapter explains how we got to this state of affairs. We will begin by looking briefly at the original constitutional design, as "completed" by the Civil War Amendments, then at the Progressive Era and the New Deal "constitutional revolution" that followed, resulting in the demise of both the doctrine of enumerated powers, the very centerpiece of the Constitution, and the nondelegation doctrine, under which "all legislative power" is supposed to be vested in the Congress. After those principles were abandoned, owing to political forces and judicial deference, the courts themselves came to play handmaiden to the aggrandizement of executive power, as we will see next.

Against that background of general legal developments, we will then turn to the kinds of environmental issues that arose with the Industrial Revolution, which pose special but not unsolvable problems for our system of government. Those environmental issues are best addressed, however, not by abandoning the Constitution's basic principles but by adhering to them. To illustrate how we have not done that, and how the modern executive state has come to rule over environmental matters, we will look finally at several recent statutory schemes that have delegated so much power to the executive branch as well as the judicial decisions that have sanctioned those delegations, often in the name of science trumping politics. Yet fundamentally, the issues are only partly scientific. In fact, in the end they are basically evaluative, involving balancing competing values. Thus, under our system of constitutional government, they should be decided not by "experts" but by the American people through the process the Constitution prescribes, or so we will conclude.

The Executive State Emerges

The Original Design, as "Completed" by the Civil War Amendments

The Constitution, written in the shadow of the Declaration of Independence, was designed to secure individual liberty and responsibility through limited government. To that end, it established a government of limited powers, leaving most power with the states or, even more, with the people, to be exercised in their private capacities. The Tenth Amendment, the last documentary evidence from the founding period, makes that clear, expressly.[2] But so does the Constitution's Preamble, which shows that all power rests originally with the people, only some of which they give up to government for greater convenience and security. In the very first sentence of Article I, we see that "All legislative Powers *herein granted* shall be vested in a Congress . . . " (emphasis added). By implication, not all power was "herein granted." Article I, Section 8, enumerates Congress's main legislative powers, 18 in number—hence the doctrine of enumerated powers. Article II vests the executive power in the president, which in domestic affairs is mainly the power to "take Care that the Laws be faithfully executed." Article III vests the judicial power in the Supreme Court and in such inferior courts as Congress establishes, the power to ensure that constitutional constraints are respected. Thus the separation of powers, each branch defined functionally.

The Bill of Rights was added two years later, for extra precaution. It limited more precisely the way in which the federal government might exercise its enumerated powers. But the Bill of Rights applied originally only against the federal government,[3] reflecting the Framers' compromise over slavery, reached to ensure union. Their hope that slavery would wither away over time did not materialize. Instead, the Civil War, followed by the Civil War Amendments, ended slavery. Those amendments "completed" the Constitution by incorporating at last the grand principles of the Declaration of Independence.[4]

Progressivism and Planning

Practice has never matched promise, of course: there has never been a "golden age" of liberty and limited government—witness, among much else, the rise of Jim Crow in the South shortly after the Civil War Amendments were ratified. Nevertheless, for our first 150 years as a nation, we lived more or less under limited government. The great change came, as noted above, with the rise of the Progressive Era, the ideas of which the New Deal Court institutionalized some 40 years later. American elites, influenced by the rise of science and of the social sciences in particular, grew enamored with "social engineering." Drawing from German ideas about "good government"—Bismarck's social security scheme, for example—and British utilitarianism—the idea that policy and law should secure not our unalienable rights but the greatest good for the greatest number—those elites sought to "plan" all manner of human activities, mostly through government agencies staffed by "experts."[5]

Standing athwart that agenda, of course, was a Constitution designed for limited government, and the willingness of early 20th-century courts to uphold it, which they did—not entirely but in large measure. Things came to a head during the New Deal, however, especially after the landslide election of 1936, when President Franklin D. Roosevelt threatened to pack an uncooperative Supreme Court with six new members. The reaction in the nation was swift and intense: not even an overwhelmingly Democratic Congress would go along with the scheme.[6] But the Court got the message: it began rewriting the Constitution without benefit of constitutional amendment.[7]

Expanding Power, Contracting Rights

The Court did so in three main steps. First, in two decisions in 1937, the Court eviscerated the Constitution's legitimating principle

18

and main restraint on overweening government, the doctrine of enumerated powers. It held that under the so-called general welfare clause, a phrase in Congress's power to tax, Congress could tax and spend for the general welfare quite apart from any authority to do so under one of its enumerated powers or ends.[8] Thus was born the modern redistributive state. And it held that under the commerce clause, which was written to enable Congress to ensure free commerce among the states in light of state protectionist measures that had arisen under the Articles of Confederation, Congress had the power to regulate, for any reason, anything that "affected" interstate commerce, which of course is anything and everything.[9] Thus was born the modern regulatory state.

Second, because individual rights could still be invoked to check that expanded federal power, as well as state power, the Court in 1938 effectively bifurcated the Bill of Rights, distinguishing "fundamental" from "nonfundamental" rights.[10] If a law implicated "fundamental" rights like speech, voting, and, later, certain "personal" rights, the Court would apply "strict scrutiny" and most often find the law unconstitutional. By contrast, if a law implicated "nonfundamental" rights like property and contract, rights we exercise in "ordinary commercial transactions," it need pass only the "rational basis" test: as long as there was some conceivable basis for the law, it would be found constitutional.

Delegation and the Modern Administrative State

With those decisions, the Court institutionalized an approach to constitutional adjudication that in truth had been growing for a decade or two, "constitutionalizing" in the process the Progressive vision of active government—the very antithesis of the Framers' vision. But one step remained, which will bring us to our underlying subject, the emergence of the executive state. As legislative schemes were enacted, it became clear, of course, that Congress (or state legislatures, for that matter) could not manage all that they had brought forth. Thus was born the modern administrative state. But the problem here, once again, was with that troublesome Constitution, for recall that the very first sentence of Article I says that "All legislative Powers herein granted shall be vested in a Congress." Not only were many of the powers Congress was now exercising never "herein granted," but even those that were granted were being

19

delegated increasingly to the executive branch or to "independent agencies." In fact, in the new executive state, administrative agencies—headed by members of the executive branch or by independent officials but filled with career and hence unaccountable civil servants—were performing legislative, executive, and even judicial functions, affecting virtually every aspect of life, from the jobs we have, to the food we eat, to the air we breathe. Powers the Framers had separated were now conjoined in one branch of government.

The demise of the nondelegation doctrine is best understood in the light cast by the doctrine of enumerated powers, which says, again, that Congress has only those legislative powers that the people have granted it. Not only are *all* those powers vested in Congress, but among them there is *no* power to delegate any of them in turn to another branch of government. Any such delegation is thus *ultra vires*.[11] The Supreme Court recognized that principle early on when Chief Justice Marshall wrote in 1825, "It will not be contended that Congress can delegate . . . powers which are strictly and exclusively legislative."[12] Unfortunately, Marshall gave no further guidance on the meaning or scope of "strictly and exclusively legislative." But he added that "the line has not been exactly drawn which separates those important subjects which must be entirely regulated by the legislature itself from those of less interest in which a general provision may be made and power given to those who are to act under such general provisions to fill up the details."[13] Thus, he laid a foundation for what the Court would later call the "intelligible principle" standard: a delegation is constitutional, the Court said in 1928, if Congress lays down "by legislative act an intelligible principle to which the person or body authorized. . . is directed to conform."[14]

Judicial Deference

That standard, under which the Court in two separate decisions in 1935 found provisions of Roosevelt's National Industrial Recovery Act to be unconstitutional,[15] continues to guide courts today. But so deferential to the political branches has the Court been since the "constitutional revolution" of 1937 that the most amorphous congressional directives satisfy the "intelligible principle" standard—directives that regulations must serve "the public interest," be "just and reasonable," check "unfair profits," and so forth. In fact, the Court has been so deferential that "not a single post–New Deal statutory program has been invalidated as an unconstitutional delegation of legislative power to the executive branch."[16]

Indeed, not only has the Court deferred completely to Congress when Congress has delegated its legislative powers to executive agencies, but more often than not, the Court has deferred to those very agencies in their interpretations of Congress's broad statutory delegations. Although the record on this is mixed and often seemingly arbitrary, under the Court's main standard today, known as "*Chevron* deference,"[17] the Court in 1984 set forth a two-step process for reviewing agency interpretations of statutes. First, the Court asks "whether Congress has directly spoken to the precise question at issue. If the intent of Congress is clear, that is the end of the matter." But second, "if the statute is silent or ambiguous with respect to the specific issue," which is often the case, the Court asks "whether the agency's answer is based on a permissible construction of the statute. If Congress has explicitly left a gap for the agency to fill"—note well what follows—"there is an express delegation of authority to the agency to elucidate a specific provision of the statute by regulation. Such *legislative regulations* are given controlling weight unless they are arbitrary, capricious, or manifestly contrary to the statute" (emphasis added). Finally, the Court concluded that if a legislative delegation is implicit, "a court may not substitute its own construction of a statutory provision for a reasonable interpretation made by the administrator of an agency."[18]

In sum, the New Deal Court's evisceration of the doctrine of enumerated powers and bifurcation of the Bill of Rights vastly expanded Congress's powers and contracted individual rights. But as those powers grew and federal programs multiplied, the Court abandoned the nondelegation doctrine, allowing Congress to delegate ever more power to executive branch agencies. Finally, having deferred to Congress on both counts, the Court most often deferred to the executive branch as well, granting it wide discretion to interpret statutes and enact "legislative regulations." Thus did the modern expansive and powerful executive state come into being.

Environmentalism under the Constitution

Environmentalism and Private Law

Environmental issues were not unknown at the Founding. Isolated individuals and human communities alike use natural resources, changing the natural environment as they do. It may sound heretical today to say it, but nature and the environment have no rights: *people* have rights—uniquely human constructs designed to order relationships through enforceable correlative obligations. They have rights to live and to use natural resources in the process, provided only that they take nothing that belongs to others. Thus, the law of *property*—broadly understood as "lives, liberties, and estates"—underpins and defines those relationships.[19] And the Latin maxim *sic utere tuo, ut alienum non laedas* (use your own property so as not to harm another's) served early in our history, and continues to serve today, to guide common-law courts as they adjudicated what we would now call environmental complaints.

But "harm," defined as taking what belongs free and clear to another,[20] will afford a court a bright line only in a certain range of cases—"physical" trespass to person or property, for example. When the trespass involves classic nuisances—noise, particulate matter, odors, vibrations, and the like—or risks of various kinds, the line between one person's right to the active use of his property and another person's right to the quiet enjoyment of his is not as bright. How many decibels of noise, what quanta of particulate matter are needed before the line is crossed? Obviously, given the conflicting interests of the parties, absent an agreement between them, they cannot be judges in the case. A "public" line of some sort is needed. But that line is not written in stone, nor can it be. At different times in our history, we have drawn the lines at different places. Early on, we tended to favor active uses. Later, as we've grown wealthier, we've moved in the other direction (or we've made private or public accommodations like industrial parks to allow for a variety of tastes). But there is no precise right or wrong place to draw that public line: it reflects the tradeoffs we've wanted to make as a people at a particular time.

Closely related is the issue of the supersensitive person. Under common law, the rule in ordinary torts rightly was that you take your victim as you find him. Thus, if A hit supersensitive B, producing injuries beyond those that would have been suffered by the average person, A was liable for the full costs of making B whole. In nuisance, however, the supersensitive plaintiff did not get relief, and rightly so. For if he were to prevail in his complaint that, for example, the noise or particulate matter was injurious to him but not to others due to his sensitive condition, he could, in principle, shut down the world. Thus in nuisance cases, the "average man" standard prevailed—a reflection of the need, again, for a *public* line, one that favors neither side but reflects instead a public consensus about where to draw the line.

Environmentalism and Public Law

In a great range of cases, then, the common law, grounded in reason and custom,[21] served to adjudicate especially those environmental harms we would call "pollution." But not all environmental problems lend themselves to case-by-case common-law resolution. The Industrial Revolution, in particular, brought forth pollution affecting large numbers of people, even though none might be in a position to adjudicate the matter. And the large-numbers problem was especially acute when automobile pollution became an issue, when polluters and victims were usually the same people. All that and more marked the need to draw those public lines not on a case-by-case basis through private law but rather through statute and regulation—the need for *public* environmental law. But the move to public law did not change the underlying principles, at least in principle. Parties still had no right to pollute beyond a certain line. And they still had a right against pollution, again beyond a certain line. Although that line was now a matter for public, not private, law to determine, it still needed to reflect, more or less, the tradeoffs that might be reached by the "average man," favoring neither the active nor the quiet user, much less the supersensitive person.

Under the Constitution this public law rested mainly with the states, of course, because that is where the general police power resides—the power to secure rights and hence to protect against environmental wrongs. And there is no reason even today why much if not most environmental law should not have remained with the states, both to respect our federalist principles and to better reflect local conditions and values. Stationary sources of pollution, for example, can easily be regulated by states; and if states are insufficiently sensitive to the rights of neighboring state residents, interstate suits can address that. But state and local solutions, however much to be presumed, may be inadequate for some environmental problems, or may prove less efficient than national solutions. Thus, in at least some cases, we may want to move to national solutions.

A Federal Problem: Where's the Power?

But there is a constitutional problem in doing so: Where among Congress's 18 enumerated powers do we find the power to address environmental issues, including through means that are both necessary and proper, as required by the last of those powers?[22] Except in federal enclaves, there is no general federal police power of the kind that enables states to police environmental wrongs, much less a power to provide the public with environmental "goods" like lovely views or wildlife habitat. If the Constitution as written and amended is to be respected, and if federal environmental law is to be legitimately grounded, that is no small problem.

Federal environmental statutes today are "authorized" under the Constitution's commerce clause[23]—granting Congress the power to regulate international and interstate commerce—mainly because the Court since the New Deal has read that clause, as noted above, to enable Congress to regulate anything that "affects" interstate commerce, which makes it an open sesame for virtually anything.[24] The original understanding of the clause, however, as also noted above, was much narrower, in keeping with a Constitution for *limited* government. It was written against a background of states, under the Articles of Confederation, having erected tariffs and other such measures to protect local merchants and manufacturers from competition from out-of-state interests, which was leading to the breakdown of free trade among the states. Thus, Congress was authorized to "regulate" interstate commerce—to make it "regular" by negating state interference[25] and by doing whatever else might be necessary and proper to ensure a free and efficient national market.[26]

A Constitutional Solution?

Interestingly, however, under that original understanding, one can make a plausible case for at least some federal environmental regulation, provided the facts warrant it, unlike with so much else that today is thus "authorized." To be sure, there is no general federal police power, beyond federal enclaves, that would enable Congress to directly protect the rights of Americans against environmental wrongs or to provide broader environmental goods. But if conflicting state environmental regulations in a given area—say, auto emission standards—were to impede a free national market by subjecting auto manufacturers to exorbitant compliance costs,

24

then Congress's power to regulate interstate commerce, understood functionally as it was originally understood, could authorize federal preemption of state regulation and hence indirect environmental protection. Given the national market in automobiles, Congress would be regulating "commerce" "among" the states to ensure a more efficient market, free from state interference. There may be other such examples that would be consistent with the Constitution as originally written. But except in federal enclaves, as authorized under Article I, Section 8, Clause 17, the provision of environmental *goods* would remain with the states, consistent with state constitutions and the need to pay just compensation to owners when regulatory takings were required to provide the public with such goods.

Respect for the Constitution as written is not what we have today, however. After the New Deal constitutional revolution, the floodgates were opened for Congress to do pretty much what it wanted. And so we turn at last to a brief but critical look at how the general pattern of executive aggrandizement, discussed in the first section of this chapter, has played out more specifically in the environmental area, and then at what might be done, short of the suggestions just made, to begin restoring the separation if not the division of powers.

Federal Environmentalism Emerges

Judicial Deference, Executive Consolidation

As noted toward the end of the first section above, judicial scrutiny of agency "lawmaking" has been mixed, although deference has generally been the rule—in part because when Congress early on codified the New Deal's delegation of regulatory power through the Administrative Procedures Act of 1946,[27] it specified that courts could overturn agency policy and fact-finding decisions only if they were "arbitrary, capricious, an abuse of discretion, or otherwise not in accordance with law."[28] Thus, courts granted regulations the same presumption of facial validity that they were granting statutes, rarely finding any so arbitrary as to meet those criteria.[29] Add to that the Supreme Court's restrictive view of individual standing to challenge agency actions,[30] and the result is that "in the half century following the start of the New Deal, the separation of powers doctrine effectively died out."[31]

But not on all issues. With economic regulation, judicial deference to agency rulemaking was especially prominent. But in cases pitting economic development against the emerging environmental agenda of the 1960s and 1970s, the courts began taking a "hard look" to determine whether administrators adequately considered environmental values in their rulemaking, relaxing standing requirements in the process to enable more plaintiffs to challenge agency rulemaking.[32] Cases decided during the period frequently demonstrate the courts' deference to environmental values and the short shrift they gave to economic values, including the costs of regulation. In *Calvert Cliffs' Coordinating Committee v. Atomic Energy Commission*[33] in 1971, for example, the D.C. Circuit noted that "several recently enacted statutes attest to the commitment of the Government to control, at long last, the destructive engine of material 'progress.'" And in that same year, the Supreme Court interpreted environmental statutes similarly. Thus, in *Citizens to Preserve Overton Park, Inc. v. Volpe*,[34] the Court rejected an agency plan to build a highway through parkland in Memphis, Tennessee, stating, "The few green havens that are public parks were not to be lost unless there were truly unusual factors present in a particular case or the cost or community disruption resulting from alternative routes reached extraordinary magnitudes."[35] In so ruling, the Court expanded the Administrative Procedures Act standard for judicial review beyond "arbitrary and capricious," holding that the reviewing court must make a "searching and careful" review of the entire record, not just the portion that supported the agency's position.[36] This strengthening of the "arbitrary and capricious" standard culminated ultimately in 1983 in *Motor Vehicle Manufacturers Association v. State Farm Mutual Automobile Insurance Co.*,[37] where the Court explicitly adopted the "hard look" standard for reviewing agency action.[38]

Yet a year later, as discussed earlier, the Court gave us *Chevron* deference, so it's difficult to find any ordering principle for the Court's degree of deference to executive agencies, save for the suspicion that there may not be any such principle and that the Court, in its often fractured opinions (*Chevron* was not one), may itself be subject to political winds. Rather than review the lengthy mixed record on that question, however, it may be best to go straight to the most recent environmental case that illustrates the point, the Court's 2007 decision in *Massachusetts v. Environmental Protection Agency*,[39] where five members of the Court were not at all reluctant to insinuate themselves into a political debate over the subject to which we come at last, global warming.

By way of background, in the years following *Chevron*, presidents of both parties took a number of steps, especially through executive orders, to consolidate their control over executive agencies. Pursuant to his deregulatory agenda, for example, President Reagan issued Executive Order 12,291[40] in 1981, requiring agencies "to perform cost-benefit analyses for regulations and, within statutory limits, to select the policy that maximizes benefits compared to costs."[41] In 1993, President Clinton issued Executive Order 12,866,[42] which delegated authority to the Office of Information and Regulatory Affairs to review agency rules to ensure that they conformed to the president's regulatory priorities. And in 2003, President Bush's Office of Management and Budget issued a bulletin that mandated rigorous peer review of all "significant regulatory information" on which an agency policy determination was based[43] and barred any scientist funded by the agency (but not industry scientists) from participating in the peer-review process,[44] which was widely seen as an effort to politicize agency science.[45]

Massachusetts v. the EPA

That sets the stage for *Massachusetts v. EPA*. Section 202(a)(1) of the Clean Air Act requires that the EPA administrator "shall by regulation prescribe . . . standards applicable to the emission of any air pollutant from any class or classes of new motor vehicles or new motor vehicle engines, which in his judgment cause, or contribute to, air pollution which may reasonably be anticipated to endanger public health or welfare."[46] In 1999, several environmental organizations and others petitioned the EPA, asking the agency to initiate rulemaking to regulate greenhouse gas emissions from new motor vehicles under that section. After lengthy considerations, based on extensive public comments on the petition and a report on the science of climate change from the National Research Council of the National Academy of Sciences,[47] the EPA declined, saying that it lacked statutory authority to do so.[48] And it added that even if it had authority, it would decline to regulate in order not to interfere with international climate change negotiations.

Those groups plus 12 states then appealed the EPA decision, losing in the D.C. Circuit. Before the Supreme Court, there were two main questions: Did at least one of the states or groups have standing to bring the suit? And if so, was the EPA's decision reasonable under *Chevron* such that the Court should defer to the agency's decision?

Justice Stevens, writing for himself, the Court's three other liberals, and Justice Kennedy, gave away the answers with his very first words: "A well-documented rise in global temperatures has coincided with a significant increase in the concentration of carbon dioxide in the atmosphere. Respected scientists believe the two trends are related."[49] From there it was a straight line to the conclusions. To have standing to get to the merits, Massachusetts had to show that it had a "concrete and particularized" injury that was "actual or imminent" and "fairly traceable" to the defendant, and that a favorable decision would redress it.[50] The state pointed to its shoreline, which might be threatened over the next 100 years by the effects of global greenhouse gas emissions, only a small fraction of which might be addressed by the EPA's regulation of mobile source emissions. That was good enough for Stevens.

On the merits, standing having been established, Stevens threw deference out the window, despite the lack of any evidence that Congress intended the Clean Air Act to address global air pollution issues like climate change or greenhouse gas emissions. In fact, Congress had repeatedly addressed climate change by authorizing and funding studies, "by encouraging 'non-regulatory' measures to address greenhouse gas emissions, and by the Senate's unanimous expression of disapproval of the Kyoto Accord in 1997"; yet there was never any indication, through all of that, "that anyone in Congress, for or against regulation of greenhouse gas emissions, thought that the Clean Air Act already authorized the EPA to regulate those emissions."[51] Despite that, Stevens found that greenhouse gases like carbon dioxide are air pollutants covered by the act, that the EPA must determine whether they endanger human health, and, if they do, that the EPA must regulate them.

The Endangerment Finding

That ruling sent the EPA back to the drawing board. On December 7, 2009, with a new administration overseeing the agency and the Copenhagen climate change summit just getting under way, the EPA's much-anticipated "Endangerment Finding" was released, concluding that "the evidence provides compelling support for finding that greenhouse gas air pollution endangers the public welfare of both current and future generations."[52] Make no mistake, the implications of this finding are far-reaching. As stated by the Climate

28

Law Institute report we cited at the outset: "The finding required in the context of automobile emissions is similar or identical to findings in other sections of the Clean Air Act that trigger regulation of greenhouse gas emissions from ships, aircraft, power plants, factories, and other sources. Such a finding also compels the issuance of nationwide pollution caps for greenhouse gases."[53]

Thus has the Court played handmaiden to the aggrandizement of executive power. Judicial abdication during the New Deal enabled Congress to delegate its legislative powers to the executive branch. Judicial activism just now has compelled a president who hardly needed compulsion to turn the global warming agenda into binding public policy.

A President with All the Authority He Needs

Several statutes can now be read as authorizing President Obama's EPA to regulate greenhouse gas emissions in the name of preventing global warming. Especially in the wake of *Massachusetts v. EPA*, the Clean Air Act provides President Obama the most direct tool to limit carbon dioxide emissions from both stationary and mobile sources and likely far beyond. Atmospheric pollution controls in other statutes, including the Clean Water Act, the Endangered Species Act, and the National Environmental Protection Act, provide further sources of authority. In addition to domestic authority, President Obama could conceivably use his foreign affairs power to bind the United States to emission reductions, but given the president's considerable authority under domestic law, such measures are unlikely to be needed.

The Clean Air Act

Since *Massachusetts v. EPA*, the Clean Air Act[54] provides perhaps the greatest source of authority to regulate carbon dioxide emissions.[55] The act was designed to empower the federal government to limit emissions of air pollutants from all sources. The act grants the EPA administrator the authority to designate a compound as an "air pollutant," determine a maximum permissible level of that pollutant in the air, review state-level plans to control emissions of that pollutant from stationary sources, and set standards to regulate directly emissions from mobile sources.[56] The act defines an "air pollutant" as any "air pollution agent or combination of such agents, including any physical, chemical, biological, radioactive substance or matter which is emitted into or otherwise enters the ambient air."[57] The act does not specify each pollutant to be regulated but rather requires the EPA administrator to produce a list of "criteria air pollutants" that includes "each air pollutant, emissions of which, in his judgment, cause or contribute to air pollution which may reasonably be anticipated to endanger public health or welfare."[58]

Listing a pollutant as a criteria air pollutant requires the administrator to set National Ambient Air Quality Standards for that pollutant, delineating maximum allowable concentrations of that pollutant in the air.[59] These standards operate on a state and local level to cap the maximum permissible concentrations in those areas.[60] In response to those limits, each state must create a state implementation plan (SIP) detailing its plans to meet NAAQS standards.[61] Noncompliance with NAAQS standards allows the federal government to withhold highway funds otherwise provided to states and municipalities,[62] creating a strong incentive on states to develop SIPs meeting NAAQS requirements. Despite the significant rulemaking authority granted to the EPA administrator, the Supreme Court has previously upheld the NAAQS program as constitutional under the nondelegation doctrine.[63] Moreover, the Court has explicitly barred the EPA administrator from considering the economic cost of pollution regulations in promulgating NAAQS requirements.[64]

While EPA's ability to set NAAQS standards and to review state implementation plans for compliance gives EPA a great deal of control over the ultimate result of such regulations, it does not permit EPA to force states to implement a cap-and-trade system. The Clean Air Act allows, but does not require, states to use "economic incentives such as fees, marketable permits, and auctions of emissions rights" in their plans.[65] Of course, a state could always institute such programs of its own volition.

Stationary sources. The Clean Air Act includes several measures to control pollution emissions from both stationary and mobile sources. In addition to NAAQS requirements, the Clean Air Act regulates stationary sources of pollution directly under Title I's new source performance standards (NSPS) and new source review (NSR) program, as well as under Title V's permit requirements. NSPS requirements impose uniform emission standards on all stationary sources of pollution throughout the nation.[66] Similarly, the NSR program requires permits for emissions of noncriteria air pollutants (the prevention of significant deterioration [PSD] program) and for emissions of criteria pollutants in areas where such emissions already exceed national caps (nonattainment new source review (NNSR).[67] Currently, as a noncriteria pollutant, carbon dioxide is subject only to the PSD program. Since the endangerment finding will require the EPA administrator to list carbon dioxide as a criteria air pollutant, however, if EPA decrees that current ambient air levels of carbon dioxide exceed maximum acceptable levels, the stricter NNSR requirements will apply to emitters of carbon dioxide.[68] Such requirements would likely impose large costs on emitters, handicapping industry significantly.

Since many stationary emitters of carbon dioxide, such as small manufacturing facilities, hospitals, hotels, retail stores, shopping malls, office buildings, and even commercial kitchens, do not emit significant concentrations of air pollutants other than carbon dioxide, regulating carbon dioxide under the Clean Air Act will expand the scope of federal regulation dramatically.[69] Under the text of the Clean Air Act, any source emitting more than 25 tons of air pollutants per year must obtain a permit from EPA. Since carbon dioxide is emitted in much greater quantities and by many more sources than other pollutants, applications for the permits required under the PSD program and under Title V will skyrocket once the government begins regulating carbon dioxide under the Clean Air Act.[70]

EPA is not equipped to handle that explosion in permit requests.[71] Accordingly, it has proposed a "tailoring rule" to accommodate its expanded regulatory activity. To limit the number of permit applications for EPA to review, the tailoring rule would temporarily increase the threshold permit requirement from the current level of 100–250 tpy (tons per year) of emissions to 75,000 tpy in 2013. That threshold would eventually be decreased to 25,000 tpy (and possibly even lower) over time.[72]

Although a tailoring rule would accommodate EPA's bureaucratic incapacity, allowing an administrative agency to amend the clear text of a statute passed by Congress would violate the separation of powers in a way never before permitted by the Supreme Court.[73] Citing this threat to the separation of powers, the Southeastern Legal Foundation has filed a lawsuit seeking to enjoin EPA's application of the Clean Air Act to carbon dioxide.[74] SLF argues that since Clean Air Act provisions are not severable, if EPA cannot enforce the act as written, it cannot enforce it at all. But even if this suit is successful, voiding the tailoring rule would not prevent EPA from regulating carbon dioxide. At best, a victory would temporarily enjoin regulation of stationary sources until such time as the agency employs enough bureaucrats to handle the huge number of applications. At worst, a victory would empower the agency to prohibit emissions for however long it takes the agency to grant a permit, which would effectively destroy the American economy.

Mobile sources. As noted above, the Clean Air Act also grants EPA the power to regulate pollution from mobile sources, including cars, trucks, airplanes, and ships.[75] Section 202(a) provides for the regulation of air pollutant emissions from new motor vehicles,[76] while Section 213 reaches emissions from oceangoing vessels and Section 231 reaches emissions from airplanes.[77] Since EPA has long regulated motor vehicle emissions in a top-down fashion, imposing additional requirements on automobile manufacturers is a relatively simple task for the bureaucracy (although compliance by manufacturers may be a different story). Moreover, the Clean Air Act's interconnected statutory language means that an endangerment finding under one title all but requires regulation under other titles as well, including Title II, which addresses mobile emissions sources.[78] Given EPA's endangerment finding for stationary sources, "the adoption of new vehicle emission standards is only a matter of time."[79]

But President Obama's EPA has authority to regulate mobile emissions sources beyond that provided by the Clean Air Act. Until now, EPA has regulated motor vehicle emissions primarily through corporate average fuel economy (CAFE) standards. Since 1975, CAFE standards have required that automakers produce vehicles meeting certain fuel economy requirements.[80] In an effort to decrease gasoline consumption, Obama recently proposed to raise CAFE standards for cars, light trucks, and SUVs, to achieve an average fuel economy of 34 miles per gallon by 2016.[81] And more recently still, EPA published a notice of intent to raise that "to as much as 62 miles per gallon by 2025."[82]

The Clean Water Act

The Clean Water Act provides another vehicle through which President Obama can act unilaterally to try to prevent global warming.[83] Atmospheric carbon dioxide is eventually absorbed into rivers, lakes, and oceans at a rate directly proportional to the rate of emissions into the air.[84] Waters become more acidic as a result of this absorption, threatening many species of marine life.[85] It is noteworthy, however, that for most of the past several hundred million years, atmospheric carbon dioxide concentrations have exceeded those of today and those projected for the 21st century.[86]

The Clean Water Act is designed to prevent such threats.[87] The act's stated purpose is to "restore and maintain the chemical, physical, and biological integrity of the Nation's waters."[88] The act requires EPA to set water quality standards and orders states to implement plans in conformity with such standards "for the protection and propagation of fish, shellfish and wildlife and for recreation."[89] Under the Clean Water Act, states must also identify "impaired" waters exceeding EPA standards,[90] for which the state must set more stringent pollution limitations.[91]

EPA has begun to formulate new water quality standards that include measures to prevent ocean acidification.[92] These new standards will empower EPA to use Clean Water Act measures to restrict carbon dioxide emissions and will explicitly authorize the president to use his foreign affairs powers to the same end. This broad executive power to eliminate pollution, no matter the cost, typifies the absolutist legislation enacted in the name of the environment.[93]

The Endangered Species Act

The Endangered Species Act also provides a source of domestic authority useful in the president's crusade to stop global warming.[94] The act is administered by the U.S. Fish and Wildlife Service and the National Oceanic and Atmospheric Administration. Those agencies are responsible for listing a species as "threatened" or "endangered," depending on the degree of peril it faces from habitat loss, disease, or "other natural or manmade factors affecting its continued existence."[95] Every federal agency must use its authority to "carry out programs for the conservation" of listed species.[96] The Endangered Species Act defines "conservation" as "recovery to the point where the Act's protections are no longer necessary."[97]

The Endangered Species Act forbids anyone to "take" any listed species—a prohibition that applies with equal force on government-owned land and private property.[98] The statute defines the term "take" broadly to include any activities "to harass, harm, pursue, hunt, shoot, wound, kill, trap, capture, or collect, or to attempt to engage in any such conduct."[99] The Supreme Court has also adopted an expansive reading of this mandate, holding in *Babbitt v. Sweet Home Chapter of Communities for a Great Oregon* that this prohibition extends to incidental harm as a result of habitat modification or destruction.[100] These broad interpretations of government power reflect the act's absolutist mandate "to halt and reverse the trend toward species extinction, whatever the cost."[101]

Despite this expansive power, the Obama administration has denied having any intent to combat climate change through the Endangered Species Act.[102] The absolute authority granted under that statute, however, may prove an attractive option for the president should he encounter resistance in curtailing carbon dioxide emissions using other statutory tools.

National Environmental Policy Act

The National Environmental Policy Act,[103] intended to "prevent or eliminate damage to the environment and biosphere,"[104] imposes high procedural hurdles on many areas of federal activity. NEPA demands that the federal government prepare a detailed environmental impact statement (EIS) projecting and assessing the environmental consequences of every piece of proposed legislation and "other major Federal actions significantly affecting the quality of the human environment."[105] The EIS also mandates an analysis of alternatives to mitigate any potential environmental harm, requires a period of public comment, and typically delays federal action from 18 to 36 months.[106]

In addition to procedural requirements, NEPA includes an important substantive requirement—it specifically directs federal agencies to consider proposed activities' likely effects on climate change. NEPA orders agencies to "recognize the worldwide and long-range character of environmental problems and, where consistent with the foreign policy of the United States, [to] lend support to initiatives, resolutions, and programs designed to maximize international cooperation in anticipating and preventing a decline in the quality of mankind's world environment."[107]

The president exercises significant control over just which environmental impacts are considered in the NEPA process. He is thus empowered to inject carbon dioxide emission reductions into many areas of government action. Although many federal agencies have their own NEPA regulations,[108] the President's Council on Environmental Quality issues guidelines on the implementation of the NEPA review process. Twelve environmental groups recently petitioned the council to set out regulations governing how global warming is analyzed under NEPA.[109] Including such considerations aligns with federal court decisions holding that NEPA requires an analysis of climate change impacts.[110]

Foreign Affairs Power

Unlike in domestic affairs, where the president's main function is to see that the laws are faithfully executed, in foreign affairs the president, who speaks and acts for the nation, has wide power to conduct foreign policy and make treaties and other agreements.

Treaties. Article II of the Constitution authorizes the president, with the "advice and consent" of the Senate, to "make treaties" with foreign nations.[111] To be binding, however, a treaty must be ratified by two-thirds of the Senate[112]—a high hurdle.[113] The Kyoto Protocol,[114] for example, the most recent major treaty on climate change, was not even submitted to the Senate for ratification, notwithstanding that the United States signed it.[115] Thus, absent Congress's overwhelming support, the ratification obstacle limits the usefulness of treaties to a president seeking to bind the United States to any international climate change initiative.

Moreover, many treaties are not "self-executing," which is an added hurdle. A self-executing treaty needs no congressional action beyond ratification to take effect domestically: once Congress signs off, the treaty is the law of the land. By contrast, a non-self-executing treaty requires domestic legislation to take effect. Ratifying the treaty may bind the United States internationally, but it does not force Congress to pass the legislation necessary to give the treaty domestic effect.[116] That extra step exposes non-self-executing treaties to the delays and political compromises inherent in the legislative process.

But while President Obama may face difficulties in entering a new climate change treaty into force, several existing treaties provide the basis for executive agreements that would enable him to commit the United States to carbon dioxide emission reductions.

Executive agreements. The difficulties in ratifying treaties and the necessity of obtaining international participation in measures designed to address global warming encourage presidents to pursue international cooperation using executive agreements.[117] Executive agreements circumvent the advice-and-consent hurdles imposed on the treaty process and allow the president to enter into binding arrangements with foreign powers with little congressional participation.[118] Despite the fact that the Senate Foreign Relations Committee has urged the president to negotiate international climate change agreements through the Article II treaty process,[119] the president's nearly unrestricted authority to bind the United States through executive agreements suggests that they will serve as his international instrument of choice. To develop the nation's climate change policy, President Obama could enter into a "congressional-executive" agreement based on authority delegated to him under existing statutes or treaties. Or he could enter into a "sole executive" agreement that may be enforceable domestically even in the face of congressional disapproval.

Congressional-Executive Agreements Pursuant to Statute

A "congressional-executive" agreement is a binding commitment made by the president pursuant to a statute or treaty passed by Congress. Because passing a statute authorizing the president to enter into an international agreement requires the approval of only a majority of both houses of Congress—rather than two-thirds of the Senate—congressional-executive agreements are easier to enact than treaties. Congressional approval can either precede the signing of such an agreement or be granted by a vote after the fact. On several occasions, however, the Senate has objected when *ex post* agreements have been submitted as executive agreements rather than Article II treaties.[120]

The existing domestic environmental laws previously discussed already provide several bases for congressional-executive agreements to limit carbon dioxide emissions. The Clean Air Act expressly directs the president to "undertake to enter into international agreements" to "protect the stratosphere,"[121] although this provision is specifically targeted to prevent depletion of the ozone layer.[122] To protect international waters, the Clean Water Act includes a provision declaring that "the President, acting through the Secretary of State and such national and international organizations as he deems appropriate, shall take such action as may be necessary" to ensure that foreign countries act to prevent the contamination of national and international waters "to at least the same extent as the United States does under its laws."[123] Likewise, the Endangered Species Act directs the secretary of the interior and the secretary of state to "encourage ... the entering into of bilateral or multilateral agreements with foreign countries to provide for" the conservation of listed species.[124]

In addition, Congress set out a basic framework for U.S. climate change policy in the Global Climate Protection Act.[125] That act indicates that the United States should "identify technologies and activities to limit mankind's adverse effect on the global climate" by "slowing the rate of increase of concentrations of greenhouse gases in the atmosphere in the near term" and "stabilizing or reducing" those concentrations in the long term.[126] To reach these goals, Congress directed the president to "work toward multilateral agreements" on climate change[127] and ordered the secretary of state to work with the president and the EPA administrator to engage in multilateral agreements consistent with federal law.[128]

Statutes authorizing scientific and technological partnerships with foreign countries can also be interpreted as sanctioning agreements to prevent climate change. The 1979 Foreign Relations Authorization Act directs the president to "assess and initiate appropriate international scientific and technological activities which are based upon domestic scientific and technological activities of the United States Government and which are beneficial to the United States and foreign countries."[129] Similarly, the 1979 International Development Cooperation Act authorizes the creation of an Institute for Scientific and Technological Cooperation "subject to the foreign policy guidance of the Secretary of State and whose task is 'to assist developing countries to strengthen their own scientific and technological capacity.'"[130] The act further directs the president to "make and perform contracts and other agreements with any individual [or] institution, ... and with governments or government agencies, domestic or foreign."[131]

The International Development and Food Assistance Act of 1977 confers additional authority on the president, although it should be noted that programs authorized by this legislation would require congressional funding before taking effect.[132] The act empowers the president "to furnish assistance ... for developing and strengthening the capacity of developing countries to protect and manage their environment and natural resources . . . including reforestation, soil conservation, and other activities to rehabilitate degraded forest lands."[133] The act also grants the president authority to furnish assistance "on such terms and conditions as he may determine, to enable [developing] countries" to develop energy resources,[134] including "renewable energy sources for rural areas."[135]

While not authorizing emission caps, executive agreements on science and technology promote the development of renewable energy sources, efficient heating and cooling systems, and low-emission vehicles—investments designed to reduce the economic and political costs of future emissions restrictions in the United States.

Congressional-Executive Agreements Pursuant to Treaty

Existing treaties provide other sources of authority. Like statutes, treaties ratified by the United States represent Congress's blessing to enter into executive agreements in furtherance of treaty objectives.

The 1992 United Nations Framework Convention on Climate Change seems the most likely candidate to authorize executive agreements on climate change. That treaty, which has been ratified by Congress, established measurement, reporting, and verification requirements under which parties must develop, update, and report "national inventories of anthropogenic emissions . . . of all greenhouse gases. . . , using comparable methodologies to be agreed upon by the Conference of the Parties,"[136] and must describe the country's mitigation actions and plans to implement the convention.[137] Despite this strong language, the UNFCCC is not self-executing, and Congress has not implemented legislation to give it domestic effect. In fact, when reviewing the UNFCCC for ratification, the Senate Foreign Relations Committee noted its expectation that any future decision applying legally binding emission reduction targets and timetables under the UNFCCC would require the Senate's advice and consent.[138] Although this resolution is not legally binding, it indicates Congress's disapproval of emission targets enacted without that body's consent, and likely discouraged Obama from seeking to bind the United States to emission reductions at the 2009 Copenhagen climate change summit.[139]

But existing domestic legislation does empower Obama to honor other UNFCCC obligations. The Energy Policy Act, for example, created a framework to implement the treaty's monitoring and reporting requirements.[140] Insofar as this legislation represents congressional authorization to monitor and report emissions, Obama may use this approval to implement more robust monitoring and reporting requirements in future executive agreements.[141]

Treaties governing aviation, however, do currently empower the president to enact executive agreements in order to limit greenhouse gas emissions from aircraft.[142] Most notably, the Convention on International Civil Aviation, which entered into force in 1947, established the International Civil Aviation Organization as a UN agency responsible for coordinating and regulating international air travel.[143] The Aviation Convention requires parties to "collaborate in securing the highest practicable degree of uniformity in regulations, standards, procedures, and organization in relation to aircraft, standards, [and] procedures."[144] As noted previously, the Clean Air Act requires EPA to issue emission standards for airplane engines emitting dangerous air pollution.[145] In combination with the Clean Air Act, then, the Aviation Convention requires the United States to promulgate airplane engine emission standards consistent with ICAO standards.[146] As a result, the Aviation Convention permits Obama to enter into executive agreements binding the United States to airplane engine emission reductions.

These statutes and treaties provide President Obama ample authority to enter into binding congressional-executive agreements restricting greenhouse gas emissions. Although the current Congress may actually disapprove of carbon dioxide emission caps, these statutes constitute Congress's support for presidential action in the environmental sphere. As Justice Robert Jackson famously stated, when acting under an express delegation of power from Congress, the president's authority is "at its maximum," and he may "be said . . . to personify federal sovereignty."[147]

Sole Executive Agreements

The president can also enter into binding international agreements without Congress's consent. The president's authority to enter into a "sole executive agreement" arises from the general vesting of executive power in the office of the president,[148] the president's duty to "take care" that the nation's laws be faithfully enforced,[149] and the president's "foreign affairs" power.[150] In the international realm, there is no dispute that sole executive agreements are as equally binding as Article II treaties.[151]

The weight of their authority under domestic law, however, remains a topic of much debate.[152] Although the Supreme Court has long held that sole executive agreements prevail over contrary state laws,[153] the Court's recent decision in *Medellín v. Texas*[154] suggested that a sole executive agreement might not be binding domestically unless it is self-executing. Indeed, there is consensus that the president's independent foreign affairs power in such situations is limited,[155] and the "limits are difficult to determine and to state."[156] Independent presidential power is at its greatest in agreements relating to the military, the recognition of foreign governments, and settling international claims. The power is more limited in other areas, including climate change.[157] Under Justice Jackson's delineation of presidential power, presidential action in the face of congressional silence occupies a "zone of twilight" where presidential and congressional powers overlap.[158] Jackson also noted that when the president acts contrary to Congress's express or implied will, his power is "at its lowest ebb."[159]

A review of previous sole executive agreements confirms that presidents typically employ such agreements in areas where presidential power is at its zenith. State Department records reveal that the most common areas in which executive agreements are used are the military (27 percent), international assistance and development (18 percent), nuclear energy and safety (9 percent), aviation (6 percent), and scientific cooperation (6 percent).[160] Another study produces similar findings: the military (14 percent), trade (9 percent), scientific cooperation (6 percent), postal matters (6 percent), and debts (6 percent) were most often the subject.[161]

With regard to global warming regulation, the Senate resolution disapproving of the Kyoto Protocol could be seen as an assertion of the Senate's authority over (and even objection to) executive agreements to reduce carbon dioxide emissions.[162] But that interpretation is challenged by the fact that the Senate resolution is limited in scope to international agreements "which would require the advice and consent of the Senate to ratification," and therefore does not apply to executive agreements.[163]

Should President Obama sign a sole executive agreement pledging to cap carbon dioxide emissions, the Case Act would require him to notify Congress of any such agreement within 60 days of execution.[164] Congress could then pass legislation invalidating the agreement, but it would likely need to do so with enough votes to override a presidential veto.[165] Given the president's ample authority to act both domestically and internationally under existing statutes, it seems unlikely that Obama would seek to wage such a war with Congress when less confrontational tactics are more than sufficient to achieve his policy goals.

Conclusion

In sum, with the demise of constitutional restraints during the New Deal and the massive expansion of congressional power that followed, much of it delegated to the executive branch, President Obama today faces very few obstacles in implementing the global warming agenda. The Progressive Era, enamored of science, sought to bring about rule by "experts" ensconced in government planning bureaus. We have that pretty much today. As a result, environmental decisions involving not simply science but, at bottom, value-laden tradeoffs are made by relatively few unaccountable bureaucrats concentrated in the executive branch, with only sporadic and uneven judicial and congressional review.

Yet those decisions and the questions they address arise in a political context. Concerning all the people, they are quintessentially political questions that should be decided by the most political of our branches of government, the Congress. To be sure, the president represents all the people, and he has legislative "power" in the form of the veto, but it is the Congress that represents the variety of interests in the nation; constitutionally, it is the Congress in which all legislative power is vested. Accordingly, although it may be necessary for executive agencies to administer, execute, and even draft environmental laws, regulations, and rules, it is also necessary that Congress give its final approval of those provisions and take responsibility for them if the Constitution's separation-of-powers principle, as originally understood, is to be respected.

In the short run, if it so chose, Congress could enact legislation to check executive actions with which it disagreed, or it could refuse to fund various regulatory schemes, even if that meant overriding a presidential veto. And of course the people can always elect representatives who will take their oaths of office more seriously. In the longer run, however, the problems are deeper and more systemic, as this review of history and law has shown. We have strayed far from our Constitution of limited government with powers divided between federal and state governments and separated among the three branches of the federal government. There is nothing in the Constitution that precludes us from enacting measures to protect the environment, but it must be done in the right way, consistent with the Constitution's provisions for limited government. We need to revive not only the nondelegation doctrine but the doctrine of enumerated powers, including the division of powers between the federal and state governments. The resurrection of those principles would bring value-laden environmental questions closer to the people affected by them, restoring government of, by, and for the people.

2. A Hot Political Climate: Recent Evolution of Global Warming Policy and Regulation

Patrick J. Michaels

Roger Pilon's contribution to this volume is truly scary because it shows the breathtaking concentration of power now in Washington and the remarkable reach of both the executive and legislative branches of the federal government into our daily lives, facilitated by the permanent civil service that resides in Washington's bureaucracy.

The federal government has increasingly gravitated toward overarching global warming policy in recent years, enhanced by the election of Barack Obama in 2008. This chapter details the recent evolution of global warming policy, with specific reference to several important—and somewhat unforeseen—events that took place while legislation was under consideration.

The rush to policy and the increasing intrusiveness of global warming into our lives and governments have been accompanied by a remarkable breakdown in the community most cited in support of these policies: climate scientists. The revelations of the "Climategate" e-mails and the subsequent exposure of the politicized science of the United Nations' Intergovernmental Panel on Climate Change could not have come at a less opportune time for policy hawks.

Three weeks after the e-mails hit the front page, world leaders assembled in Copenhagen at a much-anticipated meeting of the signatories of the UN's 1992 Framework Convention on Climate Change. For years, environmental pundits pointed toward the December 2009 meeting as where the world would finally agree to binding and scientifically meaningful limits on

(continued on next page)

43

(continued)

carbon dioxide and other greenhouse gases. The meeting was an abject failure, aided and abetted by Climategate and ominous rumblings about the unraveling of the IPCC.

As Copenhagen started, President Obama announced that his Environmental Protection Agency found "endangerment" of human health and welfare from atmospheric greenhouse gas increases and signaled that—whatever might or might not happen in our legislature—the United States would act to reduce its emissions.

As Copenhagen ended, in complete failure, Barack Obama flew off into the night, the engines of Air Force One firewalled in an attempt to beat a record-setting blizzard descending on the White House. The sight of the presidential jet landing in a near whiteout after the true wipeout at Copenhagen eerily predicted the evolution of global legislation that would unfold in the next year.

But that's not the way things were, just half a year before Copenhagen. . .

The Political Climate

June 26, 2009

Around 7:00 p.m. on Friday, June 26, 2009, the U.S. House of Representatives passed, on a 219–215 vote, the American Clean Energy and Security Act of 2009, also known as H.R. 2454. The vote was delayed and timed to avoid the Friday evening news cycle, effectively short-circuiting any serious coverage until the next week.

ACES ran to 1,427 pages, 300 of which were added in the wee hours of June 26. No member could possibly have read the bill that ultimately came up for a vote.

ACES mandates a reduction of 83 percent in total emissions of carbon dioxide in less than 40 years. Given historical and prospective population data, by 2050 the average American will be allowed the carbon dioxide emissions of the average citizen in 1867 (see Figure 2.1).

44

Figure 2.1
PER CAPITA CARBON DIOXIDE EMISSIONS IN THE UNITED STATES,
1800–2050

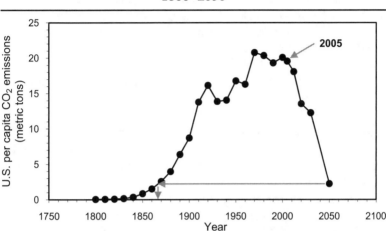

SOURCES: Figures for 1800–2005 are from U.S. Energy Information Agency, http://www.eia.doe.gov; subsequent figures are from H.R. 2454.

The mechanism to accomplish this emission reduction is known as "cap-and-trade." ACES sets a "cap" on annual carbon dioxide emissions. Large emitters are given a "permit," defined by their 2005 release. The law reduces the amount of carbon dioxide "permitted" each year, from 3 percent below 2005 values in 2012, to 83 percent by 2050. These are "caps." If a company emits less than its permitted value, it can sell the remainder to another that needs to emit more. That's a "trade."

ACES is 1,427 pages of tedious micromanaging of almost every aspect of our economic life. Immediately after its passage, at least no one had to ask, "Where's the outrage?" Within a few days, President Obama's "approval index," calculated by the polling firm Rasmussen Reports as "strongly approve" minus "strongly disapprove," went negative *and has never since been positive.* This permanent change of sign occurred before health care hit the legislative radar screen.

Is ACES intrusive? Among other things, it requires domestic automakers—now largely owned by the federal government anyway—to produce massive numbers of so-called plug-in hybrid vehicles.

The first of these will be the Chevrolet Volt, which hit the road late in 2010. It can be charged up overnight. On a good day, it will run for 40 miles on its lithium-ion battery pack. On a hot day, requiring air conditioning, or a cold, rainy day, requiring defogging, wipers, and lights, it will go maybe 25 miles or so.

While the House was debating cap-and-trade, General Motors wasn't telling the truth about the car. GM repeatedly said that when the Volt runs low on charge, an internal combustion engine will serve as a generator—not directly powering the wheels.

In October 2010, the month before actual production models were to hit the street, GM fessed up that indeed the gas engine would move the car mechanically when the battery was low or the vehicle was at high speed. This makes the Volt nothing new—just a much-gussied up Toyota Prius–type hybrid, where the engine also powers the wheels when the battery does not.

The president's much-debated "stimulus" package awarded each purchaser of the Volt a cool $7,500. This was justified because it was represented as a true breakthrough vehicle, all-electric rather than hybrid. General Motors simply did not tell the truth in pursuit of a handout for the buyers of its new, very expensive ($41,000 plus taxes, etc.) car.

As of this writing, Volts are actually on the road. People are getting about 30-35 miles on pure battery power. Then the internal combustion engine kicks in. In this state, which is where the real-world cars are likely to spend most of their time, the auto testing firm Edmunds.com got an unremarkable 31mpg. The hybrid Prius beats the heck out of this, with most owners getting in the high 40s under normal conditions. Why the subsidy?

In terms of its reach into every aspect of life, ACES is by far the most intrusive piece of energy legislation ever passed by either the House or the Senate. See for yourself at http://thomas.loc.gov/cgi-bin/bdquery/z?d111:h2454; the table of contents *alone* is 10 pages long.

ACES mandates very expensive electricity and energy sources. It requires new technological infrastructures for things that people simply may not want or for products that may not perform. For example, utilities must provide a national array of charging stations for the plug-in hybrids, even though such vehicles do not exist in any economically viable form that can survive without a federal subsidy, and there is no guarantee that people will buy them anyway if they are ever produced in large numbers.

Coal is our most abundant source of domestic energy, which is why approximately half our electricity is created by its combustion. Even though ACES calls itself an "energy security" act, it virtually guarantees that there will be no new coal-fired power plants in our future (and it will result in the shutdown of those that operate now). That's because ACES requires that any new facility "capture" half the carbon dioxide that is emitted from the combustion of coal, and then "store" it somewhere (underground?). This procedure has *never* been demonstrated as being commercially or technologically viable on a national scale.

No problem. ACES levies a new tax on electricity generation (i.e., a new tax on the consumers of electricity), which will be used to fund the development of carbon capture and storage. The funds will be disbursed through the Edison Electric Institute, the Washington lobbying organization for investor-owned utilities.

Why should coal producers object? Carbon capture and storage take *energy*, and lots of it. If it takes two or three times as much coal to produce the same amount of electricity, what's not to like? Assuming coal's main competition in the generation business—natural gas— would also be required to capture the carbon dioxide it releases from combustion, then we simply have to use more of both fuels.

Funding research on carbon capture through the utility lobby is but one example, out of hundreds, of the way ACES works. It buys off virtually every special interest that one can imagine having any-thing to do with energy and power . . . with your money.

In another example, ACES creates a large infrastructure for etha-nol, which buys the support of big agriculture. Originally the George W. Bush "solution" to global warming, and expanded by the 110th Congress, corn-based ethanol actually results in increased carbon dioxide emissions, as shown by Timothy Searchinger and others in *Science* magazine in 2008.[1]

Why? High-yielding corn production is very fossil fuel intensive. Synthesis of nitrogen fertilizer consumes about 2 percent of the world's energy per year. Mechanical tillage of enormous acreages required for large-scale ethanol production consumes more fuel. Diversion of land from background forest or prairie obviously destroys a natural "sink" for carbon dioxide. The list goes on.

By mandating and subsidizing technologies that people normally would not adopt, ACES creates infrastructure and "jobs." But how many does it destroy? Its manifold subsidies have to come from someone—that is, personal and corporate taxpayers—which leaves everyone with less money to spend on goods or otherwise employing people.

ACES is not an original experiment; Spain performed it over the past three years. President Obama has repeatedly stated that he views Spain as the model nation for the construction of "green jobs." There's some temporary truth to this.

Spain massively subsidized solar power, paying anyone who put up a solar panel about 75 cents per kilowatt-hour. For comparative purposes, the average cost of electricity in the United States is about 10 cents, and the average cost of solar power here is around 30 cents (which is why solar cannot function without huge taxpayer subsidies).

This nonsense created a remarkable burden. As noted by Gabriel Calzada Álvarez of Spain's King Juan Carlos University, the excess cost of electricity—passed on to the consumer—resulted in a $774,000 bill for each Spanish "green job."[2]

Solar panels became cash registers. So much so that they dragged down the rest of Spain's economy, putting the country into a major financial deficit. Spain had to reduce the subsidies, the green jobs vanished, unemployment was last seen at 19 percent, and (not surprisingly) it spent itself into financial peril resembling that in Greece. The amount of solar energy produced has actually declined, as did the profitability of virtually all the world's manufacturers of solar-power technology.

One would think that the president should be more careful about citing Spain as a role model for the United States, or that ACES wouldn't mandate outrageously expensive energy. But ACES requires that 6 percent of our energy come from "renewables" by 2012 and 20 percent by 2020. That *doesn't* count hydroelectric facilities built before 1988 (which means every large existing facility), which supply about 9 percent of our electricity. Given that the authors of ACES know that environmental opposition to any new major hydro facility will be both strong and successful, wind and solar power will make up the lion's share of the 20 percent.

Currently, 1.8 percent of our power comes from wind and a mere 0.3 percent comes from solar. Somehow, these two are going to have

Figure 2.2
GLOBAL WARMING UNDER "BUSINESS AS USUAL," WAXMAN-MARKEY U.S. ONLY, AND WAXMAN-MARKEY FOR THE KYOTO PROTOCOL NATIONS

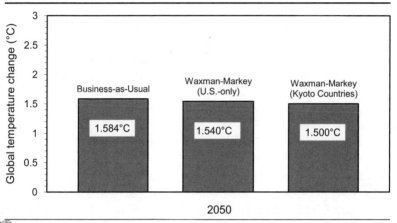

SOURCE: "The American Power Act: Climatologically Meaningless," *World Climate Report* (blog), http://www.worldclimatereport.com/index.php/2010/05/13/the-american-power-act-climatologically-meaningless; T.M.L. Wigley. "The Kyoto Protocol: CO_2, CH_2, CH_4, and climate implications," *Geophysical Research Letters* 25 (1998): 2285–88.

NOTE: Left, 50-year warming projected by the IPCC with no emissions restrictions; middle, warming projected in the United States (and nowhere else) if the United States adopts ACES; right, warming projected if all nations that had obligations under the Kyoto Protocol adopt ACES.

to add up to nearly 20 percent in 10 years, which will force people to purchase much more expensive energy than they normally would have.

Finally, what would ACES actually do for the climate? The answer is obvious: nothing detectable. In 1998, Tom Wigley, then at the National Center for Atmospheric Research in Boulder, Colorado, published a very useful algorithm that can calculate the effects of various emission reduction proposals on global warming. An example is shown in Figure 2.2, which gives the warming expected from "business as usual," i.e., no mandated reductions; ACES adopted by the United States only; and ACES adopted by the entire developed world.

Even in the last case, which is highly unlikely, global warming is reduced by a mere 0.08 degree Celsius (0.14 degree Fahrenheit) by 2050, from 1.58 degrees Celsius to 1.5. This amount is literally too small to measure. Similarly dismal figures result if the analysis is extended all the way to 2100.

(It's worth noting that this scenario assumes that the "sensitivity" of the earth's surface temperature to a doubling of atmospheric carbon is 2.5 degrees Celsius [4.5 degrees Fahrenheit]. I have demonstrated in other recent books that this figure is very likely to be too high.[3])

The Senate Punts Cap-and-Trade

The aforementioned change of President Obama's "approval index" from positive to negative immediately after the passage of ACES was hard for any politician to ignore.

So, instead of ACES, the Senate chose to take up health care. Cap-and-trade lapsed and lapsed. Sen. Barbara Boxer (D-CA) said her Environment and Public Works Committee would have a bill ready when the Senate returned after Labor Day 2009. Then it was delayed until October. Finally, Boxer moved the bill onto the Senate floor in November. Even the most rudimentary head counting showed it far short of the 60 votes required to stop debate and force an up-or-down vote.

In December 2009, Senators Graham (R-SC), Kerry (D-NH), and Lieberman (I-CT) then proposed an alternative that more specifically targeted electrical generation for cap-and-trade. No actual bill was produced, but they promised one in April 2010. After a series of fits and starts, they finally said the bill would be released on Monday, April 26. But on April 25, Senator Graham walked away from his own bill because Majority Leader Harry Reid (D-NV) said that immigration reform—not climate change—would be the Senate's next priority. Without Graham's token Republican support, 60 votes again became impossible.

Besides the obvious unpopularity of cap-and-trade as passed by the House, the Senate was buffeted by other events far outside of its control: Climategate, Copenhagen, Washington's blizzards, the destruction of the IPCC's credibility all occurred in rapid succession. Behind them all was the threat that the EPA would step in and regulate by presidential fiat.

Climategate—the collective name given to a horde of about 160 megabytes of over 3,000 e-mails, additional text, and computer code that were somehow moved from the server at the Climate Research Unit at the University of East Anglia—was the first unforeseen disaster:

> We feel that climate science is, in the current situation, too important to be kept under wraps.
>   We hereby release a random selection of correspondence, code, and documents.

The file in question was named FOIA.zip (Freedom of Information Act). It is unclear whether it was so titled after it was originally moved in mockery of the CRU's continued blocking of Freedom of Information Act requests for its raw (rather than what it called "homogenized") climate data, or whether that was the original title of the file on the East Anglia server. The identities of the person, people, or organizations that moved the file away from its parent server have never been determined and/or revealed.

Here I detail a small selection of the e-mails that had clear political impact.

"Hide the Decline. . . "

Phil Jones was (and still is) the head of the CRU when he wrote this November 16, 1999, e-mail to Ray Bradley, Mike Mann, and Malcolm Hughes, the authors of the original "hockey stick" paper (described in the accompanying sidebar):

> . . . I've just completed Mike's Nature trick of adding in the real temps to each series for the last 20 years (ie from 1981 onwards) and from 1961 for Keith's to hide the decline.

The trick Jones and Mann performed was to hide a decline in temperatures appearing in tree-ring data in the latter part of the 20th century (see Figures 2.4 and 2.5 in color insert). Without the "trick," the tree-ring records exhibit what dendrochronologists (tree-ring scientists) delicately call "the divergence problem."

While Climategate in general, and the "hidden" data in particular, didn't receive much attention from the legacy media, they were all over the new media, including cable television. There was never any denial on the part of Jones that the "decline" was in fact not "hidden."

The "Hockey Stick"

Until 1999, the reigning paradigm in climate history was that (a) the current era is warm, (b) there was a global cold period, the "little ice age," encompassing the 17th, 18th, and early 19th centuries, in which the average temperature was about 1–1.5 degrees Celsius (1.8–2.3 degrees Fahrenheit) lower than the average for the 20th century, and (c) there was a "medieval warm period" from roughly 800 to 1200 AD that was about a half of a degree (Celsius) warmer than the last century. This paradigm was based on literally hundreds of different indicators.

In 1999, Michael Mann and Ray Bradley, then of the University of Massachusetts, and Malcolm Hughes, from the Tree-Ring Laboratory at University of Arizona, attempted a simultaneous analysis of a number of "proxy" climate variables (mainly tree rings, which grow wider in warm, wet conditions and are narrow when it is cold and dry) and came up with a totally different result.

It was called the "hockey stick" because its long handle corresponds to 900 years (from 1000 to 1900) of little temperature variation, and its blade represents 100 years (1900 to 1999) of rapid temperature rise (see Figure 2.3 in color insert). The "hockey stick" made its debut in an article in the journal *Geophysical Research Letters*, which built on a 1998 paper by the same authors in the journal *Nature*.[4]

When presented by the United Nations' Intergovernmental Panel on Climate Change, Mann (who was a "lead author" on the IPCC section dealing with climate history) had no problem grafting the "multiproxy" temperatures to real ones observed in the late 20th century.

That certainly makes things look quite remarkable in recent years. So where did the little ice age and the medieval warm periods go?

According to extensive analyses by two Canadian researchers, Steve McIntyre and Ross McKitrick, they didn't go anywhere, but were in fact lost as artifacts of the statistical techniques employed in developing the hockey stick.[5]

(continued on next page)

(continued)

Tree rings are not thermometers. They largely explain growing season (summer) temperatures, which naturally vary much less than those in the winter. In addition, they generally explain only half (or less than half) of the variability in observed temperatures. In other words, at least half of temperature variability is *unrelated* to tree-ring widths. Tree rings and thermometer data certainly have very different statistical properties, and it is not a good scientific practice to present the two together as some type of continuous record.

Tree-ring-derived temperatures tend to indicate a decline in temperature in the late 20th century, rather than the observed rise measured from thermometers. Hence the need to "hide the decline."

As attention to cap-and-trade shifted from the passed House version to various proposals in the Senate, each senator was aware that, should the Senate bring up cap-and-trade, "hide the decline" wouldn't be far behind.

Hide the Data. . .

Phil Jones to Mike Mann, February 3, 2005:

> The two MMs [McIntyre and McKitrick] have been after the CRU station data for years. If they ever hear there is a Freedom of Information Act now in the UK, I think I'll delete the file rather than send to anyone.

Phil Jones to Bradley and Hughes (two authors of the original "hockey stick" paper), February 21, 2005:

> PS I'm getting hassled by a couple of people to release the CRU station temperature data. Don't any of you tell any body that the UK has a Freedom of Information Act!

The data in question are the original weather station data that formed the long-term surface temperature history published by the CRU. While there are three "independent" versions of this history that have been constructed (one is from the CRU, and others have been generated by the National Aeronautics and Space Administration and the U.S. National Climatic Data Center), the CRU version is the one most cited and used by working scientists.

In the early 1980s, the CRU, funded by U.S. taxpayers via the Department of Energy, began to assemble this history. The CRU record is known in climate slang as the "Jones and Wigley" history, because the first refereed summaries of it, published in the mid-1980s, were by East Anglia's Phil Jones and Tom Wigley.

It's a major effort to develop a climate history for the United States; doing so for the world is Herculean. The reason is, historically most countries had neither the resources nor the inclination to monitor climate per se in any organized fashion. Even here in the United States, where some organized efforts can be traced to the mid-19th century, reporting stations fade in and out, instrumentation changes, and observational techniques change (such as moving the time of observation for the daily high and low temperatures from near sunrise to near sunset).

There's inherent bias in long-term records. Weather-reporting stations tend to have been originally established at points of commerce, which in the 19th century meant along rivers. Cold air flows into river valleys at night, creating especially low temperatures in the winter when compared with the surrounding countryside. Often, official stations for a city eventually move from a downtown location to a major airport, as occurred in the early and mid-20th century. Those "major" airports soon became outmoded as longer runways and space were needed for first-generation jet aircraft.

As an example, Chicago's official station moved from downtown to Midway Airport, a more residential neighborhood with fewer tall buildings that impede ventilation. But Midway couldn't handle jets, so the official station eventually moved to (then) very rural Orchard Park, which became O'Hare International (hence its call letters, ORD). Anyone who has been to O'Hare knows it's hardly rural any more!

So, Chicago's "official" climate history begins in a crowded downtown that can't disperse the heat of the day, moves to an urban airport away from downtown, moves to another airport in the countryside that eventually becomes another urbanized site. Without some type of adjustment, the changes in site characteristics would erroneously indicate that Chicago's climate suddenly cooled when the official station left downtown, then cooled even more as it left the city entirely, and then warmed as O'Hare's environs increasingly urbanized.

Accounting for all these changes is clearly a very subjective operation. Jones and Wigley originally eyeballed neighboring records to see if one had an increase in temperature while the other did not, which would indicate artificial urban warming. But this method is very insensitive to any artificial warming in recent years that just doesn't jump off the page. Then there are the problems of the station moves, which can create artificial "discontinuities."

Obviously, free exchange of data is at the core of healthy science, as is curiosity on the part of competitive researchers and the need to replicate results independently. Consequently, McIntyre and McKitrick were simply doing what most scientists normally do when they requested the original raw data that went into the temperature histories.

For some reason, Jones was clearly worried that McIntyre could demand the raw data via a Freedom of Information Act request, which is why he threatened to destroy the data in his February 3, 2005, e-mail. (It turns out he had already lost plenty of it.)[6]

Another example of the need for independent analyses appeared within a month of the release of the Climategate e-mails. The Institute of Economic Analysis, a small Moscow think tank, published a white paper indicating that the CRU Russian data selection was biased.[7] CRU used only a quarter of the available data, and when the larger set was used, warming since the late 19th century was reduced about 0.7 degree Celsius (1.3 degrees Fahrenheit), as shown in Figure 2.6 (see color insert).

The Moscow study was not peer reviewed and therefore was of little practical use. But the obvious difference between the institute's and CRU's records indicates the need for scientists and other interested parties to be privy to the original data that go into our global climate histories.

The Copenhagen Fiasco

In December 2009, the parties to the 1992 United Nations Framework Convention on Climate Change met in Copenhagen. The purpose of the meeting was to come to a new, binding international agreement limiting emissions of greenhouse gases to replace the failed Kyoto Protocol to the Framework Convention on Climate Change. Climategate could not have happened at a more inauspicious time for those supporting a new treaty.

The old Kyoto Protocol mandated a carbon dioxide emissions reduction of 5.2 percent below 1990 levels for industrialized nations, averaged over the period 2008–2012. Emissions rose by more than that value. Kyoto was a major policy failure.

It could never have been otherwise. Even if it had been completely successful, Kyoto would have had no detectable effect on global surface temperature. If one again assumes that the "sensitivity" of temperature to a doubling of atmospheric carbon dioxide is (a questionably high) 2.5 degrees Celsius (4.5 degrees Fahrenheit), the aforementioned work by Tom Wigley shows that full international compliance would have resulted in a reduction in warming of 0.07 degree Celsius (0.13 degree Fahrenheit) per half century.

Kyoto was a waste of effort simply because China and India, two very large carbon emitters, were exempt (China is now the world's largest, having passed the United States in 2006). Without their participation, any new protocol is similarly futile.

Despite absolutely misleading headlines, such as the one in the November 27, 2009, *Washington Post*—"China Sets Targets for Emission Cuts"—the Chinese did *not* propose cuts in their emissions. Instead, they stated that they would reduce the *intensity* of their emissions, which is the amount of carbon dioxide emitted per unit of gross domestic product, by 45 percent from 2005 to 2020.

The fact is that emission intensity naturally drops as economies develop and mature. The more inefficient an economy is initially, the larger the change in intensity, and China just happens to be the world's most inefficient large economy. Its emission intensity actually *rose* by 14 percent between 2000 and 2005. The 45 percent drop in part reflects countering this remarkable anomaly. In fact, the U.S. Energy Information Administration projects that under "Business-as-Usual" (i.e., development without any mandated emission reductions), Chinese emission intensity would drop by 45 percent between 2005 and 2020.[8] So despite the *Post*'s headline, China in fact agreed to do *nothing*.

The *Times of India* was as misleading as the *Post* concerning Indian emissions, headlining on January 31, 2010, "India Keeps Copenhagen Pledge on Emissions Cuts," when in fact India agreed to reduce its emission intensity a mere 20–25 percent by 2020. If India merely continued its GDP growth of 2008, its economic output would grow by more than 100 percent over the same period. Instead of having four times its 2005 emissions in 2020, it will have three times. This is not an emissions "cut"!

President Obama went to Copenhagen and failed to even secure a commitment to make a commitment to emission cuts from China, India, Brazil, and South Africa. After declaring success, he fled the scene in Air Force One in an attempt to beat what turned out to be a record-setting December snowstorm back to Washington. He didn't (see Figure 2.7 in color insert).

All the Copenhagen participants were to submit an emission schedule (which didn't even have to include reductions) by January 31, 2010. That date came and went with little fanfare and with the vast majority of the participants submitting absolutely nothing. The head of the Framework Convention on Climate Change, Yvo de Boer, resigned on February 18.

Obviously, no one can isolate whether or not Climategate figured in the intransigence of the rapidly developing large emitters. But not a day went by during the Copenhagen meeting without a new Climategate story or revelation. Having said that, one can state with certainty that the lack of any substantive agreement in Copenhagen further incentivized the Senate to avoid considering cap-and-trade.

Climategate had kicked the blogosphere into high dudgeon. Influential icons such as McIntyre's http://www.climateaudit.org and Anthony Watts's wattsupwiththat.com carried at least a story a day. At the same time, both blogs began to run outside contributions on major problems with the UN's Intergovernmental Panel on Climate Change, providing even more cover for those who saw cap-and-trade as a political liability.

The Decline of the IPCC

Climategate and Copenhagen certainly threw up a lot of political roadblocks for the Senate to negotiate on its way to passing its version of cap-and-trade. But, of course, it would always have the IPCC to rely on to provide scientific cover.

Or so it seemed. The IPCC itself suffered a series of disastrous reversals in 2009 and 2010 that began with the Climategate e-mails.

From Phil Jones, head of the CRU to Mike Mann at Penn State, May 29, 2008:

RE: IPCC & FOI

> Can you delete any e-mails you may have had with Keith
> re AR4? [this is the Fourth Assessment report of the IPCC,
> published in May 2007] Keith [Briffa, another CRU scientist]
> will do likewise. He's not in at the moment—minor family
> crisis. Can you also e-mail Gene [Wahl] and get him to do
> the same? I don't have his new e-mail address. We will be
> getting Caspar [Amman] to do likewise.

This is a request by Jones to Mann to delete any e-mails that he had with CRU scientist Keith Briffa with regard to the Fourth Assessment Report (AR4), fearing that there might be some FOIA requests concerning correspondence about that influential 2007 document.

What is odd is that the IPCC places the specific reviewer comments in the public record, so whatever Jones is so concerned about is *not* any peer-review commentary on the report. It is noteworthy that Eugene Wahl (a paleoclimatologist with the National Oceanic and Atmospheric Administration) and Caspar Amman (a climate modeler with the U.S. National Center for Atmospheric Research) had authored a paper supporting Mann's "hockey stick," and it was having a difficult time in peer review. Ultimately, as revealed in the Climategate e-mails, publication deadlines were indeed manipulated to allow it to be cited in the 2007 IPCC report.

More than any other of the Climategate e-mails about the IPCC (and there are many), this one was particularly harmful. The review process for the AR4 began in 2005 and closed months before its publication in May 2007. Consequently, whatever Jones felt that he and Briffa had to destroy was on their computers for years and was clearly something that was on their minds. What the correspondence was between Jones, Mann, Briffa, Wahl, and Amman about the AR4 (or, perhaps, to the authors of the AR4?) has never been revealed, despite multiple "investigations" of the CRU, Jones, and Professor Mann.

Problems with the 2007 IPCC Report

The IPCC divides its reports into products of three "working groups": climate science (Working Group 1), effects of climate change (WG2), and mitigation and adaptation (WG3).

The WG2 chapter on Asia contained the following statement with regard to the massive Himalayan icecap, the largest nonpolar glacial system in the world:

The likelihood of them disappearing by the year 2035 and perhaps sooner is very high if the Earth keeps warming at the current rate.

Equal Treatment for Equal People?

Climategate emboldened a number of people on all sides of the global warming issue to begin to submit FOIA requests for e-mails of scientists who might be required to provide them if asked. One "excuse," for example, would be that a scientist had some type of taxpayer support for his or her research, which applies to just about everyone in the business.

Back around the time of publication of the first "hockey stick" papers, I was the first person given permission by my department to contact Mike Mann in order to recruit him to the University of Virginia faculty. Silly me, I thought intellectual diversity would be good for our reputation.

Our recruitment was successful, and Mike Mann was on the faculty from 1999 through 2005, when he left for Penn State over a job dispute. So naturally there were a lot of e-mails in the Climategate time frame (1998–2009) that Mike had written and received at U.Va., and many of them were likely germane to any investigation of his conduct.

A member of the Virginia House of Delegates, Bob Marshall (R-Prince William County), sent a FOIA request to U.Va. for Mann's relevant e-mails in early December 2009. U.Va. informed Marshall that they were no longer available because Mann was a former employee, and it is normal procedure to purge the e-mails of retired or former faculty from the university's server.

Then, on December 17, Greenpeace submitted a FOIA request for my e-mails from U.Va. U.Va.'s Public Information Office informed me that it intended to comply.

One problem—I'm a former employee, too, having accepted a buyout package in June 2007.

So in January 2010, I asked Elizabeth Wilkerson, special projects officer at U.Va.'s Office for Public Affairs, why U.Va. would retain my e-mails while having purged Mann's. She informed

(continued on next page)

> *(continued)*
>
> me that mine were kept "in a different place" from Mann's. I informed her that Mike and I were in the *same* department (Environmental Sciences) and that this would seem unlikely. Since then, I have received virtually no communication from U.Va. concerning my e-mails or Greenpeace's FOIA request.
>
> In fact, U.Va. did not tell the truth to Delegate Marshall. The e-mails were on the Environmental Science Department server, something the central university administration certainly knew.

The citation is a nonrefereed 2005 document from the World Wildlife Fund. WWF cited a news article in the (nonrefereed) science periodical *New Scientist*. *New Scientist* cited a nonrefereed article by Dr. Syed Hasnain, from the "Working Group on Himalayan Glaciology."

The depth of the Himalayan glacier complex is up to several hundred feet. It would be simply impossible to melt it in 25 years. An "urban legend" immediately sprang up that the IPCC had simply transposed 2305 and 2035, but this proved not to be true at all.

It was put in on purpose.

In an interview with the London *Sunday Mail*, published on January 24, 2010, Dr. Murari Lal, who was responsible for the IPCC WG2 chapter on Asia, acknowledged that the IPCC knew the 2035 figure was not from the refereed literature. "We knew the WWF report with the 2035 date was "'grey literature.'"

The Indian government was quite aware that the IPCC was misstating the behavior of the Himalayan glaciers and commissioned its own study by Dr. V. K. Riana, [9] which was immediately denounced as "schoolboy science" and "voodoo science" by Rajenda Pauchari, the head of the IPCC. Riana found absolutely no evidence that the Himalayan glaciers would largely disappear in 25 years; in fact, he noted that several of the Himalayan glaciers were growing.

Lal told the *Sunday Mail* that the gray literature citation was put in for political effect: "It related to several countries in this region and their water sources. We thought that if we can highlight it, it will impact policy-makers and politicians and encourage them to take some concrete action."[10]

Several scientists had criticized the 2035 statement during the review process for the WG2 document; their comments were obviously ignored, given that the figure 2035 remained in all the IPCC drafts and revisions, including the final copy.

This fact leads to a most interesting question that has never been discussed: did the senior climatologist for WG2 read any drafts of the document before publication?

That climatologist is Martin Parry, who is well known in academic circles, having done a fair amount of research on climate and agriculture. Anyone with even the most rudimentary knowledge of climate science knows that the 2035 figure is wrong. One is therefore forced to hypothesize that Parry, who is listed as the first author of the WG2 document, did not even read it closely enough to have seen that number.

The IPCC used yet another non-peer-reviewed study by WWF to scare people into believing that very slight changes in rainfall would destroy the Amazonian rain forest, when it stated:

> Up to 40% of the Amazonian forests could react drastically to even a slight reduction in precipitation; this means that the tropical vegetation, hydrology and climate system in South America could change very rapidly to another steady state, not necessarily producing gradual changes between the current and the future situation (Rowell and Moore, 2000).

Rowell and Moore (2000)[11] is not a refereed citation.

In reality, the Amazon forest is quite resilient. Two years before the AR4 was published, the Amazon experienced one of the driest years in its recorded climate history. While lakes dried up and river flows were severely reduced, satellite data found little if any change in the volume or appearance of the tropical forest.[12] It is pretty safe to say that there were a large number of IPCC authors and reviewers who knew of the 2005 drought and also had firsthand experience in the forest itself. One is then left to wonder how a nonrefereed document with little resemblance to the reality being observed at the time of the IPCC report's review was allowed to stand through all the revisions and ultimately be published in the final version.

The "Synthesis Report" of the IPCC is supposed to summarize all three working group reports for use by policymakers. It contains this statement on African agriculture: "By 2020, in some countries, yields from rain-fed agriculture could be reduced by up to 50%."[13]

Again, Parry could not have read work with his own name on it. His consulting group, Martin Parry Associates, produced two reports (at a cost of approximately $125,000 to the British government) on African agriculture that had a "worst-case" scenario by 2080 (not 2050) of "up to a 30%" reduction in yields.[14] This erroneous statement—about the 50 percent loss in yield by 2050—was often invoked by none other than Pauchari. Addressing a group of students attending a "model climate summit" in Potsdam in September 2009, Pauchari said, "I speak to you in the voice of the world's scientific community," and that "in some countries of Africa yields from rain-fed agriculture could be reduced by up to 50 percent."[15]

As is becoming numbingly repetitive, Pauchari was relying on yet another non-peer-reviewed paper, this time from the "Climate Change Knowledge Network." The citation given in WG2 is:

> Agoumi, A., 2003: Vulnerability of North African countries to climatic changes: adaptation and implementation strategies for climatic change. Developing Perspectives on Climate Change: Issues and Analysis from Developing Countries and Countries with Economies in Transition. IISD/Climate Change Knowledge Network, 14 pp.

Beginning to notice something about the errors? They're all exaggerations, and they have no basis in the refereed literature. No one has yet found a factual statement in the AR4 that is the opposite— an underestimate of climate change or its effects based on a nonstandard citation.

There's more:

> The Netherlands is an example of a country highly susceptible to both sea-level rise and river flooding because 55% of its territory is below sea level where 60% of its population lives and 65% of its Gross National Product (GNP) is produced.[16]

This statement is completely unsourced. The IPCC then blamed the Dutch Environment Ministry for the information, which is fine, but again, where is the peer-reviewed citation? Just because a government bureaucrat says something doesn't make it true.

Ultimately, the same ministry issued a clarification stating that 26 percent of the Netherlands is below sea level and 29 percent is subject to riverine flooding (which adds up to 55 percent).

River flooding has very little to do with global warming. Inland rivers exceed their banks because of heavy rainfall events rather than sea level rise. But there's no evidence for any increase in European storminess. Writing in the journal *Climate Dynamics* in 2008, Christoph Matulla and coauthors found absolutely no sign of an increase in storminess as surface temperature of the planet rose in the 20th century.[17] Lars Barring and Hans von Storch found the same in 2004, published in the journal *Geophysical Research Letters*.[18]

So, even the "clarified" statement is misleading.

Finally, another major gaffe, this time in the WG1 report pertaining to observations of hemispheric sea ice, from Chapter 4, "Observations: Changes in Snow, Ice, and Frozen Ground":

> There is a significant decreasing trend in arctic sea ice extent of $-33 \pm 7.4 \times 10^3$ km^2 yr^{-1} (equivalent to $-2.7 \pm 0.6\%$ per decade), whereas the Antarctic results show a small positive trend of $5.6 \pm 9.2 \times 10^3$ km^2 yr^{-1} ($0.47 \pm 0.8\%$ per decade), which is not statistically significant.[19]

So the reader is left with the impression that there is a significant decline in Northern Hemisphere sea ice but no change (i.e., not a statistically significant one) in the Southern Hemisphere.

This misconception gets played further in the "Executive Summary" for Chapter 4 (the only part, say, a congressional staffer might read):

> Satellite data indicate a continuation of the $2.7 \pm 0.6\%$ per decade decline in annual mean arctic sea ice extent since 1978. The decline for summer extent is larger than for winter, with the summer minimum declining at a rate of $7.4 \pm 2.4\%$ per decade since 1979. Other data indicate that the summer decline began around 1970. Similar observations in the Antarctic reveal larger interannual variability but no consistent trends.[20]

The overall "Summary for Policymakers" for the WG1 report— which is by far the most "read" portion of the report said:

> Antarctic sea ice extent continues to show interannual variability and localized changes but no statistically significant average trends, consistent with the lack of warming reflected in atmospheric temperatures averaged across the region.[21]

63

Figure 2.8
EXTENT OF SOUTHERN HEMISPHERE SEA ICE, 1979–2010

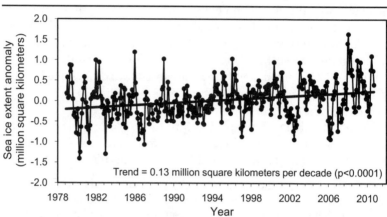

SOURCE: *Cryosphere Today*, http://arctic.atmos.uiuc.edu/cryosphere/.

NOTE: Satellite measurements beginning in 1979 clearly show a statistically significant (probability of greater than .9999) increase in Southern Hemisphere sea ice.

This is wrong. Satellite data indeed show a statistically significant *increase* in the extent of Antarctic sea ice. Figure 2.8 shows the data from *Cryosphere Today*, a daily update of sea ice published at the University of Illinois.[22]

The AR4 did not include references to any previous study that showed that Antarctic sea ice trends were increasing in a statistically significant way, including Cavalieri and others (1997)[23] and Parkinson and others (1999).[24] Nor did the AR4 include a reference to Zwally and others (2002) in the *Journal of Geophysical Research*, which found:

> The derived 20 year trend in sea ice extent from the monthly deviations is $11.18 \pm 4.19 \times 10^3$ km^2yr^{-1} or $0.98 \pm 0.37\%$ (decade)$^{-1}$ for the entire Antarctic sea ice cover, which is *significantly* positive.[25] [emphasis added.]

Instead, the IPCC used a non-peer-reviewed reference, in this case "an updated version of the analysis done by Comiso (2003)." Comiso (2003) is a mere book chapter, not a refereed journal article:

Comiso, J. C., 2003: Large scale characteristics and variability of the global sea ice cover. In: *Sea Ice—An Introduction to Its Physics, Biology, Chemistry, and Geology* [Thomas, D. and G. S. Dieckmann (eds.)]. Blackwell Science, Oxford, UK, pp. 112–142.

There are a few more things worth considering.

Josefino Comiso (the author of the above-mentioned book chapter) was a contributing author of the AR4 chapter on snow and ice, so the coordinating lead authors (a rung above) probably just turned directly to him to provide a non-peer-reviewed update.

It gets worse. Comiso subsequently published a paper (along with Fumihiko Nishio) in the *Journal of Geophysical Research* in 2008[26] that added only one additional year to the IPCC analysis (i.e., through 2006 instead of 2005), and once again found a *statistically significant* increase in Antarctic sea ice (see Figures 2.8 and 2.9):

> When updated to 2006, the trends in ice extent and area ... in the Antarctic remains slight but positive at 0.9 ± 0.2 and 1.7 ± 0.3% per decade.

These trends are, again, by anyone's reckoning, statistically significant.

And just in case further evidence is needed, a 2009 paper by Turner and others[27] (of which Comiso was a coauthor), concluded:

> Based on a new analysis of passive microwave satellite data, we demonstrate that the annual mean extent of Antarctic sea ice has increased at a statistically significant rate of 0.97% dec^{-1} since the late 1970s.

This rate of increase is nearly *twice as great as the value given in the AR4* (from its non-peer-reviewed source).

So, the peer-reviewed literature extant at the time of the AR4, as well as that published since the release of the AR4, shows that there has been a significant increase in the extent of sea ice around Antarctica since the time of the first satellite observations in the late 1970s. And yet the AR4 somehow "assessed" the evidence and determined not only that the increase was only half the rate established in the peer-reviewed literature but also that it was statistically insignificant as well. The increase in sea ice in the Antarctic was downplayed in preference to highlighting the observed decrease in sea ice in the Arctic.

As noted earlier, there's no analogous opposite to the UN's gaffes. Nowhere do we read that the IPCC *under*estimated the magnitude of climate change or its effects using a gray literature source. We can be pretty sure—given the amount of attention that the errors noted above have received—that people have been looking; obviously they have found none.

So that leads to an interesting proposition, namely, that one can say with statistical confidence that indeed the IPCC is biased. In all five instances above, the IPCC says something is happening that is actually worse than portrayed in the peer-reviewed literature. In other words, they are all in the same direction while every mistake should have an equal probability of being in the "worse" or "not as bad as" direction.

That equal probability is the same as getting a head or a tail on an individual coin toss. So what is the chance of throwing five heads or tails in a row? It is .03. Normally, scientists say something is statistically significant when the probability of it occurring by chance is .05 or less. So there you have it. The UN is biased. Significantly.

EPA's "Endangerment" Finding

Finally, the Senate was absolved of any responsibility for expensive emissions regulation by the Environmental Protection Agency.

On April 2, 2007, the Supreme Court handed down its landmark decision in *Massachusetts v. EPA*, in which it determined that the Clean Air Act Amendments of 1990 required that EPA determine whether or not carbon dioxide was a "pollutant," meaning something that endangered human health and welfare. If it found an "endangerment," then EPA would, under the law, be required to regulate (reduce) our emissions of it, unless specifically exempted by an act of Congress.

EPA is an agency of the executive branch of our government, so it was not surprising that the George W. Bush administration passed the ball forward, choosing not to explicitly find carbon dioxide a pollutant, but when the Obama administration came to Washington, it was not long before EPA indeed first "proposed" an endangerment finding in April 2009. Finally, on December 7, 2009, the first day of the ill-fated Copenhagen climate change summit, EPA did issue an endangerment finding.

The timing was obvious. The American Clean Energy and Security Act passed the House the previous June, but there was no pending legislation in the Senate. If Obama was to go to Copenhagen with any credibility, he had to assure other nations whom he wanted to agree to emission reductions that indeed the United States would cut its carbon dioxide as well and in a significant fashion.

So Obama essentially had a promise that there would be some carbon dioxide regulations coming from some branch of our government. And clearly, he was remarkably unconvincing, as the only "agreement" to come out of Copenhagen was a promise that the participating nations would specify some nonbinding "goals" for emission reductions by the end of the next month (which were waived; see previous mention).

EPA's December finding was based mainly on two compendia that claimed to be comprehensive reviews of the scientific literature on global warming: the Fourth Assessment Report of the IPCC (whose follies were just noted) and the 2009 "synthesis report" from the U.S. Climate Change Science Program,[28] both obviously political entities. EPA extracted from both reports the following language:

> Most of the observed increase in global average temperature since the mid-20th century is very likely due to the observed increase in anthropogenic GHG [greenhouse gas] concentrations.

Soon after the IPCC report, David Thompson and several others (including Climategate's Phil Jones) published a paper in *Nature*[29] showing a cold bias in measurement of sea surface temperatures from the early 1940s through the mid-1960s. This adjustment has yet to be incorporated into the temperature history.

At the time of the IPCC report, Canada's Ross McKitrick and I published a paper in the *Journal of Geophysics*[30] showing a clear and systematic "nonclimatic" warming—from changes in land use and problems with station maintenance—in temperatures measured at weather stations. This adjustment was also not factored into the temperature history.

Earlier in 2010, Susan Solomon of the National Oceanic and Atmospheric Administration published a bombshell in *Science*[31] in which she argued that the lack of recent warming was likely due to fluctuations in water vapor way up in the stratosphere—changes that bear no obvious relationship to greenhouse gas (GHG) emissions. This means that an additional, unanticipated fraction of the observed temperature trend is due to something other than greenhouse gases.

In 2008, V. Ramanathan of the Scripps Institute of Oceanography (along with University of Iowa's Greg Carmichael) summarized the scientific literature on the emissions of black carbon (aka "soot") and concluded they were responsible for about 25 percent of global warming.[32] Carbon particles are *not* GHGs. This is an additional non-greenhouse gas factor producing warming.

It is true that black carbon (soot) is also a result of the combustion of fossil fuels, but it also results from the combustion of pretty much anything, such as a forest or prairie. Eliminating fossil fuels would certainly reduce soot. However, removing carbon dioxide from the effluent of coal-burning or natural gas–burning power plants and storing it somewhere (so-called carbon capture and storage—which itself demands an incredible amount of energy and infrastructure, subsidized in the American Clean Energy and Security Act) would leave the soot warming effect intact.

Taken together, all of these account for a considerable fraction of the observed trend since the mid-20th century, and, depending upon the way their influence is calculated, could in fact be responsible for around one half of the observed warming. However, it is a subject of a vigorous debate as to how to make these adjustments.

While the resolve in the Senate was certainly weakened by Climategate, Copenhagen, and the IPCC brouhahas, what was the result of EPA's endangerment finding?

The Senate knows that cap-and-trade isn't particularly popular and that it is very expensive. While it's popular to bluster in Washington that "if the Senate does not act, EPA will," why would the Senate think that is such a bad deal? EPA takes the onus away and lands it squarely in the Oval Office, where only one person stands for election every four years, as opposed to 33 senators every two. In addition, judging from the 2009 and 2010 midterm elections, President Obama isn't viewed as particularly helpful to Democratic gubernatorial or senatorial candidates. So how upset will they be to see him go? The bottom line is that an unexpected constellation of inconvenient events—the patent unpopularity of cap-and-trade legislation passed by the House, Climategate, Copenhagen, and the loss of IPCC credibility—all while the Senate was considering legislation, made it pretty much improbable that it would ever pass a bill like the House's ACES. EPA's endangerment finding made it impossible.

3. Bias in the Peer-Review Process: A Cautionary and Personal Account

Ross McKitrick

The second chapter in this volume goes to the core of what we consider to be the canon of science, which is the peer-reviewed, refereed scientific literature. McKitrick's and my trials and tribulations over journal publication are similar to those experienced by many other colleagues. Unfortunately, the Climategate e-mails revealed that indeed there has been systematic pressure on journal editors to reject manuscripts not toeing the line about disastrous climate change. Even more unfortunate, my experience and that of others are that the post-Climategate environment has made this situation worse, not better. It is now virtually impossible to publish anything against the alarmist grain. The piles of unpublished manuscripts sitting on active scientists' desks are growing into gargantuan proportions. Surely, one day, there will be an incentive and an initiative to put them in the public domain—probably after people realize the enormous costs that will accrue in futile attempts to stop planetary warming.

One interpretation of the infiltration of global warming into so many aspects of our political life is that the United Nations' Intergovernmental Panel on Climate Change, by claiming to be the "consensus of scientists," is actually defining a "paradigm" in the sense of the late historian of science Thomas Kuhn. To Kuhn, paradigms are overarching logical structures, and the work of "normal science" is the care and feeding of paradigms with data and research findings that confirm that indeed the paradigm is a correct representation of scientific reality.

Kuhn notes that paradigms are very resistant to change, despite data or experiments that don't "fit." In his 1962 classic *The Structure of Scientific Revolutions*, he states:

(continued on next page)

(continued)

> "In science, ... novelty emerges only with difficulty, manifested by resistance, against a background provided by expectation. Initially, only the anticipated and usual are experienced even under circumstances where anomaly is later to be observed.[1]

Consequently, I wasn't very surprised when the IPCC dismissed, without appropriate logic or citation, findings about systematic errors in global temperature records that Ross McKitrick and I had published in the peer-reviewed literature. Nor was I surprised at how resistant the scientific community was to publishing those results or important follow-on work.

This is the story of those difficulties with the IPCC and with the keepers of the paradigm. It is a story of how the core of the science literature is becoming one-dimensional. How much this has to do with the grief caused to editors by the Climategate gang will never be known; it's equally possible that the responsible editors were quite sympathetic with the authors of the e-mails and simply wanted to demonstrate their fealty by excluding work that the Climatgaters wouldn't like from their journals.

This is a problem with profound consequences. The abject difficulty of publishing virtually anything that concludes that warming is likely to be lower than the current mean projections of the IPCC is creating a remarkable bias in climate science. Unfortunately, policymakers and the political class cannot see what is happening because the absence of these publications gives the appearance of unanimity of science that is not there.

Starting in 2007, I spent two years trying to publish a paper to refute an important claim in the IPCC's Fourth Assessment Report (called AR4 in the climate community). The claim in question was not just wrong but was based on fabricated evidence. Showing that the claim was fabricated was easy: It suffices merely to quote the section of the report, since no supporting evidence is given. But unsupported guesses may turn out to be true. Showing that the IPCC claim is also *false* took some mundane statistical work, but the results were clear. Once the numbers were crunched and the paper was written, I began sending it to science journals.

Having published several against-the-flow papers in climatology journals, I did not expect a smooth ride, but the process eventually became surreal. In the end, the paper was accepted for publication, but not in a climatology journal. Fortunately for me, I am an economist, not a climatologist, and my career doesn't depend on getting published in climatology journals. If I were a young climatologist, I would have learned that my career prospects would be much better if I never wrote papers that question the IPCC. The skewing of the literature (and careers) can only be bad for society, which depends on scientists and the scientific literature for trustworthy advice for wise policy decisions.

I decided to take this story public because of what it reveals about the journal peer-review process in the field of climatology. Whether climatologists like it or not, the general public has taken a large and legitimate interest in how the peer-review process for climatology journals works, because it has been told for years that it will have to face lots of new taxes, charges, fees, and regulations because of what has been printed in climatology journals. Because of the policy stakes, a distorted peer-review process is no longer a private matter to be sorted out among academic specialists. And to the extent the specialists are unable or unwilling to fix the process, they cannot complain that the public credibility of their discipline suffers.

The Background Issue: Temperature Data Contamination

Climate data are *supposed* to be a measure of something that does not, in most places, even exist. In most (inhabited) places around the world, the temperature outside would only be the climate if you happen to live where no one has ever changed the surroundings, either through deforestation or agriculture, road building or urbanization, or any other modification of the landscape. Otherwise, some of the temperature changes can be attributed to the local modifications.

Even if you can find undisturbed locations, you might not have records that go back very far. Or you might have a long sequence of records collected using different instruments that need to be joined somehow. Or you might have records with gaps in them, or records that weren't all sampled at the same time of the day, or other such problems.

Most likely, you will have temperature data series collected in places that were gradually built up over time through urbanization. Further, the long-term site may not be a randomly chosen representative of a region. If located at an original point of commerce, the site will likely be along some type of watercourse, as rivers were important for commercial transportation in the early 19th century. So most long-term records, at least at their beginning, are likely to be for valleys where cold air pools at night, giving them a climatic history potentially different from the wider area in which they are located.

Producing a long time series of climate data requires making a lot of assumptions about how the various dribs and drabs of temperature data around the world need to be adjusted and tweaked in order to reveal the continuous "climate signal," as it is called. In other words, all the changes in the recorded temperatures that are caused by things other than climate change need to be filtered out of the data: urbanization, deforestation, equipment modification, and so forth. These conditions are called "inhomogeneities."

It would be fine if the climate signal were large and the inhomogeneities were small. But the reverse is true. We are looking for changes measured in tenths or hundredths of a degree per decade, using data from weather stations where the inhomogeneities can easily shift the record by several degrees. So the adjustment rules matter. Whenever you see a climate data series, such as the so-called global temperature, bear in mind that what you are seeing is the output of a model, not a reading from a scientific instrument. Thermometers produce some of the basic input data, but the models take over from there. Maybe the models are just right, applying perfect adjustments and not a bit more. Maybe they really do filter out all the inhomogeneities, yielding an output series so precise that we can talk meaningfully of changes on the order of a few hundredths of a degree per decade, confident that it's a pure climate signal.

The IPCC certainly thinks so. In its Fourth Assessment Report,[2] as in the previous three, the claim that its data are properly adjusted to remove nonclimatic contamination was invoked several times. It is an essential, bedrock assumption behind all key IPCC conclusions. Global temperature trends were presented in Table 3.2 on page 243 of volume 1 of the AR4. The accompanying text (page 242) states that the data uncertainties "take into account" biases due to urbanization.

The executive summary to the chapter (page 237) asserts: "Urban heat island effects are real but local, and have not biased the large-scale trends. . . . [T]he very real but local effects are avoided or accounted for in the data sets used." The influential "Summary for Policymakers" stated:

> Urban heat island effects are real but local, and have a negligible influence (less than 0.006°C per decade over land and zero over the oceans) on these values.[3]

The supporting citation was to Section 3.2. Make a note of that: Section 3.2 will turn out to be important.

Chapter 9 of the AR4 provides the summary of evidence attributing warming to greenhouse gases. The problem of surface data contamination is set aside as follows:

> Systematic instrumental errors, such as changes in measurement practices or urbanisation, could be more important, especially earlier in the record (Chapter 3), although these errors are calculated to be relatively small at large spatial scales. Urbanisation effects appear to have negligible effects on continental and hemispheric average temperatures (Chapter 3).[4]

Again, the case for ignoring the issue of data quality problems consists of a citation to Chapter 3 of the AR4.

Many scientists believe the climate data are just fine. To take one example, a paper in the *Journal of the American Statistical Association* used surface climate data to test some properties of climate models.[5] Like countless papers before them, the authors had to consider, if only for a brief moment, whether the climate data on which their analysis rested were garbage or not. They dispensed with the question as follows:

> Inhomogeneities in the data arise mainly due to changes in instruments, exposure, station location (elevation, position), ship height, observation time, urbanization effects, and the method used to calculate averages. However, these effects are all well understood and taken into account in the construction of the data set.[6]

Ah, there you go. A little further on in their paper, after they had observed some discrepancies between model-generated and

73

observed trends (which they label D_i), the authors explain why they do not attribute those discrepancies to data contamination:

> [Climate] scientists have fairly strong confidence in the quality of their observational data compared with the climate model biases. Therefore, we assume that the effect of observational errors to D_i is negligible.[7]

There's your proof: appeal to authority. But I am old-fashioned enough to want to know *why* they are so confident. Have they really drilled into the issue? Let's be clear what the stakes are in all of this. If the effects are *not* well understood and they are *not* taken into account in the construction of the data set, then *all* the analysis using climate data over land may be flawed. That includes all the studies that claim to have detected global warming and attributed it to greenhouse gases.

A key basis for the IPCC's claim comes from the Climate Research Unit at the University of East Anglia. The CRU provides the CRU-TEM surface climate data set relied on by so many researchers and by the IPCC. The CRU webpage http://www.cru.uea.ac.uk/cru/data/hrg/ references several data products. One series is called CRU TS 1.x, 2.x, and 3.x. These data sets are interesting for our purposes because they are not subject to adjustments for nonclimatic influences. Users are explicitly cautioned not to use the TS data for the kind of climatic analysis found in IPCC reports. The 1.2 release of this product[8] contained FAQs related to time series analysis.[9] The first question, and its answer, are reproduced in part below.

> Question One
>
> Q1. Is it legitimate to use CRU TS 2.0 to "detect anthropogenic climate change" (IPCC language)?
>
> A1. No. CRU TS 2.0 is specifically not designed for climate change detection or attribution in the classic IPCC sense. The classic IPCC detection issue deals with the distinctly anthropogenic climate changes we are already experiencing. Therefore it is necessary, for IPCC detection to work, to remove all influences of urban development or land use change on the station data. In contrast, the primary purpose for which CRU TS 2.0 has been constructed is to permit environmental modellers to incorporate into their models as accurate a representation as possible of month to month

74

climate variations, as experienced in the recent past. Therefore influences from urban development or land use change
remain an integral part of the dataset. We emphasise that
we use all available climate data. If you want to examine the
detection of anthropogenic climate change, we recommend
that you use the Jones temperature dataset. This is on a
coarser (5 degree) grid, but it is optimized for the reliable
detection of anthropogenic trends.

The link attached to Jones' name leads to http://www.cru.
uea.ac.uk/cru/data/temperature/, the homepage for the HadCRUT
data products (the land-only portion is CRUTEM). The clear implication is that users will find therein data that have been adjusted to
remove nonclimatic influences. Readers are referred to some academic papers for the explanation of the process. Those papers don't
actually tell you how it is done; they mostly tell you that *something*
was done and that the remaining inhomogeneities are small. For
instance, Jones and others explain the adjustments this way:

> All 2000+ station time series used have been assessed for
> homogeneity by subjective interstation comparisons per-
> formed on a local basis. Many stations were adjusted and
> some omitted because of anomalous warming trends and/
> or numerous nonclimatic jumps (complete details are given
> by Jones et al. [1985, 1986c]).[10]

The cited papers from the 1980s are technical reports to the U.S.
Department of Energy, referring to the construction of data sets
that took place in the early 1980s. They are irrelevant since we are
concerned with temperature data collected after 1980. In the early
1980s, they would not have known what adjustments would be
needed for data collected in the late 1990s. And in any case, another
CRU paper published in 2005 states that to properly adjust the data
would require a global comparison of urban versus rural records,
but classifying records in this way is not possible since "no such
complete meta-data are available." So in that paper, the authors
apply an assumption that the bias is no larger than 0.0055 degree
per decade. Round that up to 0.006 degree, and you have the basis
for the IPCC claim I quoted earlier from the "Summary for Policymakers" that urban heat islands "have a negligible influence (less
than 0.006°C per decade over land)."

Absence of Evidence versus Evidence of Absence

Various researchers have looked at the question of whether the CRU data are biased and have come to mixed conclusions. The CRU cites the 2004 work of David Parker, who argues that the CRUTEM data are not contaminated with nonclimatic biases.[11] Parker is a UK Met Office scientist who coauthors with CRU staff. So it is not exactly independent work. The papers base their conclusions on the failure to find a difference between warming on windy nights versus calm nights. (Nights tend to be warmer in cities because the built-up land impedes the flow of ventilating winds.) But this is a problematic style of argument. Sometimes a researcher fails to find an effect because the effect really isn't there. But sometimes the effect is there and the study was just poorly designed, or the statistical analysis was sloppy, or the researcher looked in the wrong place. That is why an argument based on the failure to find an effect is tentative at best.

What one needs to ask in such contexts is, first, whether the method that didn't find the effect is generally viewed as the right way to look for it and, second, whether other researchers looked at the same problem in a different way and *did* find an effect. The answer to the first question is no. Papers have been published in good journals arguing that the method that didn't find the effect might fail to find it even if it is there.[12]

And the answer to the second question is yes: two different teams, working independently, published strong evidence of the effect. So taking scientific literature regarding the CRU surface temperature data as a whole, it is legitimate to point to the Met Office study that failed to find evidence of contamination. But it is not legitimate to stop there.

I was on one of the teams that published evidence of the effect. I worked with George Mason University climatologist Patrick Michaels. Just before we published our results in 2004 in the journal *Climate Research*, a team of Dutch meteorologists (Jos de Laat and Ahilleas Maurellis) published a paper showing that they had also asked the question in a different way and found the effect.[13] They and we also published follow-up papers extending our results on new data sets.[14]

Here is what Pat and I did. We started with two temperature data sets, each with observations from 1979 to 2000 for 218 locations around the world. The first data set, which we got from the National Aeronautics and Space Administration, was, like the TS data, unadjusted for inhomogeneities. We fit a linear trend at each location. That gave us a spatial pattern of temperature trends. Then we got data on climatological variables for the same 218 locations that would plausibly explain the pattern of trends. We obtained the spatial pattern of temperature trends as measured by weather satellites in the lower troposphere, as well as measures of local mean air pressure and a dryness indicator, latitude, and proximity to a coastline.

Then we added data on socioeconomic variables. In the unadjusted data, we expected to find that indicators of local industrial activity, data quality, and other socioeconomic variables would affect the observed temperature trends. We used multiple regression analysis to show that this was, indeed, the case. The correlations were very strong, even after controlling for the climatic and geographic effects.

Then we took the CRU data—the adjusted series that everyone says is free from such signals. The correlations were smaller but still large and statistically significant. The spatial pattern of trends in CRU temperature data does not appear to be measuring just climate: it is partly measuring the spatial pattern of industrialization.

Our paper was published in *Climate Research* in 2004.[15] There was some excitement when a blogger found a minor error in our computer code (we had released the code at the time of publication), but we sent a correction[16] to the journal immediately and showed that the results hardly changed. A comment was submitted to the journal claiming that our results failed an independent validation.[17] But that test was overly extreme: it consisted of using only Southern Hemisphere data and a subset of explanatory variables and showed that the resulting estimation did not form very good predictions of the omitted Northern Hemisphere data. Nobody had ever used a test like that before. We were able to show that our model passed a more reasonable and conventional cross-validation test.[18]

De Laat and Maurellis published a second paper in 2006[19] extending their earlier findings. Pat and I did as well, in 2007,[20] in the *Journal of Geophysical Research*, but it did not appear until after the IPCC had issued a deadline for the appearance of new papers that could be cited in its report. Nonetheless, taking our paper and the two Dutch papers together, as well as the papers questioning the method that had failed to find evidence of contamination, the peer-reviewed literature now presented a strong case that the CRU surface temperature data were compromised by nonclimatic biases. The studies also suggested that the contamination effects added up to an overstatement of warming.

E-Mail, July 8, 2004

The scientist who runs the CRU and takes primary responsibility for the quality of the data is Phil Jones. According to the Climategate e-mails,[21] on July 8, 2004, Phil Jones wrote to Michael Mann:

> From: Phil Jones <p.jones@xxxxxxxxx.xxx> To: "Michael E. Mann" <mann@xxxxxxxxx.xxx> Subject: HIGHLY CONFIDENTIAL Date: Thu Jul 8 16:30:16 2004
>
> Mike, Only have it in the pdf form. FYI ONLY—don't pass on. Relevant paras are the last 2 in section 4 on p13. As I said it is worded carefully due to Adrian knowing Eugenia for years. He knows they're wrong, but he succumbed to her almost pleading with him to tone it down as it might affect her proposals in the future! I didn't say any of this, so be careful how you use it—if at all. Keep quiet also that you have the pdf.
>
> The attachment is a very good paper—I've been pushing Adrian over the last weeks to get it submitted to JGR or J. Climate. The main results are great for CRU and also for ERA-40. The basic message is clear—you have to put enough surface and sonde observations into a model to produce Reanalyses. The jumps when the data input change stand out so clearly. NCEP [National Centers for Environmental Prediction] does many odd things also around sea ice and over snow and ice.
>
> *The other paper by MM is just garbage—as you knew. De Freitas again. Pielke is also losing all credibility as well by replying to the mad Finn as well—frequently as I see it.*
>
> *I can't see either of these papers being in the next IPCC report. Kevin and I will keep them out somehow—even if we have to redefine what the peer-review literature is!* Cheers
>
> Phil
>
> Prof. Phil Jones Climatic Research Unit Telephone +44 (0) 1603 592090 School of Environmental Sciences Fax +44 (0) 1603 507784 University of East Anglia Norwich E-mail p.jones@xxxxxxxxx.xxx NR4 7TJ UK

I have italicized the juicy part. "MM" is McKitrick and Michaels, that is, Pat's and my 2004 paper. De Freitas is Chris de Freitas, the editor who handled our paper. De Freitas has been head of science and technology and a vice chancellor at the University of Auckland. Jones is alluding to him because de Freitas had earlier handled a paper that questioned another doctrine of the IPCC, namely, that the medieval era was colder than the present. The Climategate e-mails contain many heated exchanges around that issue wherein people like Jones and Mann discuss whether to launch a campaign to destroy the reputation of *Climate Research*. In the earlier instance, the controversy prompted the publisher of *Climate Research* to conduct a review of the handling of the file, which concluded that de Freitas had done a good job. But by then, the well was poisoned, and several editorial board members quit.

The refereeing process Michaels and I went through was long and detailed. We had four referees, and initially none of them liked the paper. It took three rounds to settle all the objections before they approved publication, and de Freitas had made it clear he would not proceed without the support of all the referees.

Not that the name of the editor has anything to do with anything. One of the patterns I have encountered in response to this work has been that critics begin by saying, "I don't believe your results because of *X*," where *X* is some technical objection. But when I respond by showing either that *X* is irrelevant or that when I take it into account, the results don't change, the critic replies, "I don't care, I still don't believe them."[22] In other words, the stated objection is usually just a red herring: the critics just hate the results.

In 2006, I presented the findings of a follow-up study using a new and larger database, which yielded nearly identical findings, at a conference at Los Alamos, New Mexico. Chris Folland of the UK Met Office stood up and objected to the results, saying that they were a fluke due to strengthened atmospheric circulation effects over Europe, which I hadn't controlled for. So I asked, if I take Europe out of my sample and I get the same results, would you believe them then. After a moment's thought he said, "No, I still wouldn't believe them."

When our *Climate Research* paper came out in mid-2004, many of our critics pounced on the programming error and said, in effect, we're *wrong* because there was an error in the calculation of the cosine of latitude. But when we fixed that and the results held up, they still refused to believe them. They moved on to say we were wrong because we hadn't applied an adjustment for "error clustering," which is a legitimate concern for the kinds of data we used and because our sample was not truly global.

So when I did the analysis for the follow-up study, I used a clustering adjustment on the error term, and the results remained very strong. That paper was published in the *Journal of Geophysical Research—Atmosphere* in 2007. The critics who had pounced on the cosine error and the error clustering issue moved in again, rejecting the new findings by saying that we had a problem of spatial autocorrelation, which means the trends in one location are influenced by the trends in the surrounding region, which can bias the significance calculations.

The source of that objection was Rasmus Benestad, a blogger at realclimate.org, the online organ populated largely by principals in the Climategate e-mails, but he didn't present any statistical proof of the problem. So I wrote a program that tested for spatial autocorrelation, ran it, and showed that the results were not affected by it. And if I applied an adjustment for it anyway, the findings remained the same. I even submitted my response to the *Journal of Geophysical Research*, but the editor wrote back and said that he couldn't publish it because it was a reply to a comment that no one had submitted. Good point, I thought, so I e-mailed Rasmus, sending him my paper and the editor's note and suggesting he write up his blog post as a proper comment and send it to the *JGR*, so his comment and my reply could be sent out for peer review. Rasmus wrote me back on December 28, 2007, saying that he would think about it, adding:

> But I should also tell you that I'm getting more and more strapped for time, both at work and home. Deadlines and new projects are coming up. . . . [ellipsis in original]

Yes, yes, time pressures: I understand. I guess blogging takes up a lot of time. Well, it's been three years, and he still hasn't sent his comment to the *JGR*. I published the material elsewhere.

So when Jones said my paper was "just garbage" and referred to "De Freitas again," it's not as if he'd have taken a different view had the editor been someone else. I can't find any indication that

Jones has ever given a careful read to either of our papers on the subject. His reaction is purely emotional. Granted, a man is entitled to his emotions and biases, but the problem is that Jones had by this point accepted the IPCC's invitation to serve as a coordinating lead author.

As a coordinating lead author, he would be reviewing the published evidence on, among other things, the question of whether the CRU data were contaminated with nonclimatic inhomogeneities. Now it's true that the IPCC had put him in the conflict of interest. The IPCC needed someone to write a section of the report that would examine Jones's papers, as well as those of Jones's critics, and then offer a judgment on whether or not Jones was right. So it asked Jones to write the section. You would think that an agency bragging about having 3,000 brilliant scientists involved with it could figure out how to avoid such conflicts of interests.

Over time I have simply stopped being surprised by such conduct from the IPCC. In other words, I have stopped expecting ethical behavior from the IPCC. A commitment to ethical behavior would lead an organization to take every precaution against conflicts of interest and bias. An organization committed to high standards of impartiality and fairness would never even have contemplated asking Jones to be an author of chapter 3. The leaders of the IPCC, on the other hand, have likely never noticed how inappropriate the choice was; such is their blind spot.

In any case, once Jones accepted the IPCC's invitation, he gave up the right to be biased on behalf of the CRU. Yet in the e-mail sent a year before the IPCC expert review process would begin, he was already signaling his determination to block any mention of a paper that had provided significant statistical evidence that the data he supplied to the IPCC were potentially contaminated.

Keeping It Out of the IPCC

As it turns out, Jones did keep it out of the Fourth Assessment Report, at least for a while. The first draft of the report that went to reviewers contained no mention of either McKitrick and Michaels or the de Laat and Maurellis papers. (Jones was certainly aware of my paper since he mentioned it in the e-mail a year earlier.) I objected to the omission, as did another reviewer (Vincent Gray from New Zealand). The second draft was still silent on the subject. So I objected even further and wrote a longer challenge to the section. Expert review closed in June 2006. As of that point, there was no mention of the 2004 paper in the AR4.

Reviewers did not get to see the lead authors' responses to our comments until long after final publication. The response dossier contained the following reply to my first draft comments:

> Rejected. The locations of socioeconomic development happen to have coincided with maximum warming, not for the reason given by McKitrick and Mihaels [sic] (2004) but because of the strengthening of the Arctic Oscillation and the greater sensitivity of land than ocean to greenhouse forcing owing to the smaller thermal capacity of land. Parker (2005) demonstrates lack of urban influence.

David Parker, the UK Met Office scientist mentioned earlier, wrote that response. (I learned this as a result of a successful Freedom of Information Act petition by David Holland of the United Kingdom, who finally secured release of the review editor records for chapter 3 of the AR4 in May 2010, three years after the report was published.) Parker was a lead author for chapter 3, working under the direction of Phil Jones, one of the two coordinating lead authors. Parker's report to Jones was brief: "I have rejected the McKitrick and Michaels 2004 with appropriate reasons!"

If you have any doubts about the inbred nature of the IPCC, this episode should dispel them. Jones works at the CRU producing climate data. Jones takes note of the work of Jones's coauthor Parker, who has published a paper saying Jones's data are not contaminated. Jones then takes on the role of IPCC coordinating lead author, in which capacity he takes delivery of Jones's data and uses them to derive chapter conclusions. Before the start of the IPCC process, Jones notes with contempt a paper by an outsider critical of the quality of Jones's data set and boasts to a friend that he will keep it out of the IPCC report. Jones's coauthor Parker does the deed, relying on evidence published by Parker to justify rejecting criticism of coauthor Jones's data. This is what the IPCC means when it refers to its "comprehensive and objective" peer-review process.

As to the "appropriate reasons," the part about the strengthening of the Arctic Oscillation is bizarre on many levels. The Arctic Oscillation is a multidecadal cycle in prevailing winds over the Arctic region that can affect the severity of winters in high-latitude regions. Our study used data on locations around the world, including the southern end of South America and Australia. The IPCC report doesn't even attribute warming patterns in the *Arctic* to the Arctic Oscillation, let alone patterns in the farther reaches of the Southern Hemisphere. And the comparison of land and ocean is irrelevant. Our study looks only at the land areas, because there is no industrialization over the open ocean!

Because all mention of our work and that of de Laat and Maurellis had been kept out of the IPCC drafts, I assumed it would likewise be kept out of the published edition. So it was not until late 2007 that I became aware that the following paragraph had been inserted on page 244 of the Fourth Assessment Report:

> McKitrick and Michaels (2004) and De Laat and Maurellis (2006) attempted to demonstrate that geographical patterns of warming trends over land are strongly correlated with geographical patterns of industrial and socioeconomic development, implying that urbanisation and related land surface changes have caused much of the observed warming. *However, the locations of greatest socioeconomic development are also those that have been most warmed by atmospheric circulation changes (Sections 3.2.2.7 and 3.6.4), which exhibit large-scale coherence. Hence, the correlation of warming with industrial and socioeconomic development ceases to be statistically significant.* In addition, observed warming has been, and transient greenhouse-induced warming is expected to be, greater over land than over the oceans (Chapter 10), owing to the smaller thermal capacity of the land. (emphasis added)

The first point to dispense with is the reference to Sections 3.2.2.7 and 3.6.4 in support of the claim that "the locations of greatest socioeconomic development are also those that have been most warmed by atmospheric circulation changes." There is nothing whatsoever in either section that supports the point. In neither section is there any discussion of industrialization, socioeconomic development, urbanization, or any related term. Section 3.2.2.7 presents a spatial map of warming trends since 1979. The accompanying text states:

> Warming is strongest over the continental interiors of Asia
> and northwestern North America and over some mid-lati-
> tude ocean regions of the [Southern Hemisphere] as well as
> southeastern Brazil.

These are the regions of greatest socioeconomic development? The continental interior of Asia suffered economic decline after 1990, and northwestern North America is sparsely populated alpine forest, so the claim is rather unlikely to be true. Certainly Section 3.2.2.7 does not try to argue the point. Section 3.6.4 is a discussion of the North Atlantic Oscillation and the Northern Annular Mode, two oscillation patterns related to air pressure systems in the Northern Hemisphere. The section discusses seasonal weather patterns associated with these oscillation systems. Again, there is no mention of spatial patterns of socioeconomic development, industrialization, urbanization, or any related concept. Hence, the citations to these sections serve only to mislead casual readers into thinking there is some kind of support for the statements.

The second point concerns the claim that the correlation in question "ceases to be statistically significant." Statistical significance is a scientific term with a specific numerical interpretation. A statistical hypothesis test has an associated p-value that indicates the probability that the score would be as large as it is if the hypothesis is false, that is, there is no effect, only randomness, in the data. If a test score has a p-value below 0.05, in other words less than 5 percent, the effect is said to be statistically significant. If p is greater than 0.05 but below 0.1, the effect is said to be weakly, or marginally, significant. If p is greater than 0.1, the effect is said to be statistically insignificant. The claim that a published result is statistically insignificant implies that the accompanying p-value exceeds 0.1. These are standard, well-known statistical terms.

The effects reported in our 2004 paper had p-values on the order of 0.002 or 0.2 percent, indicating significance. The sentence in the IPCC report is worded awkwardly, but it can be interpreted as asserting either that the correlations between socioeconomic development and temperature trends are statistically insignificant or that when controlling for the influence of atmospheric circulations, they become statistically insignificant. On the first interpretation, the statement is a plain old porkie since the p-values reported in our paper are below 1 percent. On the second interpretation, the implication is that the relevant p-value exceeds 0.1 upon introduction of variables controlling for the oscillation effects. Yet no p-values are presented, nor is there a citation to any external source, peer reviewed or otherwise, in which such information is presented, nor are readers supplied with any data, statistical tests, or evidence of any kind in support of the sentence. In other words, the claim is false.

To my eyes, it looks like the appropriate word to describe the new paragraph is either "lie" or "fabrication." Evidence sufficient to disprove either accusation can be defined precisely: it would consist of the p-value supporting the claim of statistical insignificance, the peer-reviewed journal article in which it was presented, and the page number where the study is cited in the IPCC report.

These things do not exist.

The Journal Game

The absence of supporting evidence for the IPCC claim was obvious enough, and I drew attention to it in a *National Post* (Canada) op-ed in December 2007. However, I knew that it was also incumbent on me to show in a peer-reviewed article whether or not the claim was false.

Actually, it ought to have been incumbent on the IPCC to show that its claim was *true* before dismissing the evidence of contamination in the temperature data underpinning all its main conclusions. Unfortunately, the way the IPCC works, it is allowed to make stuff up; then it's the job of its critics to prove it wrong.

So in late 2007 and early 2008, I wrote a paper that tested the claim that controlling for atmospheric circulation effects would overturn our earlier results. I obtained values of the effects of trends in the Arctic Oscillation, North Atlantic Oscillation, Pacific Decadal Oscillation, and the El Niño Southern Oscillation on the gridded surface trend pattern over the 1979–2002 interval. I redid the regression results from the 2004 and 2007 papers after adding these variables into the model. I showed that the original results did not become statistically insignificant. I wrote up the paper and sent it out for publication.

The next part of the story involves a sequence of eight journals. I am not going to discuss them in exact chronological order; I am going to start with one of the later journals in the list, the *Journal of the American Statistical Association. JASA* is the top statistical journal in the world. My paper was reviewed by two referees, an associate editor, and the editor. The editor told me that all the reviewers were impressed by the paper but because the methods were so ordinary, it lacked any cutting-edge statistical insights:

> All of us agree that the paper presents a thoughtful and strong analysis. We also agree that the nature of the paper is very different from what usually appears in JASA. The referees recommended rejection on those grounds, and the [associate editor] was ambivalent. I am also torn—technically, a JASA paper need not be methodologically fresh, but essentially all of them are, and this trend has grown stronger over time. . . . So, after some long thought, I believe everyone is better served if you submit this quite good paper to a different venue.

The associate editor wrote:

> Both referees (and I) agree that the data analysis presented in the paper is carefully and well done. Both also state, however, that the paper would be best targeted in a scientific journal (e.g., Nature or Science) than in JASA. Their reasoning is that the methods used here are mundane, based primarily in linear models and t/F significance tests.
>
> I agree with the referees that this paper has excellent prospects, and a likely greater impact, in the scientific literature. I also agree that the typical JASA A&CS [Applications and Case Studies] paper brings to bear more sophisticated statistical techniques, and that the relatively mundane methods used in the present paper make it a less than ideal fit for the journal. Accordingly, I think it is reasonable to encourage the authors to submit this paper to another venue, especially a scientific journal. As it is, this is a fine paper, but it offers little in statistical direction, even in the sense of broadening understanding of the problem or area, and would fit much better elsewhere.

One reviewer said:

> This is a careful data analysis of an important problem in climatology. The author makes a convincing case that gridded surface temperature data are contaminated by effects of urbanization notwithstanding the conclusions of the IPCC.

However, the statistical methods are mundane and quite standard. Thus, it is quite different than the usual JASA applications paper. In other words, this is a good paper for a scientific journal but less well suited for a statistics journal.

The other one said:

Although the scientific problem is interesting and important, the statistics in the paper may not be enough to fit a top statistical journal like JASA. I would suggest the author(s) try Nature/Science or a geophysical journal which might be a good fit.

This was a pretty encouraging set of responses. The associate editor and the second reviewer even suggested I should send it to *Nature* or *Science*, the most famous science journals in the world.

As it happens, I had already done so. The first journal I tried, back in March 2008, was *Science*. The editors thanked me but returned the paper without review, saying the topic was too specialized for them. I then sent it to *Nature* in April 2008. Its editors also declined to send it out for review. They returned it with the comment that there have already been numerous papers published to date arguing that land-use change has left persistent effects in the surface temperature record, and my analysis did not provide any major advance in determining the magnitude of this problem. As a result, while they did not have any doubts about the quality of my analysis (at least none that they mentioned), they did not think it was suitable for publication in *Nature* and suggested I send it to a more specialized journal.

In early May, I sent a presubmission inquiry to the *Bulletin of the American Meteorological Society*. The *BAMS* website instructs authors to e-mail the editor describing the paper before making a full submission. The editor will, presumably, advise on the suitability of the paper and will indicate whether a full submission is requested. I submitted my e-mailed proposal on May 2, 2008.

A month passed without response. On June 4, 2008, having heard nothing, I sent a second e-mail asking about the timeline for getting a response.

Another month passed with no response.

July came and I still had heard nothing, not even an acknowledgment of my e-mails. I had expected a response from the editor along the lines of, this is the most boring thing ever written in the history of humanity, and you are a bad person for having written it. I did not expect total silence. I sent another e-mail on July 1, stating that for two months I had been waiting for an acknowledgment of my proposal, so rather than wait any longer, I was sending my paper elsewhere.[23]

I then sent it to *Theoretical and Applied Climatology*, which sent it to two reviewers. The responses were mixed, and the editor asked me to prepare a revision that addressed the criticisms. One of the reviewers grasped the scope of the argument and wrote a brief review pointing out that the findings were important and the analysis was clear, so the paper should be published. The other reviewer got sidetracked on the general question of whether surface temperatures are affected by industrialization and decided that I had not provided convincing proof of that point of view. What's more, the referee decided the de Laat and Maurellis papers were not convincing, nor was my work with Michaels. There was no mention in the referee's report about the actual subject of the paper I had submitted, namely, the failure of the IPCC's conjecture. Instead, the referee decided that this submission would serve as a proxy for an entire literature that he disliked. While *Nature* had turned down the paper because so many others had already shown the existence of the problem, this referee recommended rejection because no evidence for the problem existed.

The referee made very approving remarks about the comment by Rasmus Benestad on the 2004 paper and repeated Benestad's RealClimate argument that our results were fatally undermined by spatial autocorrelation. In a report that consisted mostly of sighs of subjective disbelief ("their studies are not convincing. . . "; "I think the analysis is flawed. . . "; "I'm not convinced"), the only concrete technical objections were that we had not performed cross-validation tests and we had not fixed the problem of spatial autocorrelation. The first claim was simply wrong: we had done cross-validation testing, and it was written up in both papers. The second claim was reasonable. The version of the paper I had submitted did not contain a discussion of spatial autocorrelation. That material, remember, was held up because Rasmus Benestad still hadn't sent his comment to the *JGR*. It occurred to me at the time that the referee (who was anonymous) had a writing style rather similar in tone and phrasing to Rasmus Benestad's. But, of course, there is no way that the referee could have been Benestad since Benestad had already seen my unpublished notes showing that spatial autocorrelation was not a problem for the model results, and this referee was talking as if the problem existed. So just because the referee thought Benestad's earlier writings were the last word on the subject, and just because he had Benestad's choppy writing style and vague, disputatious way of arguing, it could not have been Benestad because the referee was writing as if he did not know that the autocorrelation issue had already been disproved.

I decided, however, that since the spatial autocorrelation material was unlikely to get into *JGR* any time soon, and since the referee had brought it up, I might as well insert a section discussing it. So in the revision, I added a section providing detailed testing for spatial autocorrelation, as well as responding to all the other criticisms. The revision was submitted in October 2008. A month later, the editor, Hartmut Grassl, wrote to say he was rejecting the paper because the referee said I had not addressed the problems. As it happens, the referee had raised some new objections to the paper, such as claiming I had used only wintertime oscillation data and that I had not related them properly to temperature trends. Of course I hadn't responded to these issues since they were not raised in the first round. Not that they had any merit. The manuscript had only one graphic (see Figure 3.1 in color insert), which I copied directly from the source at the National Oceanic and Atmospheric Administration, where I obtained the data.

You can see in the original caption that the data are not wintertime only; they cover January to December. And the definition of the data, as I had explained in the paper, is the correlation between the oscillation index and the grid-cell temperature, thus relating trends to trends, which is the appropriate metric.

The referee's other objection was that I hadn't fixed the spatial autocorrelation problem. Here I realized that the referee didn't understand the technicalities. Readers who want to see the gory details can consult my accompanying sidebar.

Answering the Technicalities: A Little Math Should You Want It!

A regression model decomposes a dependent variable (y) into a portion that can be explained by the independent variables (X) using a set of estimated linear coefficients (b), and a set of unexplained variability, called "residuals" (e). The algebraic expression is the linear matrix equation $y = Xb + e$. The significance tests are based on the ratios between the coefficients and the square roots of their estimated variances. Spatial autocorrelation can bias the variance estimates, *but only if it affects the residuals*. The formula for the variance matrix estimator V is

$$V = (X'X)^{-1}X'E(ee')X(X'X)^{-1}.$$

where $E(\cdot)$ is mathematical notation for the "expected value" of the term in brackets, or the average value you would get if you took repeated data samples. If that looks confusing, rest assured that it is just a formula that takes one batch of numbers and rearranges it to produce another list of numbers. If you can read this sentence, you could, with a bit of explanation, understand what the formula does and why. For the present purpose, all that is required is that you notice that y does not appear in it. The statistical properties of V are inherited from the properties of e, not y, since y is not in the formula. Also, in this type of model, X does not contribute randomness to V; it only acts as a scaling factor for the randomness in e. So when I tested for spatial autocorrelation, I used the standard methods, which involve testing the residuals e, not the dependent variable y.

This particular referee, however, noticed that I had tested the residuals e, and he objected that I hadn't tested the dependent variable y. And despite the fact that he had focused so many of his earlier comments on the autocorrelation issue, he confessed that he didn't understand the section in which I presented the standard, mundane methods for dealing with it:

(continued on next page)

(continued)

> I suspect most of the TAC [*Theoretical and Applied Climatology*] readership will not be able to follow the argumentation here, and I too find it hard to follow. What is the author trying to say? SAC [spatial autocorrelation] is a problem if it means a lower degree of freedom than is apparent. Again, the discussion seems to be limited to SAC in the residual. Weighting will not resolve the problem of dependency—just give the nearby data lower weights—and again, I'm concerned about SAC in the temperature field and the socioeconomic variables more than in the residuals (although the latter is also a matter of concern). Thus the specification test on pp. 8–12 is too limited to residuals and doesn't really address my concerns.

I am sure that I am not the first academic who has seen the peer-review process derailed by the arrival of a blockhead. The referee recommended rejecting the paper, and the editor, Hartmut Grassl, concurred.

Oh well, *c'est la vie*. Papers get rejected all the time, and there were other places I could send it. Getting turned down didn't bother me because the referee had actually found nothing wrong with my analysis. However, I did feel that since the referee was wrong on the issues, I should write the editor back and explain the situation and ask if he would be willing to reconsider his decision. I had received the letter rejecting my manuscript on November 5, 2008. On November 7, Grassl had a letter from me explaining the problems in the referee's report. And then I waited for a reply.

And waited.

Two weeks later, I sent an e-mail asking for confirmation that my letter had been received. Grassl's secretary confirmed that he did have it. A month later, still having heard nothing, I wrote again asking if he and the referee were considering the letter. Grassl's secretary wrote back to say she did not know why he had not responded, since he did have my letter. A month after that, I still had not heard whether they were considering the matter, and in the meantime, a new paper had appeared in the literature by Rasmus Benestad's coblogger Gavin Schmidt, repeating some of the referee's arguments against my earlier work. So I wrote a member of the editorial board and asked if he could check into where things stood. He was very apologetic that I had not received a reply and promised to look into it.

But I still heard nothing after that. On April 15, 2009, five months after sending my response, still having heard nothing from Grassl, I resent my letter and reminded him that I had heard nothing since sending it in.

I continued to hear nothing.

A week later, on April 20, 2009, I e-mailed again saying that I had submitted my paper elsewhere and I wanted no further consideration from him and his stupid journal (or words to that effect). To this day, I have never received a response from Grassl.

The outlet to which I sent my paper next was the *Journal of the American Statistical Association*. I was exasperated with the *Theoretical and Applied Climatology* referee's lack of understanding of basic statistics, and I decided to see what a real stats journal would say. My submission was sent to *JASA* in April 2009, and its response came in August. As you saw earlier, the people who knew what they were talking about liked the paper and agreed that the results were solid. Rather than finding the methods confusing and hard to follow, they found them too simple and mundane to merit appearing in *JASA*.

Taking up the *JASA* suggestion of a geophysical journal, in August 2009, I sent the manuscript to *Geophysical Research Letters*. On September 4, 2009, the editor of *GRL* returned the manuscript after having decided not to send it out for review. The stated reason was:

> The work is very narrowly focused around disputing a single sentence in the IPCC report. Indeed, you state this narrowness explicitly in the manuscript. Therefore, it is my determination that the work lacks sufficiently broad geophysical implications to meet the GRL criteria.

If only the IPCC had stretched their fabrications out over, say, a whole paragraph! I guess there is a policy at *GRL* against criticizing phony claims if they are brief. The fact that I focused my critique on only one IPCC sentence did not seem to me to make it a narrow issue, since most of the conclusions in the report depended, one way or another, on the truth of that one sentence. I replied to *GRL*, stating that my paper was being submitted elsewhere, adding:

> The IPCC was presented with published, peer-reviewed evidence of a global bias in their surface temperature data, and the only counter-argument they offered relied on a fabricated statistical test result. The fact that they wrote with brevity while inventing non-existent test results does not diminish the necessity of correcting the record. I am taken aback by your claim that you cannot see any broader geophysical implications to this question.

At this point, to recap, I had spent 18 months submitting my paper to six journals. Three had refused to review it, and one did not respond to my inquiries. Two had reviewed it, obtaining among them reports from six referees. Only one of those reviews was negative. The referee had made obviously inaccurate statements, but the editor had cut off further communication, so I could not respond.

On I went. I next submitted it to *Global and Planetary Change* on September 4, 2009. I had to edit the submission two weeks later because I had not included line numbers, so the review process did not begin until September 18.

The inevitable rejection came on December 2. The editor's cover letter read:

> Dear Dr. McKitrick,
> Unfortunately, we receive far more papers than we can publish. I regret, therefore, to inform you that we cannot consider your paper for publication.
>   However, I wish you succes [sic] in preparing your manuscript for submission with another journal. And I am confident that these reviews (appended below) will be of much help during this process.

There was only one review attached, denoted "reviewer No. 2," which accurately summarized my argument, concurred with the results, and concluded as follows:

> This short paper is well written and well organized and given the clear research question and methodology, clearly deserves publication.

The only criticisms were of a minor editorial nature. Yet the journal had rejected the paper. I wrote the editor back and asked if there were other reviews as well, but (wait for it...) to this day I have never received a reply.

However, I already knew who reviewer No. 1 was. Roger Pielke Sr., professor emeritus of atmospheric science at Colorado State University, had written me in October to describe an unusual incident. On September 30, he received an e-mail from the editor of *Global and Planetary Change* asking him to review my manuscript. Roger went to the journal website where he was able to download the paper. He got an e-mail acknowledging with thanks that he had agreed to supply a review, and a request that it be submitted by October 30.

But then the journal website stopped recognizing him when he tried to sign in again to begin the review process. So on October 1, he e-mailed the *GPC* editor asking him to resend his username and password. He received no reply to this e-mail. On October 13, he received an e-mail from *GPC* saying that he was being removed as a reviewer on the manuscript since he had taken too long. Roger objected that he had been unable to access the website because *GPC* had not provided him with a working password, but he received no further response. And it made no sense because he had been given until October 30 to submit his review, but *GPC* removed him as a referee on October 13 for supposedly taking too long.

So to add to the remarkable history of this paper, I was now confronted with a journal that had solicited two reviews, blocked one reviewer before he could reply, received a positive response from the other reviewer, and then rejected the paper on the grounds that it could not publish every paper it received.

Back to JASA

It was now clear to me that this paper was never going to be published in a climatology journal. True, I had not tried *every* possible journal, but at a certain point, the pattern becomes pretty clear. So I wrote to the editor of *JASA*, described what had happened at other journals, and asked whether the paper might be reconsidered if I added some more complicated statistics (albeit at the risk of overkill), or whether he could suggest an applied statistics journal. He discussed the first option with another editor, but they decided the outcome would not likely change given the straightforward nature of the analysis required. However, he pointed to a new journal that he and some colleagues had recently founded, called *Statistics, Politics, and Policy*, which is dedicated to bringing to bear rigorous statistical analysis on important issues with policy implications. He said the paper would be a good fit and encouraged me to submit it. I did, and in due course, the journal accepted my paper. It appeared in the inaugural issue in the summer of 2010.

Conclusion

The paper I have discussed makes the case that the IPCC used false evidence to conceal an important problem with the surface temperature data on which most of its conclusions rest. In principle, one might argue that my analysis was wrong (though most reviewers didn't), but it would be implausible to say that the issue is unimportant or irrelevant. Altogether, I sent the paper to seven journals before it went to *Statistics, Politics, and Policy*. From those seven journals, I received seven reviews, of which six accepted the findings and supported publication.

The one that rejected my findings contained some basic technical errors, but the journal editor would not respond to my letter pointing them out. *Nature, Science,* and *Geophysical Research Letters* would not even review the paper, while the *Bulletin of the American Meteorological Society* said it never received the presubmission inquiry or the two follow-up queries. *Global and Planetary Change* received one review recommending publication, blocked another reviewer before he could submit a report, and then rejected the paper.

In the aftermath of Climategate, a lot of scientists working on global warming–related topics are upset that their field has apparently lost credibility with the public. The public seems to believe that climatology is beset with cliquish gatekeeping, wagon circling, biased peer review, faulty data, and statistical incompetence. In response to these perceptions, some scientists are casting around, in op-eds and blogs, for ideas on how to hit back at their critics. I would like to suggest that the climate science community consider instead whether the public might actually have a point.

Some people might be tempted to defend climatology by saying that normal scientific procedures have broken down due to the intense policy fights and political interference. But in my opinion, that confuses cause and effect. The policy community has aggressively intervened in climate science *because* of all the breaches of

95

normal scientific procedures. The public has lost confidence in the ability of the major institutions of climatology, including the IPCC and the leading journals, to deal impartially with the evidence. It doesn't have to be this way. My own field of economics constantly deals with policy-relevant topics with major public consequences. Of course, differences of opinion exist, and vigorous disputes play out among opposing camps. But what is happening in climate science is very different, or at least it is on a much more intense scale. I know of no parallels in modern economics. It appears to be a profession-wide decision that, due to the conjectured threat of global warming, the ethic of scientific objectivity has had an asterisk added to it: there is now the additional condition that objectivity cannot compromise the imperative of supporting one particular point of view.

This strategy is backfiring badly: rather than creating the appearance of genuine scientific progress, the situation appears more like a chokehold of indoctrination and intellectual corruption. I do not know what the solution is, since I have yet to see a case in which an institution or a segment of society, having once been contaminated or knocked off balance by the global warming issue, is subsequently able to right itself. But perhaps, as time progresses, climate science will find a way to do so. Now that would be progress.

4. Global Warming, Environmental Threats, and U.S. Security: Recycling the Domino Theory

Ivan Eland

The Department of Defense remains our largest nonentitlement expenditure. Needless to say, it has seized on global warming as a vehicle to enlarge its global role. The militarization of the global warming issue is a logical outcome of its spread throughout our government and our lives.

Our last chapter showed how difficult publication of nonalarmist manuscripts in the peer-reviewed academic literature has become. The opposite is also true—it is remarkably easy to publish papers citing various and sundry threats from global warming.

This situation is especially true at the military-environmental interface. As detailed below, a voluminous literature has developed to serve as the basis for amplifying military budgets because of climate change. The recurrent theme is that our armed forces will continue to be employed worldwide in an increased role as conflict managers, even beyond where they are today. But, on inspection, this argument seems to be remarkably weak.

Global warming is now a national security issue. The White House's National Security Strategy, issued in May 2010, states:

> The danger from climate change is real, urgent, and severe.
> The change wrought by a warming planet will lead to new
> conflicts over refugees and resources; new suffering from
> drought and famine; catastrophic natural disasters; and deg-
> radation of land across the globe.[1]

How did this new threat evolve?

The Alliance between the Left and Right on Global Warming as a Security Issue

The first official U.S. use of the term "environmental security" came in 1987, and the first international meeting of national policymakers and scientists highlighting the dangers of global warming was held in Toronto in 1988 with the title "The Changing Atmosphere: Implications for Global Security."[2] Both these events occurred during the Reagan administration. But the "environment affects security" argument was amplified in the George H. W. Bush administration.

When the cold war ended, new threats were needed to justify defense expenditures. Environmental degradation was one of many. The dangers of rogue states, such as North Korea and Saddam Hussein's Iraq, were front and center in the new threat paradigm, but "environment as security" began to justify not only security spending but also increased U.S. military interventions in foreign lands.

Daniel Deudney wrote about the nexus of the environment and security in 1990 as the cold war ended:

> As the Cold War winds down, such links are increasingly popular among national security experts and organizations looking for new missions, as exemplified by US Senator Sam Nunn's recently enacted "strategic environmental research program," in which US$200 million will be spent for military efforts in environmental monitoring and research. Due to the interest and support of several foundations, numerous conferences and researchers are addressing issues of "environmental security."[3]

The link between environmental degradation and international stability was officially acknowledged in the 1991 National Security Strategy, also during the George H. W. Bush administration.[4]

During the Clinton administration, Secretary of State Warren Christopher put environmental issues near the top of the American foreign policy agenda, and many high administration officials made statements linking the environment to conflict.[5] With Vice President Al Gore's passion for environmental issues, climate change crept into the U.S. National Security Strategy in 1996,[6] which stated:

> Natural resource scarcities often trigger and exacerbate conflict. Environmental threats such as climate change, ozone

depletion and the transnational movement of dangerous
chemicals directly threaten the health of U.S. citizens. . . .
[O]ur national security planning is incorporating environmental analyses as never before.[7]

Hawks: Neoconservative, Traditional, and Liberal

Despite the George W. Bush administration's more skeptical
approach to the global warming issue, the U.S. security bureaucracies' interests, and those of its hawkish supporters on the outside,
diverged from that of the administration. In an era when "small
wars"—such as those in Iraq and Afghanistan—might not be enough
to justify historically high defense spending, those bureaucracies
and their supporters looked for additional justifications.

And not only neoconservatives, such as Republican Frank Gaffney
and Democratic Director of Central Intelligence James Woolsey, got
on the "global warming as a U.S. security threat" bandwagon. Traditional security operatives hawked climate change, too. Geoffrey
Dabelko and P. J. Simmons of the Woodrow Wilson International
Center for Scholars in Washington, D.C., concluded, "The willingness of traditional security structures—including the Department of
Defense, Department of Energy, and the intelligence community—
to adopt new green missions represents a classic bureaucratic effort
to retain comparable budgetary outlays and reap public relations
benefits."[8] Dabelko and Simmons wrote that in 1997, before the
Department of Homeland Security was created, but it too is now
incorporating global warming as a security threat.

The Center for Naval Analysis Corporation's Military Advisory
Board, consisting of 11 retired admirals and generals,

> heard arguments, some depicting near doomsday scenarios
> of severe weather and oceanic changes exacerbated by man-
> made emissions of greenhouse gases to our environment,
> others depicting a much less severe outcome as merely one
> in many observed cyclic weather patterns over time, with
> virtually no man-made component.[9]

Of the two arguments, the advisory board quickly took the "catastrophic" fork. Admiral Frank "Skip" Bowman, former director of
navy nuclear propulsion programs, argued that regardless of the
probability of occurrence of new weather patterns, the effects of

global warming could be dire and could harm U.S. security. Thus, the admiral opined that the military must ready a defense plan for such climate threats. He was far less specific, as all military people are, about how the armed forces could effectively combat such multi-front security threats worldwide.[10]

Similar rhetoric came from former army chief of staff General Gordon Sullivan, chairman of the advisory board, who actually implied that the effects of global warming were a more severe threat than the low-probability/high-consequence threat of global thermo-nuclear war with the Soviet Union during the cold war (as character-ized by the advisory board). Sullivan opined:

> The Cold War was a specter, but climate change is inevitable. If we keep on with business as usual, we will reach a point where some of the worst effects are inevitable. . . . If we don't act, this looks more like a high probability/high conse-quence scenario.[11]

A study by the Center for a New American Security and the Center for Strategic and International Studies concluded that "left unaddressed, climate change may come to represent as great or a greater foreign policy and national security problem" than the war on terror, the wars in Afghanistan and Iraq, energy security, and current economic instability.[12]

Liberal hawks were delighted to link environmental issues, such as global warming, with U.S. security needs. Kurt Campbell, currently assistant secretary of state for East Asian and Pacific affairs, edited a book entitled *Climatic Cataclysm: The Foreign Policy and National Security Implications of Climate Change* to justify the high level of U.S. military interventions overseas.[13]

In this remarkably alarmist book, Campbell and his coauthors examine three scenarios: (a) change expected by scientists for the United Nations' Intergovernmental Panel on Climate Change, (b) severe climate change, and (c) catastrophic climate change. In the latter two scenarios, global warming causes more devastating conse-quences than those expected by scientists. Conspicuously absent was a scenario in which the effects of global warming were less pronounced than those expected by IPCC scientists. In another exam-ple of the apocalyptic slant of his book, Campbell predicts that democracies could turn into autocracies if they don't deal effectively with global warming. But alternatively, authoritarian governments could face democratic revolutions if they don't get it right.

In another chapter of the same book, Woolsey exhibited a similar alarmist bias when he predicted that rising sea levels and unpredictable weather patterns would interfere with oil production from offshore platforms and in the Middle East and oil transportation via oil tankers, while failing to mention that melting Arctic sea ice opens the possibility of more oil exploration and production there, as well as more direct and secure shipping.

The liberal Campbell and one of his coauthors, the conservative Richard Weitz, paint a stark picture of the snowballing security calamities arising from global warming (all of which will be rebutted below):

> We came away with considerable clarity in our own minds: the United States can expect that climate change will exacerbate already existing North-South tensions, dramatically increase global migration both inside and between nations (including into the United States), lead to increasingly serious public health problems, heighten interstate tension and possibly conflict over resources, collapse agricultural markets and global fisheries, challenge institutions of global governance, cause potentially destabilizing domestic political and social repercussions, and spur unpredictable shifts in the global balance of power, particularly where China is concerned. The state of humanity could be altered in ways that create moral dilemmas for those charged with wielding national power, and also in ways that may either erode or enhance America's place in the world.
>
> Taken together or even one at a time, some of these challenges have the potential to overwhelm national governments and international institutions. It is difficult to anticipate just how these cascading calamities might ultimately unfold, but the prospects for destabilizing global effects are clearly on the horizon.[14]

In a different chapter of the same book, Woolsey, who is not an expert on global warming or its effects on security (and appears to have been chosen by the editor by "appeal to authority" based on his credential as former central intelligence director), also suggests a gloomy future by latching onto the book's catastrophic scenario of a sea level rise of 6.6 feet, an amount approximately *four times* greater than the current midrange estimate from the United Nations' Intergovernmental Panel on Climate Change.

> All of the ways in which human beings have responded to natural disasters in the past . . . could come together in one conflagration: rage at the government's inability to deal with the abrupt and unpredictable crises; religious fervor and perhaps even a dramatic rise in millennial end-of-days cults; hostility and violence toward migrants and minority groups, at a time of demographic change and increased global migration; and intra- and interstate conflict over resources, particularly food and freshwater.
>
> Altruism and generosity would likely be blunted. In a world with millions of people migrating out of coastal areas and ports across the globe, it will be extremely difficult, perhaps impossible, for the United States to replicate the kind of professional and generous assistance provided to Indonesia following the 2004 tsunami. Even overseas deployments in response to clear military needs may prove very difficult. Nuclear-powered aircraft carriers and submarines might be able to deploy, but aviation fuel or fuel for destroyers and other non-nuclear ships could be unobtainable. Overseas air bases would doubtless be tangled in climatic chaos, and aircraft fuel availability overseas highly uncertain. Further, the Navy is likely to be principally involved in finding ways to base, operate, overhaul, and construct ships, as many ports and harbors south of New York on the East Coast and overseas disappear or become usable only with massive expenditures for protection from the rise in sea levels.[15]

Even as he warns of the rise of "millennial end-of-days cults," Woolsey is ironically advancing a similar doomsday scenario. In addition, he seems more worried about the effects of a potential sea level rise on the American ability to police its global empire using military interventions than with the security of the United States. And therein lies the root of odd neoconservative support for the "green" agenda.

Ironically, according to Jon Barnett, associate professor in environmental studies at the University of Melbourne, worldwide militaries are big emitters of greenhouse gases and are estimated to release more of them into the atmosphere than does the entire United Kingdom. Thus, despite what the newly green neoconservatives and militarists espouse, militaries contribute to global warming rather than likely doing anything substantial to deal with the problem. In fact, although the U.S. Department of Defense claims to have lowered greenhouse gas emissions by 20 percent, Barnett cogently argues that reducing the size of its forces would do much more to reduce such gases than their ecological modernization.[16]

Some liberal hawks have even adopted the long-discredited "falling dominoes" theory used by conservatives during the cold war to talk about the cascading cataclysmic security effects of global warming. John Podesta, former Clinton chief of staff and current head of the progressive Center for American Progress (often called "Obama's think tank" by Washingtonians), and Peter Ogden, its security analyst, concoct the following snowballing doomsday scenario:

> These crises are all the more dangerous because they are interwoven and self-perpetuating: water shortages can lead to food shortages, which can lead to conflict over remaining resources, which can drive human migration, which can create new food shortages in new regions.
>
> Once under way, this chain reaction becomes increasingly difficult to stop. It is therefore critical that policymakers do all they can to prevent the domino of the first major climate change consequence, whether it be food scarcity or the outbreak of disease, from toppling.[17]

Environmentalists

The environmentalists have sought to hitch global warming policies to the politically potent U.S. security bandwagon in order to get more government attention and money for their cause. According to Geoffrey Dabelko and P. J. Simmons: "Environment and security rhetoric may also generate the funding, domestic political support, and action-oriented responses necessary to achieve sustainable development and population goals. Early writings in particular employed this rhetoric explicitly to gain support and reorder priorities." They continue: " . . . [S]pecific departments and agencies within government, as well as environmental NGOs [nongovernmental organizations] are using the term "security" simply to win more attention and funding."[18]

As an example of this blatant gambit, Oran Young, a professor at the Donald Bren School of Environmental Science and Management at the University of California, Santa Barbara, hopes that if climate change becomes a threat to American security, it will galvanize a political will to make long-term investments to limit greenhouse gases. He notes: "There are a lot of people who think that the only way we're going to make changes of the magnitude required to address this problem is to cast it as a security issue. When you talk about major changes in behavior in allocations in the budget, it's easier to accomplish if it's [perceived as] a matter of national security."[19]

Even Jon Barnett, , who is appropriately skeptical of global warming's causing conflict, curiously argues that although the "security" paradigm has failed to do so in the past, it can be used politically to get more money and attention for the global warming problem. His comments deserve quoting at length:

> Environmental security was originally written with the intention of exposing the inadequacy of militarized practices of security, the porous nature of sovereignty in the face of environmental change, and to elevate environmental problems from the level of "low politics" to "high politics" so that states would commit as much energy and resources to address environmental problems as they do to other security problems. However, the result has not been the trading off of military security for environmental security, or increased resources and energy to environmental security. Instead, environmental change problems have been militarized; the emphasis has been placed on environmental change as cause of violent conflict rather than human insecurity; and on exogenous environmental threats to the state for which unspecified Others were seen to be responsible, as opposed to attending to domestic causes of environmental change.
>
> So, understanding climate change as a security issue risks making it a military rather than a foreign policy problem and a sovereignty rather than global commons problem. . . .
>
> Despite these problems with any potential climate-change security discourse, it may nevertheless have some utility. Security communicates a certain *gravitas* that is arguably necessary in climate change policy. In that climate change is a security problem for certain groups, identifying it as such suggests that it is an issue that warrants a policy response commensurate in effort if not in kind with war. . . . Security encapsulates danger much better than concepts like sustainability, vulnerability or adaptation, and it offers a framework

in which danger can be recast as widespread risks to welfare. . . .[20] [emphasis in original]

Barnett's hope that global warming can still be effectively lashed to war brings back Jimmy Carter's attempt to do something similar by deeming U.S. independence from foreign oil as the "moral equivalent of war"; Republican Senator Arthur Vandenberg's advice to Democratic President Harry Truman to "scare the hell out of the American people" about the international communist threat during the cold war to pass Truman's program of assistance to two countries fighting communism; and Truman's secretary of state Dean Acheson's implicit admission that the administration did just that when "we made our points clearer than the truth."[21]

And as Daniel Deudney summarized the state of affairs in 1990 as the cold war ended, liberals were trying to substitute the environmental peril for defunct communist threat:

> One striking feature of the growing discussion of environmental issues in the United States is the attempt by many liberals, progressives and environmentalists to employ language traditionally associated with violence and war to understand environmental problems and to motivate action. Lester Brown, Jessica Tuchman Matthews, Michael Renner and others have proposed "redefining national security" to encompass resource and environmental threats. More broadly, Richard Ullman and others have proposed "redefining security" to encompass a wide array of threats, ranging from earthquakes to environmental degradation. Hal Harvey has proposed the concept of "natural security," and US Senator Albert Gore has spoken extensively in favour of thinking of the environment as a national security issue.[22]

Compared with the threats that have driven military planning in the past—such as the Soviet Union, China, Iraq, Iran, and North Korea—the threat to U.S. security from global warming is much more vague, nebulous, and illogical.

The Exaggerated Security Threat from Global Warming

The underlying philosophy that leads both hawks and environmentalists to inflate the security threat from global warming is the archaic notion that the United States must police the world. According to the projections of such alarmists, most of the ill effects of global warming will occur in the developing world, which is too poor to cope with it. The main effects will be felt in the belt from Saharan and sub-Saharan Africa to the Middle East, to South and Southeast Asia. In addition, some small atolls are projected to be swallowed up by rising sea levels, and the polar ice in the uninhabited Arctic is predicted to melt, possibly allowing a new route for travel and commerce.

In all of these potentially affected regions, even if global warming causes more social and humanitarian misery and conflict, it would not necessarily threaten the strategic interests of the United States. U.S. vital interests include keeping the world's few centers of wealth and technology—Western Europe and Japan—free and secure. And these are the countries that are most capable of adequately dealing with any effects of global warming that arise.

Such strategic, rich nations can deal with global warming better than their poor and less strategic counterparts because these countries usually have well-developed markets, insurance industries, transportation and communication infrastructure, and open trade of food, technology, and other important items with other countries, as well as more participative democracy.[23] In fact, the earth may actually warm at higher latitudes, in which most of the rich countries lie, even more than in the lower latitudes of the poor countries, but the rich countries will likely come through the trauma using such mechanisms.[24]

Only in the very unlikely scenario of abrupt catastrophic climate change, induced by melting of the ice sheets in Greenland and West Antarctica and not projected by the climate models driven by the United Nations' Intergovernmental Panel on Climate Change's future scenarios, would developed countries have substantial difficulty adapting to global warming. However, even global warming alarmists Peter Schwartz, a CIA consultant, and Doug Randall, of California's Global Business Network, admit that even in this more severe scenario, the United States would likely gain relative to other countries because of its wealth, technology, abundant resources, and diverse agricultural growing climates. They argue that the most intractable problem for the United States would be dampening the predicted ascendant warming-induced military tension around the world.[25] Yet the potential for mounting conflict caused by global warming or over warming-induced resource scarcities has been exaggerated (see below); and even if it weren't, the United States, because of its dominant nuclear arsenal and unusually secure position away from the world's centers of turmoil, would be secure even if there is more conflict.

Will Global Warming Induce Greater Conflict?

Even in the developing nations most adversely affected by global warming, the relationship between the environmental effects of the warming and increased conflict, as routinely pronounced by environmental security analysts, has not been demonstrated. Many environmental security analysts, at the Pentagon and elsewhere, predict global warming will decrease the quantity of arable land, food production, fresh water, and available minerals. In turn, they casually assert that competition for increasingly scarce resources will lead to increased conflicts. Malthusian logic infuses the environmental security movement.

The "conflict over scarce resources" thesis has quite a history. Adolf Hitler designed Nazi war aims to achieve resource independence. Japanese expansion came when their lack of indigenous minerals and fuels was exacerbated by a tightening embargo by the Western colonial powers, prompting Japan to invade Southeast Asia to get oil, tin, and rubber. Even in the more well-endowed United States, fears of resource scarcity, leading to the strangulation of industry, held prominence in U.S. strategic thinking at the time. During the cold war, the two superpowers competed for resources in the developing world.[26]

Yet finding evidence of the causes of violent conflict is difficult, both within and between countries. At the current state of research on the environment-conflict nexus, the effect of climate change on conflict is necessarily speculative because of insufficient evidence and large uncertainty. Although some research points to some vague connection between environmental change and conflict, other factors, such as ethnic strife, availability of armaments, institutional resilience, external indebtedness, and state legitimacy and its ability and propensity to take violent action, seem to be equally or more important than environmental factors in causing conflict.[27] For example, population migration in Sudan's Darfur region—which was caused by the loss of available farm and grazing land from an extended drought to an expanding desert—merely exacerbated existing ethnic, tribal, and religious differences and population growth as the primary causes of the conflict there.[28] Rwanda's genocide was primarily caused by ethnic tensions but might have been worsened by conflict over agricultural resources.

The late economist Julian Simon pointed out that the market can generally handle resource scarcity by an increased price for a particular item and the substitution of other, relatively cheaper items for it.[29] Campbell and Weitz (cited previously) talk about global warming's making agricultural markets collapse. But some nations' agricultural production will increase because of warming, and others' will decline. This production differential will make it profitable to sell grain from those in surplus to those in deficit. Throughout history, markets and trade have survived wars, political upheaval, natural disasters, and pandemic diseases. Where there is a willing buyer and seller, there is usually an incentive and a way to trade.

In the same vein, Ronnie Lipschutz and John Holdren noted that even in the absence of environmental degradation, wars over scarce resources are unlikely because in an interdependent world, trade is a more cost-effective way to get resources than waging war; technological advances have increased the substitutability of materials; and raw materials are now less important to economic success.[30]

Deudney notes that these factors were absent during the autarkic world of the 1930s leading up to World War II.[31] Nations had to rely on war to get resources rather than trade for them or substitute other materials. There is considerable evidence of modern resource substitutability: Since 1960, despite rapid world economic growth, the price of every raw material has held constant or declined. Because in the modern world wealth is no longer created by being resource rich but by capital accumulations via savings and more efficient methods of production—for example, resource-poor Japan is wealthy while many resource-rich countries are poor—scenarios of worsening intrastate and interstate warfare caused by a decline in world wealth via resource shortages induced by environmental degradation simply don't conform to reality.

In fact, even if societies got poorer because of environmental degradation, they might very well choose to use scarcer resources for things other than conflict. Deudney cites famous strategist Bernard Brodie as saying that in the modern era, "the predisposing factors to military aggression are full bellies, not empty ones." Poor countries can fight defensive guerrilla wars, but offensive war requires excess wealth, specialized industrial items, and complex organizational acumen.

Finally, Deudney notes that nuclear weapons, the proliferation of small arms, and a virulent sense of nationalism have made it difficult even for great powers to conquer developing countries possessing resources—as illustrated by the French defeat in Algeria, the American fiasco in Vietnam, and the Soviet debacle in Afghanistan. Deudney concludes that globalization and such dispersion of potent means of self-defense give the world system much "rattle room" to deal with environmental degradation without substantial interstate conflict. Thus, Deudney argues that environmentalists overstate the probability of wars caused by resource scarcity and environmental degradation.[32]

Worldwide, since World War II, cross-border aggression has been reduced significantly by the factors mentioned by Deudney.

What about Greater Conflict over Scarce Water and Food?

More specifically, there is little evidence for the possibility of more frequent wars caused by water shortages induced by global warming's alteration of precipitation patterns, especially in the Middle East.[33] Wars allegedly caused by water shortages were usually caused by something else, according to Lipschutz.[34] Surprisingly, the Center for Naval Analysis Corporation's Military Advisory Board agrees that no wars have been conducted solely to control water resources. The advisory board also acknowledges the argument that multinational interaction over scarce water resources has contributed to regional cooperation and peace more than to war.[35]

Deudney also argues that cooperation over water scarcity may be more likely than conflict, and Stephan Libiszewski has argued that water has been the subject of negotiation and tension reduction even in the Middle East.[36] Barnett says that in the past, water has usually been peacefully managed between states through systems of water rights and traditional customs, even in the Middle East. Furthermore, Barnett notes that water is unlikely to be a source of conflict because it is hard to enclose and because a mutual hostage situation arises from countries spending much on water management equipment that is vulnerable to attack.[37]

Barnett also argues that conflict over water has been publicized more than instances of cooperation. He notes that everyone pays attention to the conflict-ridden Middle East, but central and southern Africa have similar water scarcities and social and political fissures. Instead of warfare, however, a commission was established by Angola, Namibia, and Botswana in southern Africa to peacefully manage tensions over the Okavango River. In addition, Barnett notes that those who believe water scarcity will cause conflict selectively ignore successful water management arrangements in North America and Western Europe. He attributes the bias of focusing on conflict instead of on peaceful cooperation to the militarism and sensationalism of our culture. Barnett astutely concludes that the selective spotlight on conflict rather than on cooperation is used to justify strategic interventions in key regions, especially the Middle East, by rich nations of the North.[38]

Food scarcity, like water shortages, is a dubious cause of conflict. The blithe assertion that environmentally induced famine will cause increased conflict over scarce food supplies overlooks the aforementioned fact that widespread hunger reduces the capacity of nations or groups to make war effectively.[39]

Intrastate and Interstate Conflict versus Cooperation

Summarily, in the 1990s, the argument that scarce renewable resources contributed to intrastate conflict was widely accepted, but convincing criticism of that idea on theoretical, methodological, and policy grounds has pushed it to the intellectual margin. This criticism also disputes the prevailing view that climate change, which is predicted to increase resource scarcity, is likely to trigger conflict. De Soysa and Collier, in two separate studies, using statistical modeling, show that the scarcity of renewable resources is not correlated with political instability.[40]

Thus, green hawks have adopted a subtler mantra that "climate change acts as a threat multiplier for instability in some of the most volatile regions of the world."[41] When all the qualifiers are taken out of this sentence—"threat multiplier" rather than "threat," vague "instability" rather than "conflict" or "violence," and "some" regions, not "all" regions—it is difficult to tell what threat exists at all. They use the term "threat multiplier" because the research shows that climate change may aggravate local and regional renewable resource scarcities but itself is unlikely to cause conflict.[42] Similarly, the Pentagon's well-crafted position is, "while climate change alone does not cause conflict, it may act as an accelerant of instability or conflict. . . ."[43]

The green hawks are similarly ginger about talking about global warming causing "failed states." In 2009, according to Dennis Blair, the then-director of national intelligence, "We assess climate change alone is unlikely to trigger state failure in any state out to 2030, but the impacts will worsen existing problems such as poverty, social tensions, environmental degradation, ineffectual leadership, and weak political institutions."[44]

In fact, contention in developing countries is often not competition over scarce resources but control over the revenue stream from abundant resources.[45] For example, rebellion in Nigeria's Niger Delta is caused by a portion of the population feeling excluded from receiving the substantial revenues from the delta's plentiful petroleum resources.

Although Thomas Homer-Dixon and Valerie Percival argued that environmental scarcity might be a contributing factor to intrastate conflict, they also maintain that it is not the immediate or principal cause. Conflict is not inevitable with resource scarcity. To avoid conflict, countries can reduce dependence on the scarce resources or use them more efficiently. More important, Homer-Dixon and Percival conclude that "environmental scarcity rarely contributes directly to interstate conflict."[46]

The same is true for the mitigation of climate change, with conflict unlikely to erupt between countries disagreeing about how to reduce greenhouse gases.[47] Interstate war is much more important to U.S. security than intrastate conflict because the violence is less contained. Moreover, in general, democracies and strongly authoritarian states get involved in fewer interstate conflicts than states in political and economic transition. And that is good because wealthy, technologically powerful democracies in Japan and Western Europe not falling victim to an aggressive great power is and should be one of the pillars of U.S. security.

According to Barnett, however, even Lipschutz and Holdren[48] excessively buy into the likelihood of conflict over cooperation. They suggest that environmental problems—that is, externalities such as global warming versus the previously mentioned resource scarcity— pose the greatest threat to international security and argue that inequities between the rich nations of the Northern Hemisphere and

111

the poor nations of the Southern Hemisphere will lead to environmentally caused wars. But Barnett points out that the exploitation and oppression of the South have heretofore not resulted in its use of violence against the North, so it is unlikely that added environmental issues in the future will produce such conflicts. Barnett adds that if interdependence promotes peace when resource scarcity exists, it should do the same when externalities are afoot.[49] It might also be pointed out that since the advent of modern warfare—from the U.S. Civil War on—the richer side has won virtually all conventional conflicts, because superior technology requires money.

Most often, states have managed international environmental disasters without political ramifications or violence. In the case of Aceh, a rebellious province in Indonesia, a natural disaster even led to increased cooperation. The effects of the tsunami of 2004 were so severe in Aceh that separatists decided to hand over their weapons and seek peace with the government.[50]

Would Warming-Induced Migration Cause Increased Conflict?

A consensus does seem to exist that large migrations can occasionally cause conflict. If conflict occurs over climate change, it might be caused by such migrations induced by major sea level rise, depleted soil and water supplies, or livestock, infrastructure, and human lives lost. Yet the argument that conflict is caused by scarce resources has been largely debunked, so the main threat from migration might be from ethnic, tribal, or religious differences of the migrating population with that of the receiving region or country.

But disagreement arises over how much environmental change motivates migration. People rarely migrate for environmental reasons alone, and only very few mass migrations have ended in violence. Even CNA's Military Advisory Group admits that migrations do not necessarily have negative effects, while noting, without evidence, that in the context of global warming, they are unlikely to produce a net benefit.[51]

But migration usually benefits both the migrants and the recipient country economically, and so any conflict that arises is usually a nationalist response to the migration. Even climate change alarmists John Podesta and Peter Ogden of the Center for American Progress admit that wealthy and technologically advanced nations, such as

112

the United States, will not experience destabilizing levels of internal migration due to global warming.[52]

Developing countries are less able to cope with climate change and also more prone to intra- and interstate migration. South Asia is predicted to be the region most affected by migration from global warming. An oft-mentioned scenario is a climate change–induced sea level rise that causes millions of people in low-lying Bangladesh to migrate to nearby India and Pakistan, causing violence, as it did when Pakistan and India were first formed in the late 1940s.[53] Yet as in the 1940s, although a human tragedy, such migration and violence in or among developing countries would be little threat to U.S. security today or in the future. Thus, the solution to any such calamity is not U.S. military intervention but, along with other developed countries, acceptance of immigrants from the affected countries.

In contrast to the conventional hysterical pleas of imminent doom, most effects of global warming will likely be gradual—allowing the gradual immigration and assimilation of migratory refugees, thus dramatically reducing the chances of violence. When India and Pakistan were created in the late 1940s by an abrupt British withdrawal, the ensuing mass migration did not grant the luxury of gradual assimilation. Also new countries were being formed, and the British drew the boundaries of the new states, leaving large ethnosectarian minorities on the other sides of the borderlines—which has historically made conflict much more likely.

Most Security Threats from Warming Are Exaggerated

In sum, even if the world is more interconnected than ever via modern communication and transportation systems, not everything is closely linked; regional disasters and turmoil can exist without affecting the rest of the world very much. For example, the Sahara desert has expanded without much notice by the world's political and economic systems.[54] And even in the worst case, if global warming is most likely found to cause internal war in developing countries that are especially vulnerable to any effects from climate change, or that may be especially prone to violence because their political or economic systems are in transition, or that have a history of mass migrations (all of which are far from demonstrated empirically), it would likely be more of a humanitarian, rather than a security, issue for the United States.

Even global problems—such as the fact that two-thirds of the world's population live near coastlines that could be threatened by rising sea levels—may not affect U.S. security very much. Certainly dislocations will occur as people, transportation avenues, and industrial, energy, and port facilities and infrastructure would have to be moved inland in America and elsewhere. As shown previously, however, such relocation probably won't adversely affect U.S. security and thus need not involve the United States in more overseas conflict. Modern transportation systems could spread any warming-exacerbated diseases, but again, this is primarily a public health and humanitarian issue for the United States, not one of security.

One Possible Genuine General Security Threat from Warming

The one general threat that has some validity is the possibility of increased nuclear weapons proliferation because more countries are adopting civilian nuclear power to reduce greenhouse gases. Many developing nations will begin operating such facilities for the first time during the next few decades. Some of these countries may, as Iran and others have done, use civilian nuclear programs to complete and mask the most demanding task in building a nuclear weapon—generating fissionable material.[55] But nuclear proliferation is already occurring and will be merely exacerbated by the expansion of civilian nuclear power.

Regional Threats

Given that the academic literature categorically rejects resource scarcity as a source of interstate conflict, the old guard security community adroitly steers around this problem by simply saying that global warming can exacerbate conflict within states. According to CNA's Military Advisory Board,

> Climate change acts as a threat multiplier for instability in some of the most volatile regions of the world. Projected climate change will seriously exacerbate already marginal living standards in many Asian, African, and Middle Eastern nations, causing widespread political instability and the likelihood of failed states.[56]

It goes on to warn:

> While the developed world will be far better equipped to deal with the effects of climate change, some of the poorest

regions may be affected most. This gap can potentially provide an avenue for extremist ideologies and create the conditions for terrorism.[57]

Similarly, Admiral T. Joseph Lopez, a member of the advisory
board, warned, "Climate change will provide the conditions that
will extend the war on terror." He noted that drought, violent
weather, and ruined agricultural lands occurring in regions of the
world already prone to extremism would lead to societal changes.
He then concluded that "more poverty, more forced migrations,
higher unemployment [are] conditions [that] are ripe for extremists
and terrorists."[58] Some of these arguments have been made about
the ill effects of the devastating floods in Pakistan.

Yet to recap, the academic literature has cast doubt on even the
idea that resource scarcity contributes to intrastate instability and
conflict. And remembering the quote from Bernard Brodie, conflict
tends to arise when bellies are full rather than empty. Research has
confirmed that revolutions and increases in terrorism usually occur
when the economy is improving, not declining, but expectations rise
faster than economic progress. In fact, when countries experience a
decline in their economic fortunes, they may very well conclude
that violence and war are a luxury they can't afford. As noted previously, most migrations don't end in violence, and migrations often
benefit both the immigrants and the recipient society. So all of the
quotes above have very little to back them up in the way of evidence.
Such casual and a priori assertions litter the utterances of the old
guard security community on the security threats arising from
global warming.

Nevertheless, the security hawks, mimicking the falling dominoes
of countries succumbing to communism during the Cold War, postu-
late the same domino effect for security as a result of global warming.
Diminished food and water, increased disease, and the migrations
induced by these calamities will cause weakened and failing governments, thus leading to a spike in internal conflict and, within affected
countries, the increased need for U.S. military interventions. CNA's
Military Advisory Board predicts:

> The U.S. may be drawn more frequently into these situations,
> either alone or with allies, to help provide stability before
> conditions worsen and are exploited by extremists. The U.S.

may also be called upon to undertake stability and reconstruction efforts once a conflict has begun, to avert further
disaster and reconstitute as stable government.[59]

Thus, global warming is being used as one more convenient excuse
for U.S. interventions around the globe that may very well have
other underlying geopolitical and geostrategic rationale. Alluding
to this hidden purpose, CNA's Military Advisory Board euphemisti-
cally noted that global warming "presents opportunities for constructive engagement."[60] Such American engagement with other
countries using military means has not always been needed or
constructive.

South and Southeast Asia

South and Southeast Asia have some of the world's coasts that
are predicted to be most endangered by any rise in sea levels from
global warming because they are low-lying and heavily populated.
They include coastal regions between Thailand and Vietnam, Indonesia and the Philippines, and the coasts of India, Pakistan, Sri
Lanka, Burma, and Bangladesh.[61] Many sources predict that low-
lying countries, such as Bangladesh, or small island nations, such
as Micronesia, will be flooded or even eliminated, respectively, by
rising sea levels from global warming. These events could cause
humanitarian disasters if they are too rapid. But more likely, the
affected populations will migrate to safer places, without a threat
to U.S. security. Increased flooding could also spike insect-borne
diseases, such as malaria, but again this is a humanitarian, not a
security, issue.

Podesta and Ogden, with their global warming domino theory,
actually predict that Bangladesh could become a haven for al Qaeda
because of rising Islamic radicalism from the U.S. invasion of
Afghanistan, deteriorating socioeconomic conditions, and "environmental insecurity" brought about by global warming.[62] But terrorism
is usually caused by political factors, not environmental degradation
or resource scarcity. Again, terrorism and revolution usually occur
when countries' economies are growing rapidly but expectations
are growing faster, not when countries are desperately poor, such
as Bangladesh.

Another example of Podesta and Ogden's flawed domino theory
of global warming involves climate change's vague threat to regional

stability—for example, in Nepal. They say that global warming is threatening a "glacial outburst" in which violent discharges of melt-water destroy everything in their path. This phenomenon, they allege, could destabilize a country that is close to Kashmir, which is home to a dispute between India and Pakistan, and the contested Chinese-Indian border. So Podesta and Ogden conclude that any warming-induced instability in Nepal could unsettle the entire region of South Asia.[63] Even if these warming-induced dominoes occur, although Nepal may be strategic to India, Pakistan, and China, it is a small faraway country that is not strategic to the United States.

Sub-Saharan Africa

Most of the future increase in the demand for food is projected to come from South Asia and sub-Saharan Africa. It is also predicted that these regions, already facing food shortages, could become hotter and drier, lowering food production.[64] Yet as noted before, research shows that resource shortages don't cause increased levels of interstate conflict, and most researchers believe they are not a primary cause of intrastate conflict either. The market will work as prices rise and demand is reduced. Also, international aid is likely to be rendered, thus easing pressure for conflict.

Africa, long the only continent that the U.S. security establishment didn't regard as strategic, is now in the sights of the U.S. government. By 2015, Africa will supply 25 to 40 percent of U.S. oil—a greater percentage than the Middle East, and rising—and thus has a new U.S. military command with responsibility for it. The continent's weak governments also raise the alleged threat of terrorism taking hold in countries like Somalia and Sudan. Also mentioned are strategic minerals, such as manganese, platinum, and chrome.[65]

Yet world oil markets do work, and any disruption of oil—say, from the most important sub-Saharan African producer, Nigeria—caused directly by environmental degradation from global warming, indirect political instability deriving from the same, or any other cause will be handled via increases in the world market price. This hike would result in conservation in consuming nations and compensatory production increases in other oil producers to take advantage of the increased profits to be made. Terrorism is usually more prevalent in countries that are economically advanced rather than in poor failed states, and any terrorism that arises usually has local targets

117

unless the United States intervenes and makes new enemies. For example, in the poor nation of Somalia, U.S. intervention has been one of the primary causes of increased radicalism. Sub-Saharan Africa's strategic minerals were mentioned during the Cold War, but the continent was still regarded as not very strategic. Why this viewpoint would change in a reduced post–Cold War threat environment is dubious. Also, knowledge-based economies can now more readily substitute for such minerals.

By invoking global warming, U.S. interventionists have found yet another dubious excuse to add Africa to the list of strategic continents, thus justifying interventions that are really because of oil. The only remaining nonstrategic continent is Antarctica.

Southern Africa is also mentioned as a source of conflict over water, second only to the Middle East. In southern Africa, 15 rivers flow internationally. But as noted earlier, water has been a source of cooperation, rather than conflict, in both the Middle East and southern Africa.

Warming-induced increases in rainfall in winter, causing floods, and increased drought during the summer are predicted to cause instability in East Africa, where "failed states" and open political tensions among countries exist. Yet even if Africa is strategic because of oil (a dubious proposition), the oil is not located in East Africa. The threat of al Qaeda using Somalia as a base was largely and inadvertently created by the United States by its support of corrupt warlords, not global warming.

Middle East

Despite most evidence to the contrary (cited above), CNA's Military Advisory Board asserts that because of global warming in the Middle East, "competition for scarce resources may exacerbate the level of conflict. This is the region of the world in which the United States is most engaged in militarily."[66] Yet any measures to reduce greenhouse gases—such as a carbon tax or emissions cap-and-trade system—would reduce demand for carbon-based fuels, such as Middle Eastern oil and natural gas. To the extent that such measures are adopted, these oil-producing nations will have fewer dollars to build militaries or nuclear, biological, or chemical weapons to attack nearby countries or beyond.

The advisory board also argues that reduced precipitation will exacerbate water shortages in the region, especially in Israel, Jordan, Egypt, Oman, Iran, and Iraq.[67] Evidence cited above shows that resource shortages are not the primary cause of interstate or intrastate war and that water may be a source of cooperation rather than conflict in the Middle East. Even global warming alarmists Podesta and Ogden admit that conflict over water in the Middle East is unlikely:

> Although this threat may evoke apocalyptic images of armies amassing in deserts to go to war over water, the likelihood of such open conflict in this scenario over the next 30 years is low. There are a very limited number of situations in which it would make strategic sense for a country today to wage war in order to increase its water supply.

Podesta and Ogden echo Barnett's claim that it would be difficult to capture an entire watershed, cut off supplies to foreigners, and protect the watershed and infrastructure from sabotage.[68]

General Anthony C. "Tony" Zinni, former commander in chief of the U.S. Central Command, which overseas the Middle East, opined about the effects of global warming in countries in the region:

> If the government there is not able to cope with the effects, and if other institutions are unable to cope, then you can be faced with a collapsing state. And these end up as breeding grounds for instability, for insurgencies, for warlords. You start to see real extremism. These places act like Petri dishes for extremism and for terrorist networks.[69]

Yet even if global warming does what Zinni says, which is doubtful, it merely exacerbates rather than causes extremism or terrorism. That violence is primarily caused by political factors, such as local grievances. Furthermore, such locally focused extremists and terrorists would not attack American targets unless the United States needlessly involves itself in the local political disputes (which it often does).

Finally and most important, CNA's Military Advisory Board asserts the common wisdom that the Middle East is one of the most strategic regions in the world because it possesses 57 percent of global oil reserves and 45 percent of the world's natural gas reserves.[70] (This last assertion is particularly questionable given the remarkable abundance of shale-derived natural gas that has been discovered only recently.)

The classical economists of the 18th and 19th centuries realized that empire is not cost-effective—that is, it is cheaper to simply buy commodities and goods in the global market than it is to create great armies to ensure supplies flow from abroad to the home country. In fact, not only does the United States have to pay for its expensive military to "protect" the oil, both wars and the increased instability in the Middle East caused by the U.S. military presence there may raise oil prices to U.S. consumers.

Europe and North America

Global warming is predicted to have mainly indirect effects on wealthy regions of the world that have the most resources to deal with the direct effects, which are projected to be significant (for example, the United States and Europe could be especially affected by rising sea levels). However, richer countries can devote more resources to preparing for, adapting to, and recovering from the effects of global warming.[71] From a security standpoint, the most important U.S. allies are wealthy liberal democracies that are much less at risk from global warming, because of their adaptability, than are poorer, less strategic countries. The United States and Europe might have to take refugees and immigrants from drought-stricken regions of Latin America and Africa, respectively. Refugees may also come from rising sea levels in those places.

That is not a security threat but rather a cultural and economic opportunity. Traditionally, immigrants bringing their culture, skills, and ambition, and mixing with prior immigrants and the domestic populations in the United States have led to economic innovations. For example, some of America's wealthiest people have come from abroad. America has done a much better job than Europe in integrating new immigrants, especially Muslims. Predictions of increased radical Islamism in Europe because of warming-induced Muslim immigration shouldn't affect the security of the United States and could be alleviated merely by better European societal integration of the immigrants.

If anything, in conventional global warming scenarios, increased temperatures of a few degrees and higher levels of carbon dioxide in the air will likely increase crop yields in the middle and high

120

latitudes—that is, northern Europe, Russia, and North America. In fact, global warming will likely push up global food production.[72] If that happens, all that is needed is for markets to function freely to distribute food from these regions to areas of warming-induced food production declines in sub-Saharan Africa, the Middle East, and South and Southeast Asia.

Overall, if differential effects of global warming on various regions alter the world's power balance, more than likely the very adaptable United States will fare very well.

Japan

Japan is wealthy and has much social cohesion, so it should weather even abrupt global warming scenarios well.[73]

China and Russia

Although James Woolsey, former director of central intelligence, clearly exaggerates security threats associated with global warming, he does posit one plausible scenario of increased tension between China and Russia. In it, China needs to resettle tens or even hundreds of millions of people from its southern coasts, which have been inundated by rising seas. China eyes parts of Russia, such as Siberia, which might have some warming-induced hikes in agricultural production; is rich in oil, natural gas, and minerals; and has a sparse population to maintain control of it. Woolsey predicts that a conflict between the two destabilized nuclear powers would be likely.[74] (He neglects the fact that the thin, acidic soils that underlie Siberia are virtually useless for agriculture.)

Any such conflict could affect U.S. security. However, Russia still has, and will have for the foreseeable future, many more nuclear weapons than China, and that should cause the Chinese to be cautious. Of course, the even more nuclear-dominant United States could always mediate between the two parties.

Podesta and Ogden make the vague and questionable prediction that the effects of warming could induce more violent protests against the Chinese regime and a deterioration of its relations with the West. But they don't mention that the wealthier China becomes from its continued meteoric economic growth in the next decades, the better it, too, will adapt peacefully to a changing climate.

121

A Self-Fulfilling Prophecy?

Another reason that doomsday global warming scenarios fail as security issues is that they seem to imply sudden increases in drought, floods, severe storms, and sea level rise. In fact, under the increased concentration of greenhouse gases that is being observed, the UN's climate models predict a constant, not an increasing, rate of warming, and that is what is occurring.[75] Thus, probably the only way chaos and violence will result in the face of global warming is if the doomsday "security" thinkers create enough panic among countries' policymakers and publics to create a self-fulfilling prophecy. Much as with wars over allegedly "strategic" oil deposits, merely thinking something is strategic—in the case of global warming, water, food, or arable land—could make war over such scarce resources more likely. Panic over possible shortages of these resources might crowd out faith in markets, which have been allocating scarce resources peacefully for millennia.

Global Warming as a Way to Justify Increased Security Spending

Although an alliance exists between the left and right in characterizing global warming as a security threat, the two camps split when deciding where to spend any additional revenue generated from this exaggeration. The hawks are less interested in the ill effects of global warming and more in finding added post–Cold War threats to justify keeping military spending high. Environmentalists and liberals, however, don't believe—rightly—that armed forces can solve global warming–induced security threats.[76] Instead, they want added money to be spent on dubious alternative fuels projects, greater regulation of greenhouse gases, and so forth.

Because the previously examined security threat from global warming—unlike, for example, standard security threats like the Soviet Union, Iran, North Korea, terrorism, or the proliferation of weapons of mass destruction—is vague, military planning for unpredictable conflicts caused by even harder-to-predict effects of global warming is problematic. Even the old guard security community, as exemplified by CNA's Military Advisory Board, backhandedly admitted that the security threat from global warming is much more diffuse and ethereal than traditional security threats:

> Unlike most conventional security threats that involve a sin-
> gle entity acting in specific ways and points in time, climate
> change has the potential to result in multiple chronic condi-
> tions, occurring globally within the same time frame.[77]

Doug Randall, coauthor with Peter Schwartz of DOD's virtually fictional catastrophic global warming scenario, similarly concluded, "It is a national security threat that is unique because there is no enemy to point your guns at and we have no control over this threat."[78] Also, the Cold War was a zero-sum game, with one side's advantage being the other side's disadvantage. Global warming is an economic externality (carbon emitters don't have to pay all the costs of their emissions) in which all nations and people are poten-tially affected.[79] Military and security organizations can deal with the former but will be flummoxed in planning for the latter because it is foreign to them. Also, security organizations are secretive and oriented toward conflict, whereas transparent and cooperative approaches have been deemed best to work on transnational envi-ronmental problems.

Furthermore, temporally, global warming is a unique threat for military planning. Admiral Donald L. Pilling, former vice chief of naval operations, admitted that planning militarily to counter the effects of global warming was difficult: "One of the problems in talking about this issue is that no one can give you a date by which many of the worst effects will be occurring." He added, "If it's 2050, there isn't a guy in uniform today who will be wearing a uniform then. The Pentagon talks about future year plans that are six years down the road."[80]

Added Military Expenses to Combat Warming Are Implied

At this early juncture, it is hard to pin down the exact expenses the military will allocate to putative warming-induced conflicts. But this situation is actually nothing new. The military never publicly releases estimates of how much it spends to counter even the usual threat scenarios in various regions of the world. That's because if any threat evaporates—as the most severe threat of the Soviet Union actually did—it is harder for politicians to know how much to cut out of the budget.

Rather than propose specific new programs and budgets to deal with conflicts caused by global warming, the security bureaucracies generally see global warming as just another reason to keep defense and security spending high long after the Cold War has ended.

For example, during the Clinton administration, which was much more receptive to international environmental issues than the George W. Bush administration, the DOD and U.S. intelligence community collected and analyzed data on such issues. By combating global warming—employing monitoring devices on ships, satellites, and aircraft and using DOD labs and oceanographic and remote-sensing experts with downtime—the security bureaucracies have yet another high-profile mission to justify their budgets. Under the Obama administration, data exchange from the security bureaucracies to scientists studying global warming has been restored, and the Central Intelligence Agency has established a center to collect intelligence on global warming.[81] A law requires the security implications of global warming to be studied.[82] Others correctly point out that such activities can't help but rather use valuable assets that an overstretched military needs for more important missions—for example, fighting two wars simultaneously.

Losses of overseas bases to any sea level rise—for example, the low-lying naval bases on the island of Guam or Diego Garcia, an island in the Indian Ocean frequently used for U.S. naval projection forces[83]—could entail an expensive transfer of personnel and equipment to new facilities inland or the creation of even more costly bases at sea.

Yet, rising sea levels will occur only gradually, thus allowing adaptation: either alterations to existing bases or moving American forces to bases less affected by global warming. More important, once again, such oversea bases are only needed because the United States has taken on the outdated post–World War II role as the world's sheriff, which it can no longer afford and is reducing, rather than enhancing, the security of American citizens and territory. Global warming or not, the United States should abandon these bases and retrench its imperial overstretch in a time of yawning budged deficits and huge national debt.

There have already been allusions to the need for new equipment. Admiral Pilling noted, "Open seas at the Arctic means you have another side of this continent exposed." He added: "Between the Canadians and us, there are a handful of ships oriented for the northernmost latitudes. But there is not much flexibility or depth there."[84] Similarly, a navy report in 2001 concluded that an Arctic free from summer ice would require "increased scope of naval operations." The study also said that those expanded operations would obligate the navy to reconsider weapon systems effectiveness and other operational factors.[85] Former high-ranking military officials say that any change in ocean salinity because of freshwater ice melting could affect the performance of U.S. submarine equipment, including sonar.[86] These statements imply that the navy might eventually lobby for a new class of specialized warships or anti-submarine equipment or vessels to be used in patrolling the Arctic, even though the threat from decrepit Russian naval forces or other weak northern nations seems very slight. The navy likely would also have to improve weather forecasting techniques, communications, and search-and-rescue capabilities in the region.[87]

Even more expensive, CNA's Military Advisory Board notes that "the loss of some forward bases would require longer range lift and strike capabilities and would increase the military's energy needs." This opens the possibility that new expensive longer-range airlifters, land-based bombers, and conventional missiles would have to be purchased to compensate for U.S. overseas bases being underwater. Of course, the advisory board notes that more money would need to be spent on fuel, maintenance because of harsher operating environments, and expensive replacement systems because the extreme conditions wear out weapons systems faster.[88] Of course, all this is predicated on the United States remaining the policeman of the world, instead of retracting the U.S. defense perimeter, cutting the military budget and forces significantly, and thus reducing the military's carbon footprint.

Also, the military is publicizing its environmental responsibility, researching renewable energy systems that weapon platforms could use instead of oil-based fuels. It also touts inefficient spinoffs to the civilian sector from DOD's unique scale of research and development of such new energy technologies.[89] But it would be more cost-effective to let the civilian market develop these technologies without interference and then adapt them to military weapons rather than undertake more costly and inefficient government research and development of such systems.

CNA's Military Advisory Board also implies using the threat of global warming to get more money for regional military Combatant Commands' Theater Security Cooperation programs:

125

> Climate change threats also create opportunities for constructive engagement such as stability operations and capacity building. . . . The Combatant Command's Theater Security Cooperation Program, which seeks to engage regional states, could be easily focused on climate change mitigation. . . . The objective would be to build the host nation military's capabilities and capacity to support civilian government agencies. It also enhances good governance and promotes stability, making failed states and terrorist incursion less likely.[90]

Clearly, this argument is an almost preposterous excuse to use global warming to pump more money through DOD into the militaries of U.S. client states. Joshua W. Busby, in a report for the Council on Foreign Relations, advocates spending $100 million to fund U.S. military–to–foreign military disaster preparedness conferences, which would help foreign militaries plan for global warming but would have the ulterior motive of building military-to-military ties for other reasons, including intelligence collection. Busby also advocates prepositioning military airlift and ground transportation for future warming-induced emergencies in Africa and then using that as a model for other regions.[91]

It is unclear how spending more on a country's military will help that nation alleviate any ill effects of global warming! Because the militaries of many of these developing states are focused inward toward putting down revolts instead of outward toward countering threats from other nations, it hardly enhances good governance to beef them up. Finally, U.S. intervention and military presence (which the host countries' citizens plausibly see as having ulterior motives besides merely helping out with the effects of global warming) are usually a major factor in causing increased anti-U.S. terrorism. Illustrative of the U.S. military presence's causing increased terrorism are American experiences in generating further instability in, and terrorist threats from, Afghanistan, Pakistan, Iraq, Yemen, and Somalia. In Africa, an augmented U.S. military presence to ostensibly help out with warming-induced emergencies masks the real task of defending oil.

Another argument implies that more money will be needed for the armed forces because the ill effect of global warming at home will require more military activity there, thus taking forces and equipment away from overseas missions of an already-overstretched military. American sensitivities about a militarized police state argue against using the military at home, and its missions there should be limited. Further, the problem of overstretch could easily be eliminated by withdrawing from counterproductive and dangerous foreign quagmires and permanently reducing U.S. military presence and interventionism abroad.

Any countries ill affected by global warming, or claiming that they are, will argue for more U.S., United Nations, or World Bank help with emergencies, refugee relocation, or disaster relief. This pressure began in earnest at the December 2009 Conference of the Parties to the United Nations Framework Convention on Climate Change in Copenhagen. Since the United States funds such bilateral and multilateral aid programs, various constituency groups will use global warming to justify a higher monetary flow to those organizations. For example, a dubious climate change risk reduction fund has been proposed, which would be modeled after President George W. Bush's Emergency Plan for AIDS Relief of $15 billion and would be targeted by the United States to help governments vulnerable to climate change finance adaptation in advance of warming.[92]

Conclusion

Any ill effects of global warming probably would disproportionately fall on poorer, less strategic developing countries because rich, more strategic allied nations have more resources to adapt successfully to climate change. The security of these wealthy states from cross-border aggression by a great power is, and should be, a pillar of U.S. security. Yet research shows that warming-induced resource scarcity is unlikely to cause such interstate conflict and is even suspect in generating the lesser threat of intrastate conflict. Thus, any ill effects from warming in the developing world could possibly be a humanitarian issue but not a crisis for U.S. security. Finally, it is unclear how increasing U.S. defense forces and budgets would help combat global warming. In fact, reducing U.S. forces would cut back American carbon emissions.

5. Climate Change and Trade

Sallie James

The unintended consequences of the spread of global warming into so many aspects of our political life are manifold. Here, Cato's Sallie James explores the complex world of international trade and domestic climate change policies. Without any binding international agreements on carbon dioxide emissions, any nation places itself at a competitive disadvantage by artificially raising the price of carbon-containing energy with a tax or a cap-and-trade system.

Such disparities invite "leakage" of jobs and manufacturing to nations that do not have such emission restrictions. Consequently, policymakers have often proposed compensatory tariffs or border taxes for products originating from nations without strict and enforceable emission limitations. Unfortunately, as shown so clearly below, such policies are very likely to run afoul of international trade agreements, such as those agreed to by the World Trade Organization.

A national cap-and-trade program was passed by the U.S. House of Representatives in June 2009; however, the Senate did not consider analogous legislation. As a result, the Obama Administration is committed to regulation of greenhouse gases by by the Environmental Protection Agency. Any approach will be inadequate to address what is an international issue. U.S. emissions amounted to about 20 percent of global emissions in 2006 and are forecast to fall to about 15 percent by 2035, even without any active emission policy.[1] Clearly, U.S. actions alone will not be sufficient to combat global warming.

The mismatch between the international scope of the problem and the proposed solution presents several difficulties. First, in terms of policy effectiveness, the House bill (dubbed Waxman-Markey, after

its cosponsors) would have only negligible effects on global temperatures. Using a model developed by the National Center for Atmospheric Research, climate researcher Chip Knappenberger estimates
that after the full emission reductions envisioned by the Waxman-
Markey bill take effect, global temperatures would fall by only nine
hundredths of one degree Fahrenheit, compared with business-as-
usual projections for 2050.[2]

Second, cap-and-trade presents political obstacles: Convincing
energy-intensive industries to take on extra costs in the name of
reversing climate change has proved difficult. Concerned that their
efforts to reduce emissions will put them at a competitive disadvantage compared with firms located in jurisdictions with more lenient
emission policies, energy-intensive industries have called for government assistance.

The prospect of inaction by others while the United States acts—
and pays—to reduce emissions has precipitated misguided proposals from politicians attempting to assuage competitiveness concerns
and exert leverage on the rest of the world. Proposals have included
provisions that domestic action on climate change be conditioned
on similar regulations in competing countries; that especially energy-
intensive and/or "trade-vulnerable" industries receive free emission
permits; and that policymakers introduce import barriers on imports
from "uncapped" countries to offset energy-cost differences. The
Waxman-Markey bill incorporated some of these proposals. It
attempts to address competitiveness concerns by giving up to 85
percent of emission permits away free to certain industries and by
implementing border measures to restrict carbon-intensive imports
from countries not operating a carbon control system similar to the
one that the United States implements.

In so doing, however, the bill creates a whole host of other problems, notably by running afoul of global trade rules and exposing
U.S. industry to retaliation and copycat regulations that would negatively affect U.S. exports. Furthermore, by irritating large developing
countries that are most crucial to securing an international agreement
on climate change, the bill may undermine the very purpose for
which it was ostensibly designed. Policies that support a more open
and prosperous global economy will ultimately provide a cleaner
path to a healthier environment.

Why "Leakage" Is a Flawed Concept

When politicians—even the true believers in disastrous global warming—contemplate the economic costs of actions to mitigate climate change, they don't like what they see. They then call for even more government intervention in the form of subsidies or barriers to international competition, ostensibly to counteract the unintended progression of consequences of the earlier intervention. This is how climate change has entered the international trade policy debate.

The arguments made by proponents of barriers to trade in goods from countries that have not adopted climate change mitigation policies are, at least at first glance, compelling. Consider a factory in, say, Ohio. If actions by the federal government to combat climate change add to the factory's costs, by requiring it to buy permits to cover its emissions of greenhouse gases, then the factory will earn less profit. Alternatively, the firm might charge consumers (which could include other businesses using the products as inputs) higher prices, or cut jobs, or make other adjustments to preserve its bottom line. Either way, the factory's activities as a result of climate change policy will be the same as if a tax had been imposed. This scenario is the sense in which climate change mitigation policies are like a tax. The firm now has an extra cost to consider in its production decisions.

Let's suppose the factory was competing against a factory located in, say, China (the locations of our hypothetical rival factories are not accidental; Ohio politicians often invoke competitors in China as a threat to their constituents' livelihoods). Assume further that China, perhaps because it has convinced the world that as a developing country it should not have to curb its emissions of greenhouse gases, has no comparable climate change reduction policy in place. A factory in China producing the same product as our Ohio factory, in other words, will not be saddled with the same climate-related costs as its American counterpart. The U.S. factory will, in a commonly used phrase, be at a "competitive disadvantage" compared with the Chinese factory. As a result of its higher costs, the American factory will find it tough to compete with the Chinese factory and will shed workers or, at the extreme, close down completely. Perhaps, goes the theory, it will move its operations to China to take advantage of the lower costs there. This phenomenon is one-half of the concept called "leakage."

Environmentalists have pointed to another part of carbon leakage: the effect on the overall global level of emissions as a result of

131

[handwritten: Am is at the mercy of Mother Nature (wind blows etc) Cancels whole idea of Idustrial Rev, Western Civ etc]

factories moving from a carbon-constrained country to one with no equivalent policies. Assume that the U.S. factory operates a fairly clean venture compared with its Chinese rival (more later on why this assumption is not always valid). When it closes down, the emissions previously coming from that factory disappear along with the production. Global emissions, holding everything else constant, have fallen. Chalk one up for the environment.

When that factory opens in China, however, the "carbon leakage" theory suggests that the firm will no longer be constrained by environmental considerations. If it emits the same amount of greenhouse gases as when it operated in the United States, then total global emissions on net haven't changed at all. If it takes advantage of the new, more lax regulatory environment, emissions may be even higher than those in the factory's previous home. Total emissions, in other words, may increase as a result of differences between national climate policies.

So much for the theoretical concept of leakage. Just how large is the problem in practice? Many studies have shown that leakage— the threat of overall emission increases if firms move from highly regulated jurisdictions to less regulated jurisdictions—is a relatively minor phenomenon. Policies enacted by one country acting alone tend to cause relatively small emission increases abroad.

Brookings Institution policy scholar Jason Bordoff, for example, points out that most U.S. emissions of greenhouse gases come from parts of the economy that are not part of international trade flows. Those sectors (e.g., transport and housing) could not, by definition, move offshore in search of more lenient jurisdictions and so are somewhat immune from international competitiveness effects.[3] In general, there seems to be little evidence that firms' investment decisions, and where they choose to locate their facilities, are driven by environmental regulations. If anything, the relationship is opposite to the one suggested by environmental activists concerned about a "race to the bottom": Figure 5.1 shows that there is in fact a weak *positive* relationship between environmental standards and net inflows of foreign direct investment. Firms apparently place relatively little weight on environmental compliance costs when making their investment decisions.

Surveying the literature on carbon leakage specifically, Bordoff suggests that only about 10 percent of reduced U.S. emissions would "leak" to other countries. In other words, a 20 percent reduction in

Figure 5.1

ENVIRONMENTAL STANDARDS AND FOREIGN DIRECT INVESTMENT

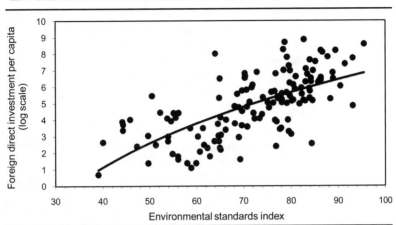

SOURCES: Yale Center for Environmental Law and Policy and Center for International Earth Science Information Network, Columbia University, with the World Economic Forum, and Joint Research Centre of the European Commission, "2008 Environmental Performance Index," http://sedac.cie-sin.columbia.edu/es/epi/; and UNCTAD (United Nations Conference on Trade and Development), http://stats.unctad.org/FDI/TableViewer/ tableView.aspx (2007 data).

U.S. emissions would see only a 2 percent offsetting increase in emissions abroad. A more recent study by World Bank researchers put the figure at about 5 percent: they estimated that the 17 percent cut in emissions to which President Obama committed[4] the United States at the Copenhagen summit would see an offsetting increase in emissions in developing countries by just 1 percent compared with business as usual.[5] The environmental motivation for preventing leakage is, in other words, somewhat overblown.

Because energy costs are typically only about 2 percent of the total costs of manufacturing industries, moreover, any leakage that does occur is seemingly resistant to the efforts of lawmakers to shield domestic competitors from competition: Firms apparently make decisions about location based on more important factors. That is not to say that those more relevant factors, such as corporate tax rates, for example, are not within policymakers' control, just that climate change–related border measures may not have much of a protective effect. Bordoff quotes an Environmental Protection Agency study on the border adjustment program of a previous climate change bill, which estimates that border measures would prevent only half a percentage point of the 10 percent leakage that would otherwise occur.[6] In other words, border measures would see the offsetting increase in emissions in the above example fall from 2 percent leakage to 1.9 percent. Border measures to prevent "leakage" are apparently as ineffective as they are hazardous to the global trading system.

If the environmental form of leakage is at most a mild concern, what about production leakage? Even if the movement of firms from a highly regulated location to a relatively lax one causes fewer emission increases than advocates claim, will jobs and output fall in climate-regulated economies?

The World Bank study cited above calculates that production and exports of energy-intensive goods would in fact fall markedly as a result of emission reduction schemes. The study found that the 17 percent emission reduction target would see production in energy-intensive industries fall by about 4 percent, and exports of those goods would fall by about 12 percent.[7]

The question then becomes, are trade measures a good idea to counteract the estimated falls in production and exports? Would placing a special "carbon tariff" on goods imported from countries that have not implemented emission reduction policies reduce the loss of competitiveness faced by American firms? In one sense, the answer may be yes. If the tariff was based on the carbon content of imports, the World Bank researchers estimated that the fall in production in energy-intensive industries would be almost halved. But to achieve this, the tariffs would have to be about 26 percent on China's imports and 20 percent on India's. Imagine a new tax of 26 percent on all imports from China and the extra costs that American families would face as a result. It is important to emphasize, too, that it is not just U.S. consumers who would face higher prices for imports: Many U.S. manufacturers would be faced with higher input costs as a result of those tariffs. By "helping" some American firms face international competition, the border measures would harm other American firms by raising their costs, just when they are facing new climate change regulations.

The picture drawn by green protectionists of trade measures negating the loss of American firms' competitiveness is clouded, however, by some inconvenient truths about the sources of America's imports of energy-intensive goods. As Table 5.1 shows, most U.S. imports of energy-intensive goods come from other relatively wealthy countries.

Moreover, most of those source countries have lower greenhouse gas emissions than the United States, have stricter greenhouse gas standards in place, or have both. China, in this sense, is not "the competition."

What about the second attractive feature of carbon tariffs: their use as "leverage" to inflict economic pressure on countries to implement emission reduction programs in order to avoid the tariff? The numbers are not promising here, either.

As Table 5.2 shows, the American market is not a huge sales draw for many of these international players. China and India, the main sources of anxiety for American industry groups, sell most of their energy-intensive goods in the domestic market or in other countries. Only 0.7 percent of Indian iron and steel, for example, is sold in the United States. The highest proportion of China's sales of energy-intensive goods accounted for by the United States is 0.9 percent, for cement. While China and India have strongly denounced the proposed imposition of carbon tariffs on their goods (more on that later), their overall sales would be little affected. The political cost of alienating these huge and growing international players—and the relatively modest U.S. sales figures suggest their objections are indeed based largely on political considerations at this stage—would appear to vastly outweigh any (spurious) benefit to American firms that would be protected by a carbon tariff at consumers' expense.

Legal and Practical Problems with Carbon-Based Trade Measures

As if the economic case against imposing carbon tariffs was not strong enough, there are compelling legal reasons that should give politicians pause. Through its membership—indeed leadership—in the World Trade Organization, the international body charged by its members with setting and monitoring the rules of international commercial engagement among them, the United States has a clear interest in seeing the integrity of world trade law maintained. The rules have so far served the United States well and have more broadly prevented a full-scale repeat of the tit-for-tat protectionism

Table 5.1
U.S. Imports of Energy-Intensive Goods

Steel

Rank	Country	Value	% Share
1	Canada	7,094	18.3%
2	China	6,604	17.0%
3	Mexico	3,361	8.7%
4	Korea	2,319	6.0%
5	Japan	2,179	5.6%
6	Germany	2,031	5.2%
7	India	1,967	5.1%
8	Taiwan	1,222	3.1%
9	Ukraine	1,189	3.1%
10	Brazil	1,121	2.9%

Total Imports
EU-27: 7,984 20.6%
OECD: 24,174 62.3%

Cement

Rank	Country	Value	% Share
1	Canada	338	42.8%
2	China	106	13.4%
3	Mexico	87	11.0%
4	Colombia	68	8.6%
5	Korea	54	6.8%
6	Taiwan	36	4.6%
7	France	22	2.8%
8	Sweden	13	1.6%
9	Greece	12	1.5%
10	Croatia	10	1.3%

Total Imports
EU-27: 63 8.0%
OECD: 549 69.6%

Paper

Rank	Country	Value	% Share
1	Canada	9,509	52.6%
2	China	2,274	12.6%
3	Finland	993	5.5%
4	Germany	954	5.3%
5	Mexico	844	4.7%
6	Japan	485	2.7%
7	Korea	412	2.3%
8	Indonesia	291	1.6%
9	Brazil	245	1.4%
10	France	229	1.3%

Total Imports
EU-27: 3,200 17.7%
OECD: 14,703 81.4%

Aluminum

Rank	Country	Value	% Share
1	Canada	7,629	58.8%
2	Russia	1,053	8.1%
3	China	741	5.7%
4	Germany	648	5.0%
5	Brazil	299	2.3%
6	Venezuela	293	2.3%
7	Argentina	278	2.1%
8	United Arab Em	241	1.9%
9	Mexico	209	1.6%
10	South Africa	183	1.4%

Total Imports
EU-27: 1,180 9.1%
OECD: 9,410 72.6%

Chemicals

Rank	Country	Value	% Share
1	Algeria	2,693	18.3%
2	Saudi Arab	2,056	14.0%
3	Iraq	1,651	11.2%
4	Venezuela	1,383	9.4%
5	Trin & Tob	1,199	8.2%
6	Canada	1,040	7.1%
7	Korea	750	5.1%
8	Libya	616	4.2%
9	Brazil	441	3.0%
10	Russia	419	2.8%

Total Imports
EU-27: 591 4.0%
OECD: 2,683 18.2%

SOURCE: U.S. International Trade Commission, Interactive Tariff and Trade Database, available from http://dataweb.usitc.gov.

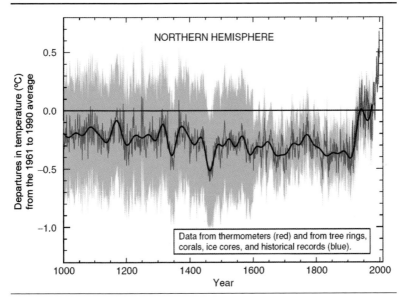

SOURCE: Intergovernmental Panel on Climate Change, *Climate Change 2001: Impacts, Adaptation, and Vulnerability* (Cambridge: Cambridge University Press, 2001).

NOTE: The blue line with gray shading depicts confidence bands. The red line is the temperature data from actual observations.

Figure 2.4
NORTHERN HEMISPHERE CLIMATE RECONSTRUCTIONS AND INSTRUMENTAL TEMPERATURES, 1000–2000

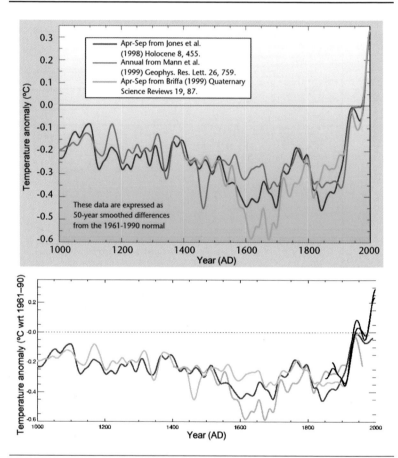

SOURCE: World Meteorological Organization, 2000, http://www.wmo.ch/pages/prog/wcp/wcdmp/statemnt/wmo913.pdf; *bottom*: Climate Research Unit, University of East Anglia, "CRU Update 2," press release, November 24, 2009, http://www.uea.ac.uk/mac/comm/media/press/2009/nov/CRUupdate.

NOTE: In the top chart, observed temperatures are grafted onto the tree-ring temperatures (green and blue lines). The bottom chart terminates different "proxy" records in 1960 (green line) and 1980 (blue line). The bottom chart was released by East Anglia in response to Climategate.

Figure 2.5
TREE-RING TEMPERATURE PROXY RECORD OF UNIVERSITY OF EAST ANGLIA'S KEITH BRIFFA, 1400–2000

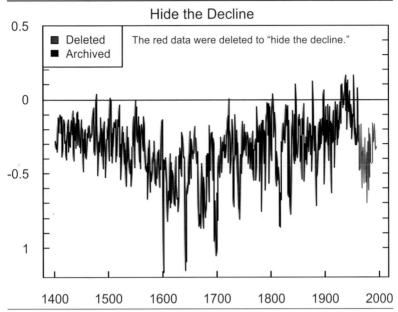

SOURCE: ClimateAudit.com website, http://www.climateaudit.com.

Figure 2.6
RUSSIAN SURFACE TEMPERATURE HISTORY, 1860–2007

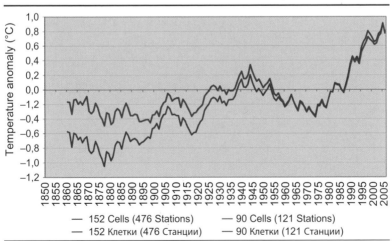

SOURCE: N. A. Pivivarova, "How Warming Is Made: The Case of Russia," Institute of Economic Analysis, Moscow, 2009.

NOTE: The red line indicates the Russian surface temperature history using the 121 CRU stations; the blue line incorporates all available 476 stations.

Figure 2.7
PRESIDENT OBAMA RETURNS FROM THE COPENHAGEN GLOBAL
WARMING CONFERENCE, DECEMBER 19, 2009

Figure 2.9
EXTENT OF ANTARCTIC ICE, NOVEMBER 1978–DECEMBER 2006

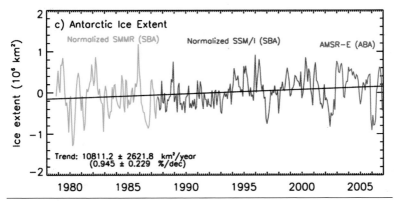

SOURCE: Josefino C. Comiso and Fumihiko Nishio, "Trends in the Sea Ice Cover Using Enhanced and Compatible AMSR-E, SSM/I, and SMMR Data," *Journal of Geophysical Research* 113 (2008): C02S07.

NOTE: These data are more smoothed than those from *Cryosphere Today*, but they give the same result.

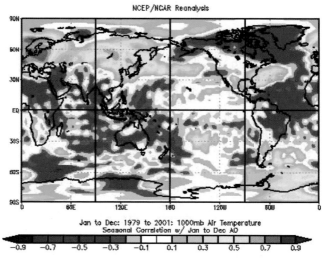

NCEP/NCAR Reanalysis

Jan to Dec: 1979 to 2001: 1000mb Air Temperature
Seasonal Correlation w/ Jan to Dec AO

NOAA/ESRL Physical Sciences Division

SOURCE: National Oceanic and Atmospheric Administration, http//:
www.esrl.noaa.gov/psd/data/correlation/.

NOTE: The referee claimed we used only winter values, and this was a basis
for rejecting the paper.

Figure 6.3
CHANGING GLOBAL MALARIA ENDEMICITY SINCE 1900: (a)
PREINTERVENTION ENDEMICITY (APPROXIMATELY 1900); (b)
CONTEMPORARY ENDEMICITY (2007); (c) CHANGE IN ENDEMICITY
CLASS BETWEEN 1900 AND 2007

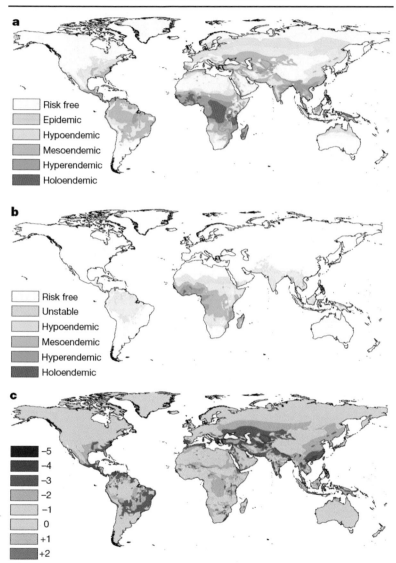

SOURCE: Peter W. Gething and others, "Climate Change and the Global
Malaria Recession," *Nature* 465 (2010): 342–45.

Figure 6.6
Guinean Students Study under the Lights of the Conakry Airport Parking Lot, June 2007

Source: Rebecca Blackwell/The Associated Press.

Figure 7.2
Anomalies of Annual Land Surface Temperature Difference from 2000–2009 Minus 1896–1905 (°C)

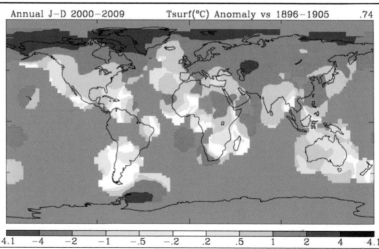

Source: Goddard Institute of Space Studies, http://data.giss.nasa.gov/gistemp/maps/.
Note: Average temperatures over the entire map are 0.74°C higher in the latter decade.

Table 5.2
How Much Leverage?: U.S. Imports as a Share of Foreign
Output, 2006-07 (Percentages)

Country/ Region	Iron and Steel	Primary Aluminum	Cement	Pulp Products	Nitrogenous Fertilizers
Brazil	8.3	5.0	1.1	10.8	3.5
China	0.5	0.3	0.9	0.1	0.5
India	0.7	0.0	0.0	n/a	0.0
Mexico	10.6	n/a	5.6	1.1	8.3
Middle East	0.1	6.5	0.2	0.0	22.1

SOURCE: Government Accounting Office, "Climate Change Trade Measures: Considerations for U.S. Policy Makers," report number GAO-09-24R, July 8, 2009.

during the Great Depression. When members of the WTO are deemed to violate the rules, the injured members can retaliate against the errant member. Any violation of WTO rules as a result of trade provisions in climate change policies could prove costly for U.S. businesses and consumers, and it is crucial that any policies to protect the environment avoid contradicting the commitments that the United States has made.

Two provisions of Waxman-Markey stand out as possibly covered by World Trade Organization agreements. First, the free allowances granted to energy-intensive industries may constitute "actionable" subsidies under the WTO Agreement on Subsidies and Countervailing Measures. Second, the imposition of import restrictions in the form of an "international reserve allowance program" may violate the nondiscrimination requirements of Articles I and III of the General Agreement on Tariffs and Trade. We will cover these two types of domestic industry assistance in turn.

Before proceeding with the analysis, though, a caveat is in order. The extent to which a trade barrier or subsidy is consistent with WTO rules is often difficult to establish in advance. While it is impossible for this chapter to cover the full range of claims that would be raised in a dispute, there are some fairly clear guidelines about which environmental or related measures would not likely conform to U.S. obligations under WTO rules. The discussion that follows is therefore only a brief outline of the types of questions

137

that a WTO reviewing body would consider in conducting its analysis and formulating a ruling.[9]

With that disclaimer in mind, let us turn our attention to the free allowances granted to address the purported problem of carbon leakage. Giving assistance to certain U.S. firms to offset, or at least help them adjust to, the increased costs associated with regulations designed to reverse climate change may constitute a subsidy under WTO rules. In this regard, it is important to note here that the WTO definition of a subsidy is broader than the conventional definition, which usually refers to government outlays. Article 1.1(a)(1)(ii) of the Agreement on Subsidies and Countervailing Measures includes in its definition of a subsidy "government revenue that is otherwise due is foregone or not collected (e.g., fiscal incentives such as tax credits)." In addition to government grants and tax exemptions for certain industries, free emission allowances to certain U.S. industries, for example, would likely fit this definition of a subsidy and would therefore be subject to the other provisions of the agreement.[10] Certainly, if the allowances are then resold on the carbon market, they would likely represent an actionable subsidy.[11]

Subsidies for nonagricultural goods are generally divided into two categories (additional rules for agricultural subsidies are provided by the Agreement on Agriculture). The first category is prohibited subsidies, which are those subsidies that are contingent on export performance or on the use of domestic content, rather than imported inputs. These subsidies are forbidden under the terms of Article 3 of the Agreement on Subsidies and Countervailing Measures. Subsidies that are not prohibited are nonetheless actionable if they cause "adverse effects" to the interests of another member, for example, by "displac[ing] or imped[ing] imports . . . in the market of the subsidizing Member,"[12] or are specific (i.e., limited) to certain industries and give a benefit to domestic producer(s) in that industry. If a subsidy is found to be actionable, the offending member must remove the subsidy or its injurious effects.

Since the WTO includes in its definition of subsidies "revenue foregone," and if the allowances were sold by the recipient firms at a profit, that would certainly be deemed a subsidy. And since the subsidies would be targeted toward some firms and not others, they would be "specific," one of the criteria for determining whether a subsidy breaks WTO rules. If the free allowances allowed the U.S.

firms to produce more than they otherwise would in a free market and harmed trade partners' interests (e.g., by lowering the world price of a certain type of product), then the WTO would likely rule the subsidy actionable. The injured member(s) would be allowed to retaliate, which has typically involved imposing higher, punitive tariffs on U.S. exports.

In addition to free emission allowances, new policies that give subsidies or consumer rebates to manufactured items that are produced in the United States would create legal problems. The Waxman-Markey bill, for example, contains a "Vehicle Manufacturing Assistance Program," which will provide financial assistance to automobile manufacturers to "facilitate the manufacture of plug-in electric drive vehicles . . . that are *developed and produced in the United States*"(emphasis added). Although many foreign carmakers have factories in the United States and would presumably qualify for those subsidies, denying them to imported cars (including those from U.S.-owned factories abroad) would seem to undermine the bill's ostensible purpose of protecting the global environment by encouraging the development of fuel-efficient cars. Those genuinely interested in protecting the environment would presumably want to encourage electric cars, no matter where they came from. Likewise, subsidies for users of renewable or "clean" energy technology would need to avoid discriminating against imports of competing goods and services in order to be at least superficially safe from legal challenge.

Bordoff makes the case that since firms make production decisions based on marginal costs and revenues, a simple transfer from the government in the form of free emission allowances will not influence production decisions. A firm that uses all its free allowances will, after all, forgo the opportunity to sell those allowances on the market and will pass on those opportunity costs to consumers. The domestic firm and its downstream consumers are thus *not* exempted from paying the full cost of emissions even if the allowance is "free" and will not have a competitive advantage over taxed importers. Importers may, as a consequence, escape the sort of "adverse effects" that would render the subsidy actionable. If free allowances are "production-decision neutral," though, giving free allowances will not be effective in preventing the reductions in output and emissions that the plan aims to achieve, even as it transfers taxpayer money to the firms' shareholders.[13]

The Waxman-Markey bill provides free emission permits to particular U.S. industries thought to be at special risk of competition from noncompliant countries, and whose energy use is relatively high, and therefore particularly vulnerable to increased energy costs. However, it may not be the benign sort of free allowance scheme outlined by Bordoff. First, the bill specifies that electricity companies, for example, must use the proceeds from selling emission allowances to keep prices low for consumers. If prices to consumers do not increase, demand will not fall, and the firms' output will remain constant (or possibly increase).

Second, it appears that emission allowances would be given on the basis of output to a certain subset of industries. Under this type of allocation, a certain number of allowances are set aside for specified industries, and each firm in the industry would receive allowances based on its share of industry output. Bordoff refers to this arrangement as "the functional equivalent of auctioning off allowances and then using the revenue to subsidize production."[14] The firms benefiting would have less incentive to decrease output absent the de facto production subsidy (indeed, they may increase production) and thus would potentially harm importers' interests.[15]

As an alternative way of helping exporters of energy-intensive products compete abroad, some researchers have proposed that exporters of energy-intensive goods get a rebate on the taxes they have paid on energy. The environmental case for that is, to say the least, very weak indeed.

When the environmental purpose of a policy is in doubt, that creates legal problems. Rebates on energy taxes or charges (or their functional equivalent) relating to emission allowances have no environmental justification as would likely be required by WTO rules: the taxes were presumably put in place to *discourage* the production of environmentally damaging goods or, more accurately, to discourage producing them in environmentally damaging ways. Rebating those taxes on the basis of output therefore reduces the price signal effect and undermines the argument that policies are aimed at protecting the environment.

The legal status of any free allowances, at least as far as the WTO is concerned, will therefore depend quite substantially on the details of how the scheme is structured. To the extent that WTO law allows for environmental exceptions to usual trade rules, there must be a clear link between the trade measure and the purpose (i.e., protecting the environment). Protecting domestic firms from import competition—even if their competitive disadvantage derives from environmental regulations—is not a legitimate purpose in this respect. As Bordoff says, "The more effective free allocation is in protecting employment and output in adversely affected sectors, the more likely it may be to violate WTO law."[16] It appears that free emission allowances can be either WTO compliant or effective in preventing carbon "leakage," but not both.

It is impossible to say a priori whether this or that manner of distributing carbon allowances is WTO compliant. But it is clear that the program of free allowances set up under Waxman-Markey offers special favors to select industries in response to overblown concerns about a loss of international competitiveness.

Carbon Tariffs

A far greater threat to the world trading system is posed by Waxman-Markey's creation of a system of import restrictions that could go into effect as early as 2020. These import restrictions, like the free allowance program, purport to deal with carbon leakage, but their broader goal is the far more ambitious one alluded to earlier: using trade restrictions as "leverage" to encourage other countries to enact carbon-control policies, rather like trade sanctions are used to try to encourage regime change or other political goals. Restricting market access in order to force other countries to do this or that is a long-standing problem in trade policy, and Waxman-Markey now threatens to apply this discredited strategy to an entirely new realm—and to open a very unpleasant can of worms in the process.

The latest scheme for using trade as a weapon under Waxman-Markey would direct the president to enter into negotiations for an international agreement on controlling carbon emissions. If no such agreement has been reached by January 1, 2018, the president is required to set up an "international reserve allowance program." The only escape hatch is if the president determines that such a program would not be in the national economic or environmental interest and both houses of Congress pass a resolution approving the president's determination.

The international reserve allowance program would be applied on a sector-by-sector basis. Specifically, the program would apply to a particular industrial sector unless at least 85 percent of imports in that sector are produced in countries that (a) have signed an international agreement with the United States that imposes restrictions on greenhouse gas emissions that are at least as stringent as those in the United States, (b) have signed a multilateral or bilateral emission reduction agreement with the United Sates for the sector in question, or (c) have an annual energy or greenhouse gas intensity in that sector that is less than or equal to that of the equivalent U.S. sector.[17] As early as 2020, imports in a covered sector would be prohibited unless the importer has obtained an "appropriate" amount of emission allowances from the international reserve allowance program. That requirement would not apply, however, to imports from (a) countries that have met one of the three criteria above, (b) countries that are classified as the least developed of developing countries, or (c) countries that are responsible for less than 0.5 percent of total global greenhouse gas emissions and less than 5 percent of U.S. imports of covered goods in the sector.

How much would the requirement to obtain emission allowances restrict trade in practice? The legislative language offers a few clues. First, the price of international reserve allowances would be set to equal the price for domestic emission allowances in the most recent auction. The idea is to equalize costs. Second, while the legislation provides no direct criteria for how to determine the appropriate quantity of allowances that a given importer would be required to obtain, it does specify that the purpose of the international reserve allowance program is to minimize carbon leakage as a result of differences between the costs of complying with Waxman-Markey and the costs of complying with other countries' carbon-emission regulations. In that regard, the legislation specifies that the quantity of allowances required would be adjusted (down to as low as zero) to take account of free allowances provided to U.S. firms in the relevant sector.

Assessing the trade impact of Waxman-Markey's system of import restrictions can be broken down into two interrelated but distinct questions. First, if it is actually put into effect, would it violate U.S. obligations under World Trade Organization agreements? Second, even if it is permissible under WTO rules, would the import restrictions otherwise do harm to the world trading system? The answer to the first question is a very fuzzy maybe. The answer to the second question is a clear and emphatic yes.

Let's examine the complicated legal questions of WTO consistency. The United States has throughout the history of the GATT/WTO agreed to—indeed, pushed for—some clear principles of international trade. First, the idea of national treatment: countries should treat imported goods the same as domestically produced goods once they have crossed the border. Second, the concept of "most favored nation," the idea that similar products (and this concept is explored further below) from any WTO member should be treated equally. The third key principle of the WTO is that members should not raise tariffs above the limits they have contractually promised to other members. Carbon tariffs pose threats to each of these long-held, important principles.

Some supporters of Waxman-Markey-type trade restrictions engage in wishful thinking and argue breezily that the import restrictions in question constitute uncontroversial "border-tax adjustments" that comply with WTO rules. Indeed, some even go so far as to say that the WTO has already basically given a green light for the restrictions. *New York Times* columnist Paul Krugman, for example, may have made his Nobel Prize–winning academic reputation arguing for the benefits of free trade, but he has recently argued that climate change is such a global-catastrophe-in-the-making that the normal economic case against protectionism doesn't apply. And he claims that WTO rules allow for his preferred course of action:

> The WTO has looked at the issue, and suggests that carbon tariffs may be viewed the same way as border adjustments associated with value-added taxes. It has long been accepted that a VAT is essentially a sales tax—a tax on consumers—which for administrative reasons is collected from producers. Because it's essentially a tax on consumers, it's legal, and also economically efficient, to collect it on imported goods as well as domestic production; it's a matter of leveling the playing field, not protectionism. And the same would be true of carbon tariffs.[18]

Krugman may be gifted at simplifying complex economic issues, but he has grossly oversimplified the legal issue here. When he says that the WTO has "looked at the issue," he is referring to a joint WTO/United Nations Environmental Programme report that merely summarizes the relevant provisions, precedents, and existing literature on the question of WTO consistency—without reaching any prescriptive conclusion at all.[19]

It is true, as Krugman states, that WTO rules permit the collection of domestic "indirect taxes"—value-added, sales, and excise taxes—on imported products. Accordingly, if a country were to impose a domestic tax on products based on the amount of carbon emitted in their production, and it then levied a corresponding tax on imports, there would be a plausible case that such a border-tax adjustment complies with WTO rules. Even here, though, there is a major complication. Under Article II2(a) of the General Agreement on Tariffs and Trade, a border-tax adjustment is permissible only when it constitutes "a charge equivalent to an internal tax ... in respect of the like domestic product or in respect of *an article from which the imported product has been manufactured or produced in whole or in part*" (emphasis added). So the question arises: does a tax on carbon emissions constitute a tax on an article from which a product "has been manufactured or produced in whole or in part"? Normally, border adjustments pertain to taxes on products or on inputs physically incorporated into products, as opposed to a waste product emitted during production (carbon in this case). While there is some WTO precedent to suggest that taxes on items not physically incorporated into the product can still be subject to a border adjustment, the question remains unresolved.[20]

However, Waxman-Markey doesn't impose a carbon tax; instead, it creates a cap-and-trade regime. And the alleged border adjustment doesn't consist of a tax, either, but rather a requirement under certain circumstances to obtain emission allowances. It is possible, of course, to argue that the requirement to obtain emission allowances domestically and for imports is the *economic equivalent* of a tax in the sense that it will increase firms' energy costs, but that is a novel and untested argument that stretches the WTO's border-tax adjustment provisions far beyond their currently understood scope. All things considered, it seems a long shot that Waxman-Markey's international reserve allowance program would be deemed a border-tax adjustment under WTO rules.

The most straightforward characterization of Waxman-Markey's import restrictions is that they consist of regulations that apply to imports from some countries but not others. And that kind of discrimination between WTO members seems to run afoul of the "most favored nation" principle incorporated in Article I of the GATT.[21] According to Article I, "Any advantage, favour, privilege or immunity granted by any contracting party to any product originating in . . . any other country shall be accorded immediately and unconditionally to the like product originating in . . . the territories of all other contracting parties." In other words, if imports from the European Union are exempt from the requirement to obtain emission allowances, imports of "like products" from China should receive the same exemption.

So the big question is, are widgets from the EU and China "like products" despite differences in the amount of carbon emitted in producing them (or differences in the emission control regulations that apply to producing them)? While there is room for debate, the answer really ought to be yes. Academic lawyer Javier de Cendra points out that no WTO ruling so far has explicitly accepted that the way in which a good is produced (called processing and production methods) is a legitimate basis for determining that goods are "unlike."[22]

Until now, that way of thinking has suited the United States very well; it has repeatedly resisted attempts by other WTO members (including the European Union) to introduce processing and production methods as relevant factors in trade policy. In fact, as U.S. trade lawyer Gary Horlick pointed out in recent Senate testimony, the attempts by Krugman and others to reinterpret WTO rules to allow them may backfire on the United States:

> It is tempting to say that we can re-interpret existing WTO rules to permit whatever measures are necessary to protect the environment. But do we really want to change those rules? The key to the U.S. economy is constant innovation. One of the important fields where we lead the world of innovation is biotechnology. . . . So far the United States has resisted efforts in Europe and elsewhere to limit our market access for our products because of how they are produced—from biotech means. But if we re-interpret WTO rules to allow trade barriers based on how things are made, we open up a can of worms—and might permit other countries to block our biotech exports.[23]

And as the WTO Appellate Body (the final authority on interpreting WTO rules) stated in an important ruling on the criteria for determining like products, "A determination of 'likeness' ... is, fundamentally, a determination about the nature and extent of a competitive relationship between and amongst products."[24] Even if physically identical or similar goods are made with varying levels of carbon emitted in the process, or under different regulatory regimes, the fact is they still compete head-to-head with one another in the marketplace. Indeed, the fact that they do is what gives rise to concerns about carbon leakage and competitiveness in the first place.

Accordingly, there is a very strong prima facie case that Waxman-Markey's system of import restrictions would violate Article I of the GATT.[25] That does not necessarily mean, however, that Waxman-Markey would violate the United States' WTO obligations overall, because Article XX of the GATT allows for exceptions from other WTO rules under certain circumstances. The exception that would most plausibly apply to Waxman-Markey is Article XX(g),[26] which reads as follows:

> Subject to the requirement that such measures are not applied in a manner which would constitute a means of arbitrary or unjustifiable discrimination between countries where the same conditions prevail, or a disguised restriction on international trade, nothing in this Agreement shall be construed to prevent the adoption or enforcement by any contracting party of measures: ...
>
> (g) relating to the conservation of exhaustible natural resources if such measures are made effective in conjunction with restrictions on domestic production or consumption.

Under existing WTO precedent, there are good arguments that, in principle, a cap-and-trade regime with an international reserve allowance program could fit within the language of Article XX(g). But under that same precedent, there are also good arguments that the specific import restrictions imposed by Waxman-Markey would *not* qualify for this exception to normal WTO rules.

In a celebrated case about U.S. trade measures designed to protect turtles from shrimp nets, the WTO Appellate Body ruled that unilateral trade measures that condition market access on adopting policies to conserve a natural resource (in that case, a ban on imported shrimp from countries that had not adopted policies designed to protect sea turtles from being accidentally caught in shrimp nets) can, in principle, fall under Article XX(g). However, the Appellate

Body also ruled that the initial U.S. import ban on shrimp as applied by U.S. authorities constituted "arbitrary or unjustifiable discrimination" and thus violated WTO rules.[27]

Looking at the details of the Appellate Body's reasoning in that case, two questions stand out as especially important in assessing the import restrictions that would be imposed under Waxman-Markey. First, will due process be observed in determining how trade restrictions are imposed? In other words, will the process be transparent and will affected countries have the right to participate in the process? Consider in this regard the Appellate Body's disapproving characterization of the process for determining which countries would be subject to the U.S. import ban on shrimp:

> The certification processes . . . consist principally of administrative ex parte inquiry or verification by [U.S. government officials]. . . . [T]here is no formal opportunity for an applicant country to be heard, or to respond to any arguments that may be made against it, in the course of the certification process before a decision to grant or to deny certification is made. Moreover, no formal written, reasoned decision, whether of acceptance or rejection, is rendered on applications. . . . Countries whose applications are denied also do not receive notice of such denial (other than by omission from the list of approved applications) or of the reasons for the denial. No procedure for review of, or appeal from, a denial of an application is provided.[28]

If the implementing regulations for imposing trade restrictions under Waxman-Markey follow a similar pattern, an adverse ruling by the WTO is likely.

Second, will the methodology for determining the amount of international reserve allowances required take due account of different conditions in other countries? Even if it were clear that carbon tariffs were allowable in principle, the *level at which they are set* will also be relevant in assessing their WTO consistency. Here again, the shrimp-turtle case is instructive. The Appellate Body found that a blanket ban on all shrimp imported from a given country amounted to unjustifiable discrimination:

> Shrimp caught using methods identical to those employed in the United States have been excluded from the United States market solely because they have been caught in waters

of countries that have not been certified by the United States.
... We believe that discrimination results not only when
countries in which the same conditions prevail are differently
treated, but also when the application of the measure at issue
does not allow for any inquiry into the *appropriateness of the
regulatory program for the conditions prevailing in those exporting
countries.*[29] [emphasis added]

Which local conditions could be relevant in the context of climate
change regulations? First, the emission control policies of the country
of origin: Is the exporting country getting due credit for its policies
even if they differ from the U.S. model? It may well be the case
that the phrase "conditions prevailing in those exporting countries"
means that the appropriate regulatory program is quite different in
scope or style from that prevailing in the United States. A second
relevant factor might be the historical carbon emissions of the country of origin: Should developing countries be held to a different
standard to account for the fact that developed countries have produced most of the carbon emissions to date? And third, the actual
carbon emissions of the producing firm: Should a firm with clean
production technology be punished just because its host country's
policies are less rigorous than its own practices? Many factories
newly built in developing countries may in fact be more environmentally efficient than older factories in the rich world.[30]

This last factor could be important from an environmental point
of view, not just in determining the legality of a policy. Assessing
the carbon footprint of a product on the basis of national averages
rather than the emissions of the individual producer will potentially
work *against* the ostensible purpose of climate change regulations.
Think about it this way: if efforts to produce goods more cleanly
impose costs on a firm, and those efforts are not recognized by a
trade partner that discriminates on a country-level basis rather than
a firm-level basis, then unilateral trade restrictions could in fact
discourage the adoption of cleaner technologies. If all firms in, say,
China, have to face the same tariff on their goods by virtue of their
factory's location, and regardless of their firm-specific emissions,
they may not invest in more expensive, new technologies. Why
produce at higher cost if you cannot gain improved market access
as a result?

148

On the other hand, and this is a factor that politicians seem not to have fully comprehended, the alternative approach—tailoring the tariff facing each firm according to its specific emission standards—poses enormous practical difficulties. Policies aimed at recognizing different production methods *within* countries in an attempt to satisfy WTO obligations promise to be an administrative nightmare. As Howse and Eliason point out, international supply chains make this task even more difficult: "The difficulty . . . [is] one of determining accurately whether a particular imported product is produced with significantly higher carbon emissions than a particular domestic product. This refers to the challenge . . . of ascertaining the carbon footprint of a particular imported product, which may have gone through production stages in several different facilities at different locations."[31] Pity the poor customs official tasked with assigning emission allowance requirements for even something as simple as a pencil on the basis of not only the country of origin but also the *firm* of origin.

In addition to the risk of violating Article XX's injunctions against "unjustifiable or arbitrary discrimination," Waxman-Markey-type schemes face a further and serious hurdle. Specifically, there is a real question as to whether the import restrictions would be found to be "relating" to the conservation of exhaustible natural resources—and even if they are, whether they nonetheless amount to a "disguised restriction on international trade." The Waxman-Markey bill appeared to say that the "appropriate" quantity of international reserve allowances should be based on differences in the cost of production between the U.S. industry and the foreign industry—as opposed to differences in carbon emissions. Thus, it seems that the import restrictions would be designed primarily to protect U.S. producers from foreign competition, not to encourage the adoption of carbon-emission regulations abroad. We learned previously that breaking the link between the trade instrument and the environmental purpose is a recipe for legal challenge. And as a practical matter, requiring importers to buy allowances based on the latest auction price is not guaranteed to equalize carbon costs if the competing domestic firm paid a different price when it bought its emission allowances.[32]

From the perspective of consistency with WTO rules, any import restrictions designed to alleviate the competitive burden borne by domestic firms (compared with their uncapped competitors) of environmental regulation are a shaky proposition indeed. All the available WTO jurisprudence to date would caution governments against framing their climate-related policies in terms of fairness to domestic producers that face competition from uncapped firms abroad. The key, it seems, is to ensure that environmental policies are focused squarely on protecting the environment. While Waxman-Markey certainly contains language that links the imposition of trade restrictions to encouraging other countries to adopt emission control policies, environmental protection—as opposed to trade protection—is clearly not the only, or even primary, focus. This mixture of motives could ultimately prove decisive in a WTO case.

Whether or not any climate-related import restrictions would end up violating WTO rules is thus a distinctly murky question. Regardless of how that issue would ultimately be decided, though, there is little doubt that unilateral U.S. import restrictions like those in Waxman-Markey would be a major setback for the world trading system—as well as international cooperation on climate change.

International Blowback

The trade implications of U.S. carbon tariffs seem fairly clear. First of all, the United States would face harsh condemnation from other countries. For a taste of how our trading partners would react, consider this recent statement by Canada's environment minister Jim Prentice:

> Trade protectionism in the name of environmental protection would be a prescription for disaster for both the global economy and the global environment. . . . Border carbon adjustments would be a thinly disguised restriction on trade and an impediment both to wealth creation and to the attainment of our collective objective, which is to address greenhouse gas emissions and to reduce them. They would constitute arbitrary discrimination. They won't work and they threaten constructive negotiations.[33]

And that's a statement from a *rich* country official. It seems clear by now that poorer, fast-growing economies will have to sign on to any international agreement on climate change if it is to be effective. How are those prospects helped by carbon tariffs? The environment minister of India recently promised to litigate any attempts by rich countries to impose carbon tariffs. Speaking to a specialist trade news source, Jairam Ramesh said:

> If they impose such a tax, we will take them to the WTO dispute settlement forum. . . . [W]e will deal [with this] through hard negotiations. Such barriers are not going to be WTO-compatible and we will fight it.[34]

He doesn't sound too conciliatory, does he?

The fact is the United States would find itself diplomatically isolated precisely when it was seeking to encourage closer international cooperation to combat climate change. Even advocates of aggressive action on climate change recognize this. Matthew Yglesias, a prominent blogger at the Center for American Progress, shrewdly analyzes how self-defeating Waxman-Markey–style trade restrictions would be:

> The bottom line about the international aspects of climate change is that the very idea of an effective response *assumes* the existence of a generally cooperative international environment. It doesn't assume the nonexistence of the odd "rogue" state here or there, but it assumes the absence of any kind of serious great power rivalries. Not just China, but also India and probably Russia, Brazil, and Indonesia, as well, are going to need to cooperate in a serious way with the OECD [Organization for Economic Cooperation and Development] nations on this. And I just don't see how you're going to get where you need to get through coercion. If anything, I think attempted economic coercion of China is more likely to wind up breaking down solidarity between the US, EU, and Japan than anything else. First, we impose our carbon tariff. Then suddenly Airbus and European car companies are getting all kinds of sales because the EU hasn't followed suit. Now not only are the Chinese mad at us, we're mad at the Europeans.[35]

Furthermore, the negative international reaction is unlikely to be confined to angry words and noncooperation. Retaliation is also a real threat. According to former U.S. trade representative Susan Schwab:

> The greater risk, however, is that import measures emanating from U.S. legislation could prompt mirror action (or simple trade retaliation) by other countries—with U.S. exports being

among the targets. This scenario could unfold long before
any potential disputes were concluded in the WTO.[36]

What if other countries decide on different, less favorable, metrics
on which to base their own "border adjustment measures"? As Table
5.3 indicates, should other countries choose to discriminate against
trade partners on the basis of, say, higher levels of per capita emissions, U.S. exports and jobs would be in grave peril. On a per capita
basis, U.S. emissions will be more than twice as high as China's by
2030, 13 times India' per capita emissions, and over 6 times as high
as those of Brazil.

Past emissions would also seem to be an equally justifiable basis
for carbon-based trade measures, since it is, after all, *cumulative*
emissions that supposedly have done the damage. Indeed, Brazil
recently joined India and China in advocating for basing emission
commitments on past emissions.[37]

The Waxman-Markey bill rests ultimate authority to impose border measures in the president. When that bill passed the House in
the summer of 2009, President Obama appeared to recognize the
dangers of using trade as a weapon in the climate change debate,
saying, "I think we have to be very careful about sending any protectionist signals out there."[38] More recently, however, the administration has shown signs of changing its mind. Obama's energy and
climate adviser Carol Browner hinted that the administration is
sympathetic to Congress's interest in using trade policy instruments
to address the concerns of trade-vulnerable, energy-intensive industries. Commenting at an event in Washington, D.C., Ms. Browner
reportedly said:

> There's going to have to be mechanisms that recognize they
> compete in a global market. . . . I think it's fair to say a final
> bill will be very mindful of the needs of these particular
> sectors of the economy.[39]

U.S. industry lobbyists will be encouraged by this about-face because
they are looking to step up the trade provisions from those contained
in the House bill. In particular, representatives of the steel industry
and the United Steelworkers trade union are calling for immediate
imposition of trade restrictions rather than waiting until 2020 as
would be the case under Waxman-Markey.[40]

Table 5.3

CARBON DIOXIDE EMISSION PROJECTIONS BY SELECTED COUNTRIES, 2006–30

Emissions in million metric tons of carbon dioxide and per capita emissions in tons per annum

Country/Region	2006 (Actual)	2006 Per Capita	2010	2010 Per Capita	2020	2020 Per Capita	2030	2030 Per Capita	Average Annual % Change (2006–30)
USA	5,902.75	19.8	6,011	18.9	6,384	18.3	6,851	18.2	0.6
OECD Europe	4,435.60	8.0	4,512	8.2	4,760	8.4	4,834	8.4	0.4
China	6,017.69	4.6	6,898	5.1	9,475	6.6	12,007	8.3	2.9
Russia	1,704.36	12.0	1,789	12.6	1,984	14.8	2,117	16.9	0.9
Japan	1,246.76	9.8	1,196	9.4	1,195	9.7	1,170	10.0	-0.3
India	1,293.17	1.2	1,349	1.1	1,818	1.3	2,238	1.4	2.3
Brazil	377.24	2.0	451	2.3	541	2.5	633	2.8	2.2
Canada	614.33	18.8	669	19.7	727	19.7	784	19.9	1.0
World	29,195.4	4.5	31,100	4.5	37,035	4.7	42,325	4.8	1.6

SOURCES: U.S. Energy Information Administration, "International Energy Annual 2006," release date June–December 2008, Tables H1 and B1, http://www.eia.doe.gov/pub/international/iealf/tableh1co2.xls and http://www.eia.doe.gov/pub/international/iealf/tableb1.xls; and U.S. Energy Information Administration, "International Energy Outlook 2008," release date June 2008, Table A10, http://www.eia.doe.gov/oiaf/archive/ieo08/excel/ieoreftab_10.xls. Population data used to calculate per capita emissions from 2010 onward are from the Population Division of the Department of Economic and Social Affairs of the United Nations Secretariat, World Population Prospects: The 2008 Revision Database, http://esa.un.org/unpp.

One final note on the damaging implications of U.S. climate change policies as they relate to trade policy. Ultimately, the border tariffs are potentially more damaging to the global and U.S. economies than the free emission allowances. They are also more likely to be legally challenged. As Horlick pointed out in his congressional testimony, prior litigation patterns point to the tariffs being the first in the firing line:

> In practice, it seems that import restrictions are much more likely to be challenged in the WTO than is financial assistance to producers, such as offsetting costs or giving away permits. Thousands of pages of non-export subsidies are reported to the WTO, but only a handful have been challenged . . . while literally hundreds of border measures have been challenged in the WTO and its predecessor GATT.[41]

Unfortunately, the prevailing domestic political winds point toward countervailing carbon tariffs, even if international politics and good economic sense, caution against them.

Why Border Measures Would Impede International Cooperation on Climate Change

Even those who may care very little for the United States' economic and trade performance, or for the integrity of the international trading system more broadly, have reason to be concerned about the use, or even the threat, of unilateral carbon tariffs on the part of rich countries against poor ones. Environmental activists who seek international action on climate change should consider the diplomatic consequences of U.S. carbon tariffs.

Most American policymakers will admit that U.S.-only approaches to reducing emissions will have no appreciable effect on global climate change. They stress the importance of reaching an international agreement on climate change, and how the cooperation of China and India is crucial for that goal. But they do much to undermine that goal by threatening trade measures on developing country goods.

Developing countries, led by China and India, have repeatedly and strongly resisted attempts to coerce them into reducing their emissions and have rejected out of hand the application of trade measures based on climate change concerns. The draft agreements leading up to the December 2009 Conference of the Parties to the

United Nations Framework Convention on Climate Change, held in Copenhagen, uniformly emphasized, at the insistence of developing countries, that developed countries "shall not resort to any form of unilateral measures including countervailing border measures, against goods and services imported from developing countries on grounds of protection and stabilization of the climate." Of course, some developed countries may wish to use countervailing border measures on the grounds not of *"protection and stabilization of the climate"* but of protecting domestic industry, but that would be likely illegal under WTO rules, as the foregoing section makes clear.

Environmentally Friendly Free Trade

There is one manner in which trade policy could be used to enhance the quality of the environment more broadly, without compromising the integrity of the world trading system or jeopardizing the world's fragile recovery from the recession. Negotiations to lower expeditiously barriers to trade in so-called environmental goods and services are stalled along with the rest of the WTO's Doha round of world trade liberalization talks, but WTO members could, if they wished, completely remove barriers to those goods immediately. Doing so does not require international agreement, of course. Any WTO member at any time can open its markets to imports without waiting for the rest of the world to catch up to the benefits of doing so. The United States could unilaterally remove its 1.3 percent tariff on imported wind turbines, for example. Many countries have so-called nontariff barriers in place, like local content restrictions that encourage the use of locally produced inputs at the expense of imported ones. If imports of these goods and services are cheaper than their domestic counterparts, then people truly concerned about the environment should promote lifting barriers to their use. Former WTO Appellate Body member James Bacchus says this about the potential to create conditions for freer trade and an improved environment:

> Eliminating the barriers to trade in green goods and services would help diffuse them worldwide at the lowest possible cost by reducing their prices. In addition, it would provide incentives and expertise needed to enable developing countries to expand their production, use and export of climate-friendly technologies.[42]

Lowering or removing barriers to environmental goods and services trade, in other words, is a promising route toward achieving environmental, economic, and development goals simultaneously.

Conclusion

Politicians have made almost an art form of trying to defy economic gravity. The climate change debate has provided numerous examples of their attempts to deny the existence of tradeoffs and unintended consequences. They want to be seen to be doing "the right thing" by the environment, and to please certain special-interest groups. But the policies they have proposed to combat climate change negatively affect other special-interest groups, whose votes and campaign contributions are at least equally valued. To extricate themselves from some of these traps, politicians have proposed a complex array of measures—some trade related—to keep favor with certain energy-intensive and trade-exposed industries that are crying foul at increased energy costs. Once again, international obligations appear to be the weak link in politicians' calculations, because those trade-related measures put the United States at risk of retaliation, litigation, or both from its global trading partners.

In principle, domestic efforts to combat climate change do not inherently conflict with global trade rules. There is leeway written into WTO rules so that, for better or worse as far as domestic policy is concerned, policymakers *can* implement environmental policies without risk of trade retaliation or upsetting the global trading system. But any trade-related measures (such as tariffs on goods from noncapped countries) need to be based strictly on the goal of protecting the environment, rather than attempting to level the playing field for domestic competitors shackled by climate change regulations. Breaking the link between the trade measure and the goal of protecting the environment is a sure invitation to WTO dispute-settlement proceedings. Attempts to coerce other countries into implementing similarly stringent regulations are also problematic. Alienating our trade partners by unilaterally imposing tariffs and subsidies that flout global trade rules will undermine efforts to obtain global cooperation on climate change and inflict unnecessary damage on the U.S. economy. Truly a lose-lose scenario.

6. Economic Development in
    Developing Countries: Advancing
    Human Well-Being and the Capacity
    to Adapt to Global Warming

Indur M. Goklany

At the December 2009 meeting of the Conference of the Parties to the United Nations Framework Convention on Climate Change, participants agreed to a goal that developed countries would provide developing nations with $100 billion annually to help them reduce carbon dioxide emissions and adapt to climate change. This wealth transfer was justified on the notion that without this largesse, developing countries are more vulnerable to climate change and are incapable of adapting and developing in the face of a warming climate, and their well-being will steadily worsen.

Here, Indur Goklany, author of *The Improving State of the World: Why We're Living Longer, Healthier, More Comfortable Lives on a Cleaner Planet*, published in 2007, examines the core assumption behind this wealth transfer: that developing nations, left to their own devices, will be unable to adapt to climate change. This notion is peppered throughout the Fourth Assessment Report of the United Nations' Intergovernmental Panel on Climate Change, its most recent assessment. Virtually every developed nation has an office, usually in the foreign ministry, devoted to "helping" developing nations "adapt" to climate change. There isn't a university course on climate change that doesn't teach that the special sensitivity of developing nations to climate change requires special measures and wealth transfer from the developed world.

So the notion of wealth transfer because of global warming is now institutionalized in our governments. But as Goklany

(continued on next page)

> *(continued)*
>
> shows below, (a) empirical data indicates that climate-sensitive determinants of well-being, far from deteriorating over the past decades for developing countries, have, in fact, improved, and (b) if the economic assumptions on which the IPCC's emissions and climate scenarios are based are correct, then the developing world will adapt just fine to climate change in the 21st century, just as it did in the last one.

Developing countries have long been deemed to be at greater risk from global warming than industrialized countries.[1] The reason for this view is twofold. First, they are poorer, and global warming is projected to exacerbate the problems of poverty that many of them face currently, problems such as malaria and other vector-borne diseases, hunger, water shortages, and vulnerability to extreme weather events and sea level rise. Second, developing countries generally lack sufficient adaptive capacity—that is, the financial, technological, and human resources—needed to cope with these problems today.[2] This deficiency is precisely why these problems have persisted there, despite having been virtually eliminated in the industrialized world.

Accordingly, the Intergovernmental Panel on Climate Change, among others, claims that global warming could, in fact, hinder sustainable development in these nations.[3] Stretching this logic further, others[4] argue that weak or poor governments may be swamped by the impacts of global warming. The resulting economic instability, they claim, could then lead to political instability, breed terrorism and conflict, and precipitate mass migration with adverse consequences for the economic well-being and national security of the United States and, following the same chain of logic, presumably other industrialized countries as well.[5] In Chapter 4 of this volume, Ivan Eland provides cogent criticism of these hypotheses.

Some even claim that we are already seeing the detrimental effects of global warming. This was asserted by the late Mary Robinson, former president of Ireland and the former United Nations high commissioner for human rights, in a report issued by the now-defunct Global Humanitarian Forum, an organization founded by Kofi Annan, former Secretary General of the United Nations:

> The impacts of climate change are being felt today in countries around the world. In some places, environmental changes such as prolonged drought and rising sea levels are threatening entire communities and even nations. If we don't take meaningful and farsighted action now to address climate change, we are not only failing those who suffer today. We are also putting at risk the well-being of our planet and future generations.[6]

This statement echoes the United Nations Framework Convention on Climate Change, which asserts that human well-being is worsening in developing countries.[7] With respect to Asia, for instance, it claims:

> There is evidence of prominent increases in the intensity and/or frequency of many extreme weather events such as heat waves, tropical cyclones, prolonged dry spells, intense rainfall, tornadoes, snow avalanches, thunderstorms, and severe dust storms in the region.... Impacts of such disasters range from hunger and susceptibility to disease, to loss of income and livelihoods, affecting human survival and well-being.[8]

At the outset, this chapter examines the veracity of these claims, exploring whether empirical trends show that climate-sensitive indicators of human well-being are indeed worsening in developing countries.

Next, it will shed light on the significant factors that affect the direction of empirical trends in climate-sensitive indicators of human well-being. This discussion will focus on the role of economic and technological development powered directly or indirectly by fossil fuel consumption.

It then examines the notion—implicit in the view that developing countries will be swamped by the future impacts of global warming—that the adaptive capacity of developing countries, which is relatively low today, will continue to be low in the future, despite the optimistic economic assumptions built into the IPCC scenarios. These economic assumptions are among the primary drivers of the IPCC's emissions and climate change projections, which are then used to estimate future impacts (and damages) from global warming. Thus, they are fundamental to estimates of the magnitude of the effects of global warming.

159

Note that economic development can be a double-edged sword. On one hand, all else being equal, higher economic development would lead to higher temperatures from global warming. On the other hand, it also means higher adaptive capacity to cope not only with global warming but also with any other problems that humanity faces.[9] In addition, one should expect that as time marches on, even if economic development does not advance, existing technologies should improve and new technologies should come on line to respond to any adverse impacts of global warming or take advantage of any positive impacts.

Such technological change, which I call "secular" technological change to distinguish it from technological change resulting from additional economic development, would occur because of the normal accretion of technology and knowledge over time. Secular technological change would further boost adaptive capacity.[10] Improvements in adaptive capacity beg the question of whether the economic development assumed by the IPCC scenarios (accompanied by technological change) will increase the damages from global warming faster than the increases in adaptive capacity and, consequently, whether global warming would hinder sustainable development or whether insufficient economic and technological development would hinder the ability to cope with future global warming.

This chapter will also examine the potential consequences on death and disease in developing countries resulting from global warming policies, mainly in industrialized countries, that encourage biofuel production to replace fossil fuels, and whether their toll exceeds that attributed to global warming itself.

Finally, it will weave these disparate strands together to articulate a coherent policy to advance human well-being in developing countries while enhancing their ability to cope with global warming.

Reality Check: Empirical Trends versus Global Warming Hype

Here, I will examine recent (decades-long) empirical trends for various climate-sensitive aspects of human well-being and contrast them against the claims and expectations that global warming is already reducing agricultural productivity; increasing hunger, death and disease, drought, and extreme events; and affecting livelihoods and well-being in the developing world.

160

Figure 6.1
CEREAL YIELD AND PRODUCTION FOR LEAST-DEVELOPED
COUNTRIES AND GLOBALLY, 1961–2008

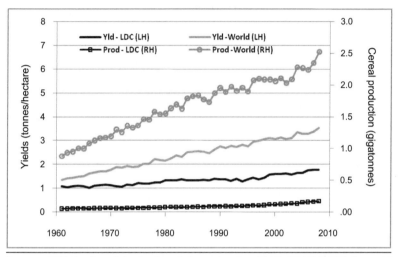

SOURCE: UN Food and Agricultural Organization, FAO STAT (2000), http://
faostat.fao.org.

Agricultural Productivity and Hunger

Proponents of greenhouse gas controls frequently proclaim that
global warming will reduce crop productivity in the developing
world, thereby exacerbating hunger and famine.[11] But contrary to
global warming hype, as shown in Figure 6.1, crop productivity and
production have clearly increased in the least-developed countries,
as well as globally, even as average surface temperatures have risen.

Because of the increase in agricultural productivity and trade
in agricultural and food inputs and outputs,[12] the portion of the
developing world's population suffering from chronic hunger
declined for decades. From 1969–1971 to 2003–2005, it declined from
33 percent to 16 percent.[13] However, it has started to rise once again,
at least temporarily (Figure 6.2). It increased to about 17 percent in
2008 and is projected to be higher for 2009. But as shown in Figure
6.1, productivity clearly has not declined. Therefore, the recent
increase in hunger cannot be because of any loss of productivity due

161

Figure 6.2
PERCENTAGE OF DEVELOPING WORLD POPULATION SUFFERING
FROM CHRONIC HUNGER, 1969/71–2009

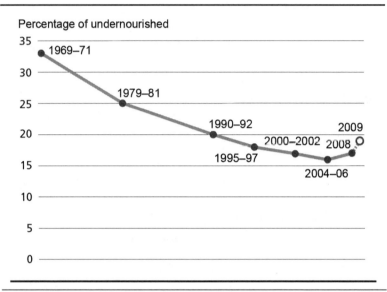

SOURCE: UN Food and Agricultural Organization, *State of Food Insecurity 2009* (Rome: FAO, 2009).

to global warming. In fact, the Food and Agricultural Organization of the United Nations ascribes the increase in hunger to the surge in food prices, the global economic slowdown, insufficient investment in agriculture, and biofuel production, which has diverted crops from food to fuel production.[14]

Ironically, the hype about global warming is responsible for the mandates and subsidies that drive biofuel production. Moreover, as investments in agriculture have dropped, spending on global warming has increased.

Disease

Advocates of stringent greenhouse gas controls expect global warming to add to the global burdens of death and disease.[15] However, average life expectancies around the world have increased from 31 years in 1900 to 47 years in the early 1950s and 69 years today.[16] For developing countries, life expectancies increased from 25–30 years in 1900 to 41 years in the early 1950s and 69 years at present.[17] In fact, in virtually every country, "health-adjusted" life expectancies currently exceed unadjusted life expectancies from just a few decades ago.[18] ("Health-adjusted" life expectancy is the life expectancy adjusted downward to partially discount the numbers of years of life that an average person would spend in a disabled or diseased condition.) In other words, people in developing countries are not only living longer, they are also healthier. Therefore, there has been less disease in the aggregate, humanity is much better able to cope with disease, or both. Disease is less of a problem today than it used to be.

Despite the UN's extraordinary claims, the ranges of the most critical climate-sensitive infectious diseases have actually shrunk as the average surface temperature warmed. Consider malaria, which accounts for about 75 percent of the global burden of disease from vector-borne diseases.[19] As indicated in Figure 6.3 (see color insert), the area in which malaria due to *Plasmodium falciparum*—the deadliest of the four protozoan parasites that cause malaria—is endemic, has been reduced substantially since 1900.[20] Endemic/stable malaria is estimated to have covered 58 percent of the world's land surface around 1900 but only 30 percent by 2007. Today, *P. falciparum* malaria is restricted largely to developing countries in the tropics. Equally important, its prevalence has decreased within its currently reduced range, with endemicity falling by one or more classes in over two-thirds of the current range of stable transmission (Figure 6.3c). Gething and others note that

> of the 66 million km² of the Earth's surface thought to have sustained stable/endemic malaria in 1900, 12%, 18% and 57% had exhibited proportional decreases in the reproductive number of up to one, between one and two, and greater than two orders of magnitude, respectively; 11% had shown no evidence of change; and 2% had shown evidence of an increase in the reproductive number by 2007.[21]

Figure 6.3, however, does not show the rebound in malaria in many developing areas that occurred in the 1980s and 1990s caused by a combination of poor policies (e.g., cessation of indoor spraying of DDT in many countries), development of resistance to drugs and insecticides, and a deterioration of public health infrastructure in

163

many African countries coincident with a period during which their economies deteriorated and AIDS was ascendant.[22]

Since then, however, matters have, for the most part, been turned around. The Living Proof Project reports that not only are malaria cases declining but the disease is killing fewer people. For example, between 2001 and 2006, deaths from malaria declined by 45 percent in Rwanda, 50 percent in Cambodia, 76 percent in the Philippines, 80 percent in Eritrea and Zanzibar, and 90 percent in São Tomé and Príncipe.[23]

Poverty

The proportion of the developing world's population living in absolute poverty (i.e., living on less than $1.25 per day in 2005 U.S. dollars) was halved from 52 percent in 1981 to 25 percent in 2005.[24] In terms of the head count, over this period, the number of people living in extreme poverty declined from 1.9 billion to 1.374 billion. The most spectacular improvements were registered in East Asia and the Pacific, where the head count dropped from 1.071 billion to 316 million. These numbers indicate that no aggregate loss of livelihood has occurred, as the United Nations Framework Convention on Climate Change suggests might be occurring due to global warming.[25]

Extreme Weather Events (Including Droughts and Floods)

Data from 1900–2008 indicate that since the 1920s, cumulative annual deaths from all extreme weather events—droughts, floods, extreme temperatures (both extreme heat and extreme cold), wet mass movement (i.e., slides, waves, and surges), wildfires, and storms (e.g., hurricanes, cyclones, tornadoes, typhoons, etc.)—declined globally by 93 percent on average, while the death rate dropped by 98 percent (see Figure 6.4).

Over this period, droughts were responsible for the bulk (58 percent) of the global fatalities due to extreme weather events from 1900 to 2008.[26] Long-term trends in global deaths and death rates from droughts, however, indicate that they peaked in the 1920s. Since then they have declined by 99.97 percent and 99.99 percent, respectively.[27] From 2000 to 2009, according to the EM-DAT, the International Disaster Database, an average of 116 people died annually due to drought, compared with 472,000 deaths annually from 1920 to 1929.[28] To place these numbers in context, currently over 58

164

Figure 6.4
GLOBAL DEATHS AND DEATH RATES DUE TO EXTREME WEATHER EVENTS, 1900–2008

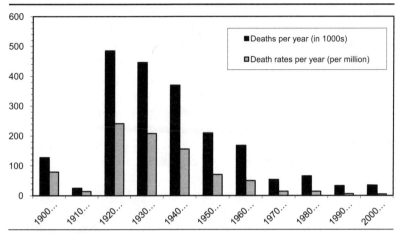

SOURCE: Indur M. Goklany, "Deaths and Death Rates from Extreme Weather Events: 1900–2008," *Journal of American Physicians and Surgeons* 14 (2009), using data from EM-DAT, 2009.

NOTE: The extreme events include droughts, floods, extreme temperatures (both extreme heat and extreme cold), wet mass movement (i.e., slides, waves, and surges), wildfires, and storms (e.g., hurricanes, cyclones, tornadoes, typhoons, etc.). Note that data for the last period are averaged over nine years.

million people die each year from all causes worldwide.[29] That is, the death toll that inevitably followed in the wake of a drought has been reduced almost to the vanishing point.

With respect to floods, the second most deadly form of extreme weather event, deaths and death rates crested in the 1930s. By 2000–2008, they were down by 98.7 percent and 99.6 percent, respectively.[30]

Notably, extreme weather events nowadays contribute only 0.06 percent to the global (and U.S.) mortality burdens in an average year. Remarkably, they have declined even as all-cause mortality has increased.[31] This decline indicates that the world, including the developing world, is coping better with risks of death from extreme weather events than with other, larger health risks.

165

Water Shortages

Not surprisingly, the possibility of water shortages leading to droughts and hunger is a recurring theme in the climate change literature.[32] Droughts, which are a manifestation of severe water shortages, have plagued humanity from time immemorial, and deaths from droughts are probably the best indicator of the socioeconomic impact of such water shortages. But as noted above, they have declined remarkably in the past century.

Also, to the extent there is a concern that global warming might have reduced access to safe water, note that between 1990 and 2006, an additional 1.6 billion people gained access to safer water[33] as the percentage of the global population with such access increased from 75.7 to 86.2, despite the increase in population and any global warming that may have occurred.[34]

Clearly, the direction of long-term empirical trends for aggregate hunger, disease, deaths from droughts, floods, and extreme weather events is inconsistent with expectations based on the general narrative regarding the effects of global warming. While the surface temperature has increased by approximately 0.7 degree Celsius since 1900 according to the IPCC's Fourth Assessment Report,[35] the agencies responsible for anthropogenic greenhouse gas emissions are, in fact, directly or indirectly responsible for reducing climate-sensitive risks faster than they are being created or exacerbated. This reduction is manifested as increases in adaptive capacity, which then increases human well-being either directly or indirectly. An alternative (and devastating) possibility is that the narrative is simply based on false expectations.

For the purposes of this chapter, whichever of these explanations (or combination of explanations) is correct is immaterial. The salient fact is that empirical reality does not match claims about deteriorating human well-being due to global warming.

Fossil Fuels and Long-Term Advances in Human Well-Being

The documented improvements since the start of the Industrial Revolution in virtually every objective measure of human well-being—poverty; life expectancy; infant, child, and maternal mortality; prevalence of hunger and malnutrition; child labor; job opportunities for women; educational attainment; income—can be ascribed to a "Cycle of Progress" composed of the mutually reinforcing,

166

Figure 6.5
THE CYCLE OF PROGRESS

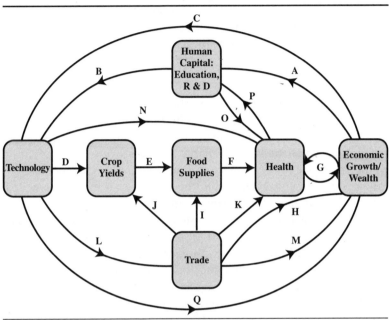

SOURCE: Indur Goklany, *The Improving State of the World: Why We're Living Longer, Healthier, More Comfortable Lives on a Cleaner Planet* (Washington, D.C.: Cato Institute, 2007).

coevolving forces of economic growth, technological change, and freer trade (see Figure 6.5 and Sallie James's chapter in this volume). And fossil fuels have been integral to each facet of this cycle.

Without the energy generated by fossil fuels, economic development would be much less; Many of the technologies that we take for granted and that have come on line since the dawn of industrialization (e.g., devices that directly or indirectly use electricity or fossil fuels) would have been stillborn; the current volume of internal and external trade, on which the global economic system depends, would be impossible to sustain. Even trade in services would be substantially diminished, if not impossible, without energy to generate electricity to power lights, computers, and telecommunications. Worldwide, fossil fuels are the major source of electricity.

In fact, no human activity is possible without energy. Every product we make, move, or use requires energy.

Fossil fuel–powered technologies underpin much of the economic development and associated improvements in human well-being that have occurred since the Industrial Revolution, as explained below.

Agricultural Production and Hunger

Global food production has, as shown in Figure 6.1, never been higher than it is today, largely due to fertilizers, pesticides, irrigation, and farm machinery.[36] But fertilizers and pesticides are manufactured from fossil fuels, and energy is necessary to run irrigation pumps and machinery.[37] This entire suite of energy-dependent technologies also enabled the Green Revolution. And in today's world, energy for the most part means fossil fuels.

The resulting increase in yields and food production helped reduce food prices worldwide, which reduced hunger by making food more affordable.[38] Additional carbon dioxide in the atmosphere has also contributed to higher yields and food production[39] because it provides carbon, the basic building block of life. Yet another factor critical to reining in food prices and reducing hunger worldwide is trade within and between countries, which enables food surpluses to be moved to food-deficit areas.[40] But it takes fossil fuels to move food around in the quantities and the speed necessary for such trade to be an integral part of the global food system, as it indeed is. Moreover, fossil fuel–dependent technologies, such as refrigeration, rapid transport, and plastic packaging, ensure that more of the crop that is produced is actually consumed. That is, they increase the overall efficiency of the food production system, which helps lower food prices and contain hunger worldwide.

Habitat Conversion

The increased efficiency of the food and agricultural sector, in addition to reducing hunger and its associated detrimental impacts on human well-being, has also contained the amount of land under cultivation.[41] Notably, conversion of habitat to agricultural uses is the single largest threat to global biodiversity.[42] Thus, fossil fuels, directly or indirectly, have also helped conserve nature.

I have estimated that between 1961 and 2002, greater use of existing and new agricultural technologies (e.g., pesticides, fertilizers, and farm machinery)—enabled for the most part, directly or indirectly, by fossil fuels—saved over 1.3 billion hectares of habitat from conversion.[43] By comparison, in 2004 the total amount of partly or wholly protected areas in developing countries was less than 1 billion hectares. That is, such technological changes saved more land for the rest of nature than did reserving land for that purpose.

Health

Having enough food is the first step to a healthy population. It's not surprising that hunger and high mortality rates go hand in hand.[44] In addition, even the most mundane medical and public health technologies depend on energy, most of which is derived from fossil fuels. Such technologies include heating for sterilization; pumping water from water treatment plants to consumers and sewage to treatment plants; and transporting and storing vaccines, antibiotics, and blood. In addition, energy is necessary to operate a variety of medical equipment (e.g., X-ray machines, electrophoresis apparatus, and centrifuges) or to undertake a number of medical procedures. Moreover, economic surpluses generated by greenhouse gas–producing activities in the United States and other industrialized countries have helped create technologies to enable safer drinking water and sanitation; developed solutions and treatments for diseases, such as AIDS, malaria, tuberculosis; and increased life expectancies through vaccinations and improvements in nutrition and hygiene.[45]

Child Labor

Not only has fossil fuel–powered machinery made child labor obsolete in all but the poorest societies, but it has allowed children to be children and, equally important, to be better educated in preparation for a more fulfilling and productive life in a technologically more advanced society.[46]

Equal Opportunity for Women and the Disabled

But for home appliances powered for the most part by electricity, more women would be toiling in the home. Moreover, power tools and machinery allow women, the disabled, and the weak to perform many tasks that would have once been reserved, for practical purposes, for able-bodied men. These devices also expand their options for employment and economic advancement. Unfortunately,

169

because of their low energy use, these benefits are limited in developing countries.

Education

Today's populations are much better educated and more productive than previous ones, in large part because of the availability of relatively cheap fossil fuel–generated electrical lighting. And education is a key factor contributing not only to economic development and technological innovation but also to personal fulfillment.[47]

As Figure 6.6 suggests (see color insert), easy access to energy for cheap and good lighting helps increase levels of education and human capital. This access, in turn, advances economic and technological development as well as health outcomes (as indicated by the Cycle of Progress, Figure 6.5) and the ability to cope with the effects of global warming.

Poverty

Economic development, powered mainly by fossil fuels, has, as noted, helped halve the proportion of the developing world's population living in extreme poverty.[48] A substantial share of its income comes directly or indirectly from trade, tourism, developmental aid (cumulatively, at least $2.3 trillion over the decades[49]), and remittances ($338 billion in 2008 alone[50]) from industrialized countries. Moreover, it would be impossible to sustain the amount of trade and tourism that occur today without fossil fuels. Much of that improvement would have been impossible but for the wealth generated in industrialized countries by fossil fuel–powered economic development.

Ironically, higher food prices, partly from the diversion of crops to biofuels in response to climate change policies, helped push 130–155 million people into extreme poverty in 2008.[51] That number is equivalent to 2.5–3.0 percent of the developing world's population. Although it was not unforeseeable,[52] this outcome is one more unintended consequence of global warming policies that were implemented based on perceptions of the importance of global warming derived from, as shall be shown below, studies that exaggerate its impacts, as well as poor policy analysis.

Disaster Preparedness and Response and Humanitarian Aid

Timely preparations and response are major factors that have contributed to the reduction in death and disease that traditionally were caused by or accompanied disasters from extreme weather events (Figure 6.4). This success hinges on the availability of fossil fuels to move people, food, medicine, and critical humanitarian supplies before and after events strike. Economic development also allowed the United States (and other developed countries) to offer humanitarian aid to developing countries in times of famine, drought, floods, cyclones, and other natural disasters, weather-related or not. Such aid, too, would have been virtually impossible to deliver in large quantities or in a timely fashion absent fossil fuel–fired transportation.

Future Adaptive Capacity of Developing Countries

As noted, economic development and available technology are two key determinants of adaptive capacity.[53] But economic development is also a fundamental "driver" of greenhouse gas emissions, the magnitude of any resulting climate change, and its future impacts. The IPCC's emission scenarios all assume substantial economic growth, especially in developing countries.[54] Here, I will examine the implications of the IPCC's estimates of economic growth on the future adaptive capacity of developing countries. I will also discuss the effects of secular technological change on adaptive capacity. I will then analyze whether and how studies of the impacts of global warming cited by the latest IPCC assessment report account for changes in adaptive capacity as both economic development and technology advance in the future.

Economic Development

Figure 6.7 provides estimates of *net* gross domestic product per capita—a key determinant of adaptive capacity[55]—for 1990 (the base year used by the IPCC's emission scenarios), 2100, and 2200, using four IPCC reference scenarios for areas that comprise today's developing and industrialized countries. The net GDP per capita is calculated by subtracting the equivalent costs per capita of global warming from the GDP per capita in the absence of any warming (that is, the *unadjusted* GDP per capita).

Note that Figure 6.7 is designed to provide a conservative estimate of the future net GDP per capita, because I intend to show that even under the most conservative assumptions, net GDP per capita will far exceed today's levels despite any climate change. Accordingly, I use the *Stern Review*'s estimates[56] for the damages (or equivalent

Figure 6.7
NET GDP PER CAPITA AFTER ACCOUNTING FOR LOSSES DUE TO
GLOBAL WARMING FOR FOUR MAJOR IPCC EMISSION AND
CLIMATE SCENARIOS, 1990–2200

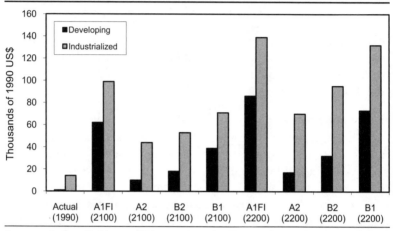

SOURCE: Indur Goklany, "Discounting the Future," *Regulation* 32 (Spring 2009): 36–40.

losses in GDP) from global warming. First, unlike most other studies, it accounts for losses due not only to market impacts of global warming but also to nonmarket (i.e., environmental and public health) impacts, as well as the risk of catastrophe.[57] Second, to develop a *very conservative* estimate for the future net GDP per capita, I use the *Stern Review*'s 95th percentile (upper bound) estimate of the losses in GDP due to global warming even though many economists believe its central estimates overstate losses due to global warming. As Tol observes, "[The *Stern Review*'s] impact estimates are pessimistic even when compared to other studies in the gray literature and other estimates that use low discount rates."[58]

In Figure 6.7, the net GDP per capita for 1990 is the same as the actual GDP per capita (in 1990 U.S. dollars, using market exchange rates, per the IPCC's practice). This assumes that the GDP loss due to global warming is negligible in 1990, which is consistent with using that as the base year for estimating changes in globally averaged temperatures (as is the case for impact studies that will be used in the following analysis). For 2100, the unadjusted GDP per capita accounts for any population and economic growth assumed in the IPCC scenarios from 1990 (the base year) to 2100. For 2200, the unadjusted GDP per capita is assumed to be double that in 2100, which is equivalent to a compounded annual growth rate of 0.7 percent, which is *less* than the *Stern Review* assumption of 1.3 percent. This scenario substantially understates the unadjusted and, therefore, the net GDP per capita in 2200. The costs of global warming are taken from the *Stern Review*'s 95th percentile estimates under the "high climate change" scenario, which is equivalent to the IPCC's warmest scenario (A1FI) that projects a global temperature increase of 4 degrees Celsius from 1990 to 2085. Per the *Stern Review*, these costs amount to 7.5 percent of global GDP in 2100 and 35.2 percent in 2200. I adjusted these losses downward for the cooler scenarios.[59]

Figure 6.7 shows that despite the various assumptions that have been designed to overstate losses from global warming and understate the unadjusted GDP per capita in the absence of any warming:

- For populations living in countries currently classified as "developing," net GDP per capita will be over 11–65 times higher in 2100 than it was in the base year, even after accounting for global warming; it will be even higher (18–95 times) in 2200.
- Net GDP per capita in today's developing countries will be higher in 2200 than it was in industrialized countries in the base year (1990) under all scenarios, despite any global warming. That is, regardless of any global warming, populations living in today's developing countries will be better off in the future than people currently inhabiting today's *industrialized* countries. This is also true for 2100 for all but the "poorest" (IPCC A2) scenario.
- Under the warmest scenario (A1FI), the scenario that prompts much of the apocalyptic warnings about global warming, net GDP per capita of inhabitants of developing countries in 2100 ($61,500) will be double that of the United States in 2006 ($30,100), and almost triple in 2200 ($86,200 versus $30,100). (All estimates are in 1990 U.S. dollars.)

In other words, developing countries will be wealthy by today's standards, and their adaptive capacity should be correspondingly higher. Therefore, even if one assumes that there will be no secular technological change—that is, no new or improved technologies will become available between the 1990s and 2100 (see below)—developing countries' adaptive capacity should on average far exceed that of the United States today. Therefore, although claims that developing countries will be unable to cope with future climate change may have been true for the world of 1990 (the base year), they are simply inconsistent with the assumptions built into the IPCC scenarios and the *Stern Review*'s own (exaggerated) analysis.

Thus, the problems of poverty that warming would exacerbate (e.g., low agricultural productivity, hunger, malnutrition, malaria, and other vector-borne diseases) ought to be reduced if not eliminated by 2100, even if one ignores any secular technological change that ought to occur in the interim. Tol and Dowlatabadi,[60] for example, show that malaria has been functionally eliminated in a society whose annual per capita income reaches $3,100. Therefore, even under the poorest scenario (A2), developing countries should be free of malaria well before 2100, even assuming no technological change in the interim. Similarly, if the average net GDP per capita for developing countries is $10,000–$82,000 in 2100 and technologies become more cost-effective, as they have been doing over the past several centuries,[61] then their farmers would be able to afford technologies that are unaffordable today (e.g., precision agriculture) or new technologies that should come on line by then (e.g., drought-resistant seeds).[62] But since impact assessments generally fail to fully account for increases in economic development and technological change, they substantially overestimate future net damages from global warming.

It may be argued that the high levels of economic development depicted in Figure 6.7 are unlikely. But if that's the case, then the economic growth rates used to drive the IPCC's scenarios are equally unlikely—which necessarily means that the estimates of emissions, temperature increases, and impacts of global warming projected by the IPCC are all overestimates.

Secular Technological Change

The second major reason why future adaptive capacity has been underestimated (and the impacts of global warming systematically overestimated) is that few impact studies consider secular technological change.[63] Most assume that no *new* technologies will come on

174

line, although some do assume greater adoption of *existing* technologies with higher GDP per capita and, much less frequently, a
modest generic improvement in productivity.[64]

*Current Practice in Impact Models to Account for Changes in Future
Adaptive Capacity*

It is possible to obtain an idea of whether, how, and the extent to
which impact assessments used in the IPCC's latest assessment
report account for changes in adaptive capacity over time through
an examination of the suite of studies that comprise the so-called
Fast Track Assessments of the global impacts of climate change.
Sponsored by the British government, these FTAs, which were state
of the art at the time the IPCC's 2007 Fourth Assessment Report
was being written, have an impeccable provenance from the point
of view of proponents of greenhouse gas controls. Many of the FTA
authors were major contributors to the IPCC's Third and Fourth
Assessments.[65] For instance, the lead author of the FTA on hunger,[66]
Professor Martin Parry, cochaired the IPCC Working Group 2 during
its latest assessment (in 2007). Similarly, the authors of the FTAs
on water resources and coastal flooding were also lead authors of
corresponding chapters in the same Fourth Assessment Report.

A dissection of the FTA methodologies shows the following:

- The 2004 water resources study by Arnell[67] totally ignores
  adaptation, despite the fact that many adaptations to water-
  related problems, e.g., building dams, reservoirs, and canals,
  are among mankind's oldest adaptations and do not depend
  on the development of any new technologies.[68]
- The study of agricultural productivity and hunger by Parry
  and colleagues in 2004 allows for (a) increases in crop yield
  with economic growth due to greater use of fertilizer and
  irrigation in richer countries, (b) decreases in hunger due to
  economic growth, (c) some secular (time-dependent) increase
  in agricultural productivity, and (d) some farm-level adaptations to deal with climate change. But these adaptations are
  based on 1990s technologies, rather than technologies that
  would be available in the future or any technologies developed
  to specifically cope with the negative impacts of global warming or to take advantage of any positive outcomes.[69] However,
  the potential for future technologies to cope with climate

climate change impact
assessments

change is great, especially if one considers bioengineered crops and precision agriculture.[70]

- Nicholls's 2004 study on coastal flooding from sea level rise takes some pains to incorporate improvements in adaptive capacity due to increasing wealth. But it makes a number of questionable assumptions. First, it allows societies to implement measures to reduce the risk of coastal flooding in response to 1990 surge conditions but not to subsequent sea level rise.[71] But this is illogical. One should expect that any measures that are implemented would consider the latest available data and information on the surge situation at the time the measures are initiated. That is, if the measure were initiated in, say, 2050, the measure's design would at least consider sea level and sea level trends as of 2050, rather than merely the 1990 level. By that time, we should know the rate of sea level rise with much greater confidence. Second, Nicholls also allows for a constant time lag between initiating protection and sea level rise. But one should expect that if sea levels continue to rise, the time lag between upgrading protection standards and higher GDP per capita will decrease over time, and may even turn negative. That is, the further we go into the future, the more likely it is that adaptations will be anticipatory rather than reactive, particularly, as societies become more affluent (as indicated by Figure 6.7). Third, Nicholls does not allow for any deceleration in the preferential migration of the population to coastal areas, as might be likely if coastal storms and flooding become more frequent and costly.[72]
- The 2004 analysis for malaria undertaken by van Lieshout and colleagues includes adaptive capacity as it existed in 1990 but does not adjust it to account for any subsequent advances in economic and technological development.[73] There is simply no justification for such an assumption. If the IPCC's assumptions about future economic development are even half right, it is, as already noted, likely that malaria will have been eliminated by 2100.

Overestimation of Impacts from Underestimation of Future Adaptive Capacity

So how much of a difference in impact would consideration of both economic development and technological changes have made?

176

If impacts were to be estimated for five or so years into the future, ignoring changes in adaptive capacity between now and then probably would not be fatal because neither economic development nor technological change would likely advance substantially during that period. However, the time horizon of climate change impact assessments is often on the order of 35–100 years or more. The Fast Track Assessments use a base year of 1990 to estimate impacts for 2025, 2055, and 2085.[74] The *Stern Review*'s time horizon extends to 2100–2200 and beyond. Over such periods, one ought to expect substantial advances in the levels of economic development, technological change, and human capital.

Retrospective assessments indicate that over the span of a few decades, changes in economic development and technologies can substantially reduce adverse environmental impacts and improve human well-being as measured by a variety of objective indicators.[75] For example, due to a combination of greater wealth and secular technological change, U.S. death rates due to various climate-sensitive water-related diseases—dysentery, typhoid, paratyphoid, other gastrointestinal disease, and malaria—declined by 99.6 to 100 percent over a span of 70 years, from 1900 to 1970.[76] Similarly, as shown in Figure 6.4, average annual global mortality and mortality rates from extreme weather events have declined by 93–98 percent since the 1920s,[77] a period of almost 90 years. Thus, not fully accounting for changes in the level of economic development and secular technological change would understate future adaptive capacity, which then could overstate impacts by one or more orders of magnitude if the time horizon is several decades into the future.

The assumption that there would be little or no improved or new technologies that would become available between 1990 and 2100 (or 2200), as assumed in most climate change impact assessments, is clearly naive. In fact, a comparison of today's world against the world of 1990 (the base year used in most impact studies to date) shows that even for this brief 20-year span, this assumption is invalid for many, if not most, human enterprises.

It should be noted that some of the newer impact assessments have begun to account for changes in adaptive capacity. For example, in a 2006 exercise exploring the vulnerability to climate change under various climate change scenarios, Yohe and others allowed adaptive capacity to increase between the present and 2050 and 2100. However, they arbitrarily limited any increase in adaptive capacity to "either the current global mean or to a value that is 25% higher than the current value—whichever is higher."[78] Such a limitation would miss most of the increase in adaptive capacity implied by Figure 6.7.

More recently, in 2007, Tol and colleagues' analyzed the sensitivity of deaths from malaria, diarrhea, schistosomiasis, and dengue to warming, economic development, and other determinants of adaptive capacity through the year 2100. Their results indicate, unsurprisingly, that consideration of economic development alone could reduce mortality substantially. For malaria, for instance, deaths would be eliminated before 2100 in a number of the more affluent sub-Saharan countries.[79] Theirs is a much more realistic assessment of the impact of global warming on malaria in a wealthier and more technologically advanced world, and one that is more consistent with long-term trends regarding the extent of malaria, as shown in Figure 6.3, rather then the estimates provided by the Fast Track Assessments.

Finally, it should be noted that it is precisely the failure to account for the combination of economic and technological developments that caused high-profile prognostications—such as Malthus's original conjecture about running out of cropland, Meadows and others' *The Limits to Growth*, and Ehrlich's *The Population Bomb*—to fizzle.[80]

Global Warming and Development

Although the IPCC notes that sustainable development "can reduce vulnerability to climate change, and climate change could impede nations' abilities to achieve sustainable development pathways,"[81] many proponents of greenhouse gas controls, on the other hand, dwell on the latter (downside) aspect of economic development while generally ignoring the upside.[82] Here, I will examine whether global warming hinders sustainable development or whether sustainable development makes it easier to cope with warming, and which effect, if any, is predominant?

It is possible to answer these questions again using results from the Fast Track Assessments of the global impacts of global warming.[83] The FTAs provide estimates of the contribution of global warming to the total populations at risk of malaria, hunger, and coastal flooding due to sea level rise for 2085. While recognizing that, realistically, 2085 is beyond the period that is reasonably foreseeable, I converted these estimates of populations at risk into mortality by comparing historical mortality estimates from the World Health Organization (for 1990, the base year) against FTA estimates of populations at risk for that year.[84]

The results indicate that under the IPCC's warmest scenario (A1FI), which gives an increase in average global temperatures of 4 degrees Celsius between 1990 and 2085, global warming would contribute no more than 13 percent of the total mortality from malaria,[85] hunger, and coastal flooding in 2085.[86] The remaining 87 percent or more is due to factors unrelated to global warming.

However, had improvements in adaptive capacity been appropriately accounted for, the 87 percent contribution from the latter would have been much smaller, but then so would have the 13 percent share attributed to global warming (probably by a like amount).

FTA results also indicate the following:

- By 2085, global warming would *reduce* the global population at risk of water shortages, although some areas would see increases.[87] This finding is contrary to the erroneous impression conveyed by the IPCC's AR4 Working Group 2 "Summary for Policymakers"[88] because that summary emphasizes the number of people that may experience an increase in water shortage but neglects to provide corresponding estimates for the number that would see a reduction in water shortage.[89] However, the finding that the net population experiencing water shortage would be *reduced* is consistent with other studies of the global impact of global warming on water resources.[90] Remarkably, this result is obtained despite the fact that Arnell does not allow for *any* adaptation and, consequently, advances in adaptive capacity that should logically occur under the IPCC scenarios![91]

- Partly due to increases in net primary productivity because of carbon dioxide fertilization, the amount of habitat devoted to cropland would be halved by global warming under the A1FI scenario, at least through 2100.[92] Since diversion of habitat to cropland is perhaps the single largest threat to species and ecosystems,[93] this means that global warming could actually *reduce* pressures on biodiversity.[94]

Thus, at least through 2085–2100, global warming may relieve some of the problems that some developing countries face currently (e.g., water shortage and habitat loss), while in other instances, the

179

contribution of global warming to the overall problem (e.g., cumulative mortality from malaria, hunger, and coastal flooding) would be substantially smaller than that of factors unrelated to global warming. Notably, economic development, one of the fundamental drivers of global warming, would reduce mortality problems regardless of whether they are due to warming or non-warming-related factors. Hence, the lack of economic development would be a greater problem than global warming, at least through 2085–2100. This outcome is consistent with Figure 6.7, which shows that notwithstanding global warming and despite egregiously overestimating the negative consequences of global warming, future net GDP per capita will be much higher than it is today under each scenario through at least 2200.

Note that Figure 6.7 also shows that through 2200, notwithstanding global warming, net GDP per capita will be highest under the warmest scenario and lowest under the poorest scenario (A2). This result suggests that if humanity has a choice of which development path it takes, it ought to strive to take the scenario that has the highest economic growth, whether or not that exacerbates global warming.[95] The additional economic development would more than offset the cost of any warming.

No less important, it is far cheaper for the world to advance economic development than to mitigate climate change by a meaningful amount.[96] This fact is consistent with the Tol, Ebi, and Yohe's 2007 analysis of various climate-sensitive infectious diseases. That analysis suggests that

> deaths will first increase, because of population growth and climate change, but then fall, because of development. . . . As climate can only be changed with a substantial delay, development is the preferred strategy to reduce infectious diseases even if they are exacerbated by climate change. Development can . . . increase the capacity to cope with projected increases in infectious diseases over the medium to long term.[97]

Thus, it is most unlikely that under the IPCC's warmest scenario, global warming will overwhelm economic development in developing countries, notwithstanding the *Stern Review*'s upper-bound damage estimates. Second, economic development should be given priority over reducing greenhouse gas emissions. It would enable developing countries to cope not only with any negative effects of climate change but, more importantly, other larger problems that they will face.[98]

Which Is Deadlier—Global Warming or Global Warming Policies?

Among the policy responses to the perceived threat of climate change are subsidies and mandates for the production and use of biofuels, including ethanol and biodiesel. As already noted, this response has been associated with an increase in food prices, which, in turn, has increased the population suffering from chronic hunger.[99] It has also added to the number of people living in "absolute poverty" worldwide, particularly in developing countries.[100]

A World Bank policy research working paper estimates that the number of people living in absolute poverty, that is, the "poverty head count," in developing countries would decline from 1.208 billion in 2005 to 798 million in 2010 because of economic development.[101] But it also estimates that higher food prices induced by biofuel production would drive an additional 32 million into absolute poverty in 2010.

Assuming proportionality between the head count for absolute poverty on one hand, and death and disease in developing countries due to poverty-related diseases on the other hand, then, per estimates from the World Health Organization's 2009 analysis of global health risks,[102] I estimated that the increase in the poverty head count in 2010 due to biofuel demand would translate into 192,000 additional deaths and 6.7 million additional lost disability-adjusted life years (DALYs).

By contrast, WHO's 2009 analysis "attributes" 141,000 deaths and 5.4 million lost DALYs in 2004 to global warming. Moreover, death and disease due to poverty are real, whereas death and disease attributed to global warming are hypothetical and, according to the researchers who developed those estimates, are based on unverified models and scientific shortcuts.[103] Thus, biofuel policies motivated, in part, by the desire to mitigate global warming may be responsible for more death and disease than climate change itself.

Summary

Despite claims that global warming will reduce human well-being in developing countries, there is no evidence that this is actually happening. Empirical trends show that by any objective climate-sensitive measure, human well-being has, in fact, improved remarkably over the last several decades. Specifically, agricultural productivity has increased; the proportion of population suffering from chronic hunger has declined; the rate of extreme poverty has been more than halved; rates of death and disease from malaria, other vector-borne diseases, and extreme weather events have declined; and, consequently, life expectancy has more than doubled since 1900.

And while economic growth and technological development fueled mainly by fossil fuels are responsible for some portion of the warming experienced this century, they are largely responsible for the above-noted improvements in human well-being in developing countries (and elsewhere). The fact that these improvements occurred despite any global warming indicates that economic and technological development has been, overall, a benefit to developing countries.

Recently, however, we have seen an upturn in the rate of hunger. However, that upturn is due not to global warming but, in part, to global warming *policies*, in particular, policies to stimulate the production and use of biofuels in lieu of fossil fuels. These policies diverted cropland away from food to fuel production, which increased food prices and, therefore, hunger worldwide. That change, in turn, also pushed a greater share of the population of developing countries into extreme poverty. Although this biofuel production–induced increase in extreme poverty is significantly less than the reduction in poverty from economic development, it raises the toll from diseases of poverty, which are among the major causes of death and disease in developing countries.

Estimates of death and disease per million people in extreme poverty derived from studies from the World Health Organization and the World Bank indicate that the increase in extreme poverty in 2010 due to biofuel production may result in 192,000 deaths and 6.7 million lost DALYs. By comparison, a WHO study attributed 141,000 deaths and 5.4 million lost DALYs to global warming (out of 59 million deaths and 795 million lost DALYs worldwide from all causes. Thus, global warming policies may be more deadly than global warming itself.

It is often argued that unless greenhouse gases are reduced forthwith, the resulting global warming could have severe, if not catastrophic, consequences for developing countries because they lack the economic and human resources to cope with warming's consequences. But this argument has two major problems. First, although developing countries' adaptive capacity is low today, it does not follow that their ability to cope will be low forever. In fact, under the IPCC's warmest scenario, which would increase globally averaged temperature by 4 degrees Celsius relative to 1990, net GDP per capita in developing countries (after accounting for losses due to climate change per the *Stern Review*'s exaggerated estimates) will be double the United States' 2006 level in 2100, and triple that in 2200. Thus, developing countries should be able to cope with climate change substantially better in the future than the United States can today. But these advances in adaptive capacity, which are virtually ignored by most assessments of the impacts and damages from global warming, are the inevitable consequence of the assumptions built into the IPCC's emission scenarios. Hence, the notion that developing countries will be unable to cope with global warming does not square with the basic assumptions that underpin the magnitude of emissions, global warming, and its projected impacts under the IPCC scenarios.

Second, global warming would not create new problems; rather it would exacerbate some existing problems of poverty (e.g., hunger, malaria, extreme events), while relieving others (e.g., habitat loss and water shortages in some places). One approach to dealing with the consequences of global warming is to reduce greenhouse gas emissions. That action would, however, reduce all global warming impacts, whether they are good (e.g., net reduction in the global population at risk of water shortage or in the habitat used for cultivation) or bad (e.g., arguably increased levels of malaria or hunger). And even where global warming provides no benefits, reducing emissions would at best only reduce global warming's contribution to the problem, but not the whole problem, since non-warming factors are also contributors.[104] With respect to mortality from hunger, malaria, and extreme events, for example, global warming only contributes 13 percent of the problem in 2085 (which is beyond the foreseeable future).

Another approach to reducing the global warming impacts would be to reduce the climate-sensitive problems of poverty through "focused adaptation."[105] Focused adaptation would allow society to capture the benefits of global warming while allowing it to reduce the totality of climate-sensitive problems that warming might worsen. For mortality from hunger, malaria, and extreme events, for instance, focused adaptation could through the foreseeable future address 100 percent of the problem, whereas emission reductions would at most deal with only 13 percent.

Yet another approach would be to address the root cause of why developing countries are deemed to be most at risk, namely, they are poor. But to reduce poverty, we need sustainable economic growth. Sustainable economic growth would not only address the climate-sensitive problems of poverty but *all* problems of poverty, not just that portion caused by global warming. It would, moreover, reduce these problems faster and more cost-effectively. No less important, it is far more certain that sustainable economic growth will provide real benefits than would emission reductions because although there is no doubt that poverty leads to death, disease, and other problems, there is substantial doubt regarding the reality and magnitude of the negative impacts of global warming, especially since most analyses ignore, for the most part, improvements in adaptive capacity. To summarize, of the three approaches outlined above, human well-being in developing countries is most likely to be advanced furthest by sustainable economic development and to be advanced least by emission reductions.[106] In addition, because of the inertia of the climate system, economic development is likely to bear fruit faster than any emission reductions.

This conclusion is consistent with Figure 6.7, which shows that despite exaggerating the negative consequences of global warming, net GDP per capita, a surrogate for human well-being, is highest under the richest-but-warmest scenario and lowest under the poorest scenario. Thus, developing countries should focus on becoming wealthier. The wealthier they become, the better able they will be to cope not only with the urgent problems they face today and will face in the future but also with any additional problems brought about by global warming, if and when they occur.

7. Global Warming and Human Health

Robert E. Davis

Indur Goklany has shown how little effect even the worst climate change scenarios ultimately will have on developing economies and how any crash program to "mitigate" global warming today will be money spent with a huge opportunity cost. Delaying development by spending today's money removes capital that can be invested in adaptation.

Here, University of Virginia's Robert Davis expands on one of Goklany's major themes: that affluent societies have better public health and that they engineer their way around weather-related deaths. The lesson is obvious: economic development, not taxation, is the key to dealing with our ever-changing weather and climate.

As shown below, global warming has clearly invaded the medical community. Its refereed literature is rife with inaccuracies about global warming and health, and, unfortunately, with our new health care program, constitutes another invasion into our lives.

Longer, more intense heat waves . . . malaria threatening populations in regions where it was never before seen . . . more and more people dying or being hospitalized from respiratory distress as urban air quality deteriorates . . . increased suffering from seasonal allergies as ragweed runs rampant through the countryside . . . the litany of human health impacts from global warming goes on and on.

It's safe to say that these (and other) health impacts either will not happen or will not be nearly as severe as the predictions. Of course, when some future prediction doesn't happen, we have usually long since forgotten the forecast in the first place, as we've moved on to being concerned about all the new predictions being proffered!

The statement that global climate change is a complex problem sounds like standard rhetoric from the thousands of scientists dealing with the issues, but it is, in fact, true. Earth's climate system involves the complex interplay of sun, ocean, land, and air that controls weather, and moving from weather to long-term climate adds additional complexities. But the introduction of human systems makes a complex problem all the more chaotic.

Let's begin with three basic, and perhaps (at first glance) contradictory, truths about this issue:

- Global warming *will* affect human health across the planet;
- The extent of this effect is unknowable; and
- No one in earth's history ever has (or ever will have) died or been hospitalized from global warming.

The story of human health impacts from climate change follows a very predictable script that is repeated ad nauseam, regardless of the disease or other cause of death. As an example, here's one disease that has been linked to climate change, selected completely at random—tick-borne encephalitis (TBE).

TBE is caused by a virus for which ticks act as both a disease transmission vehicle (commonly referred to as an insect "vector") and a storage facility. The disease is primarily transmitted to humans via tick bites in summer when ticks are most active. TBE increased from 1976 to 2008 in Europe where the disease is endemic[1] (see Figure 7.1). Why? The obvious answer is "climate change." It is a simple fact of modern times that whenever anything in nature has worsened over time, the first place to look for an explanation is climate change. The implicit assumption here is that everyone knows that the climate is changing, that climate change is always bad, and that it affects almost everything. This assumption has been part of the K–12 curriculum (and beyond) for the past three decades. One merely has to fill in the blanks and there is yet another climate change impact to throw onto the heap. This is particularly easy to do as much of the world warmed between 1976 and the present, although at markedly different rates and more so in some seasons and times of day than others. You correlate one upward trend (TBE infections) to another (temperature), and you've got yourself a climate change impact.

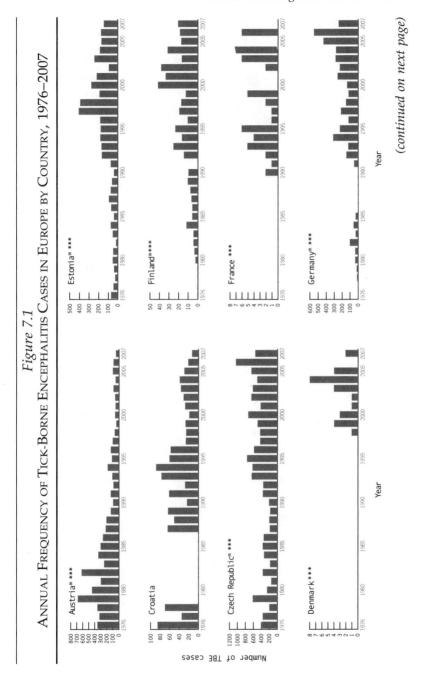

Figure 7.1
ANNUAL FREQUENCY OF TICK-BORNE ENCEPHALITIS CASES IN EUROPE BY COUNTRY, 1976–2007

(continued on next page)

187

Figure 7.1 (continued)

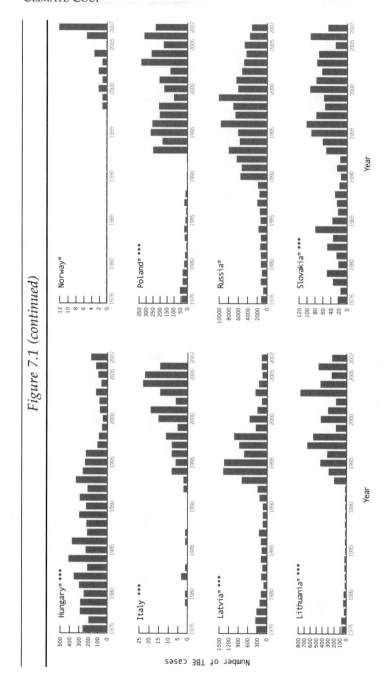

Figure 7.1 (continued)

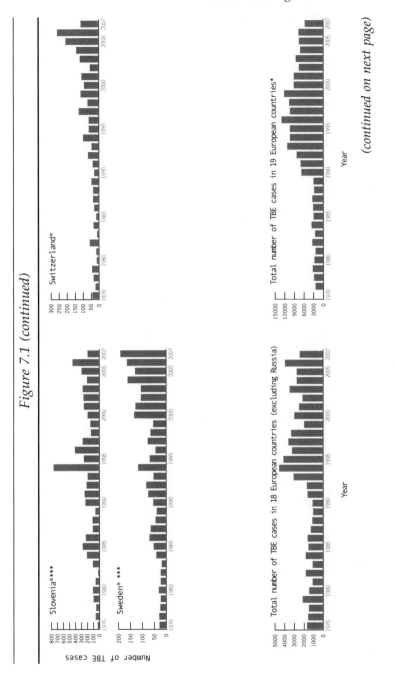

(continued on next page)

Figure 7.1 (continued)

*Austria, Croatia, Czech Republic, Denmark, Estonia, Finland, France, Germany, Hungary, Italy, Latvia, Lithuania, Norway, Poland, Russia, Slovakia, Slovenia, Sweden, Switzerland

**The numbers represent reported individual cases of TBE and not incidence, as in most countries the risk for TBE is restricted to some areas or regions and therefore a calculation of the incidence for the entire country might lead to false interpretations.

***European Union Member State

m = mandatory notification

SOURCE: J. Süss, "Tick-Borne Encephalitis in Europe and Beyond: The Epidemiological Situation as of 2007," *Eurosurveillance* 13 (2008): 1–8.

NOTE: Overall counts are in the bottom two figures.[2]

But this exercise gets a lot trickier once you begin to really explore the underlying processes. Ticks apparently thrive in warmer and wetter environments, and in much of Europe, temperatures and precipitation increased over the period of record. These conditions also help increase tick populations as they overwinter and help extend their comfortable range (both poleward and into higher elevations). But some countries have extensive vaccination programs. In Austria, for example, where TBE is endemic, most of the inhabitants receive vaccinations, and so the trend is markedly downward (Figure 7.1, top left-hand graph), rendering climate change irrelevant. Increased attention to the disease over time (because of our perseveration on climate change) may also inflate the number of cases reported. After the fall of the Iron Curtain, behavioral, socioeconomic, and data-reporting changes could also affect the trends. The Soviet Union, after all, had no unemployment until it fell, just as Lithuania had no TBE until it chased the Soviets out.

Let's now delve into the bizarre realm of predicting tick behavior. Here is an example from Jochen Süss, head of the National Reference Laboratory of Tick-Borne Diseases, in which he attempts to ascribe the observed changes to climate:

> The reasons for the increase of TBE cases over a period of 30 years throughout Europe and their decrease in most of the countries in 2007 are unknown. However, there may be an association with the exceptional weather conditions in 2007 (in Central Europe). After the extremely warm winter 2006/07, the ticks were active very early in the year (February/early March) and had certainly lost some of their energy due to their constant activity. The urgently required search for a host for a blood meal, however, was hampered in April by the extremely warm and dry weather conditions. As a rule, the ticks had to retreat to the leaf litter as a humidity reservoir. In the summer of 2007, strong precipitations *(sic)* led to a reduced exposure of humans due to a reduced rate of outdoor activities. It is also supposed that the development cycle (larva-nymph) of *Ixodes ricinus* was changed in a so far unknown way by the mild winter and the weather conditions that followed.

So ticks prefer warm, wet conditions. The winter of 2006–07 was warm, and the active ticks wasted their energy running around looking for hosts from which to suck blood but apparently could not find any. When April was warm (good for ticks) but dry (bad for ticks), the hungry little bloodsuckers retreated under the leaves, where they could find no food. But when it was wet later in the summer and the ticks emerged from their leafy hideaway, they found few humans to drain, as everyone stayed indoors because it was raining. So despite the fact that the climate in 2007 was mostly ideal for ticks, TBE was generally low *because of the climate*.

Süss actually deserves applause for attempting to craft a reasonable (and perhaps even plausible) story about TBE transmission and climate. He might even be correct!

But we'll never know. For TBE to infect a human, you need an infected tick that comes in contact with an infected human, bites the human, and transmits the virus. You have plenty of virus-free ticks, plenty of ticks that never get within biting distance of humans, and plenty of woods-loving humans who routinely check their exposed skin for ticks. Furthermore, to relate increases in TBE to climate, you need to establish that both higher temperature and higher precipitation bring more TBE-infected biting ticks in contact with more humans than you would expect had conditions been colder and drier.

Which brings us back to the original list. It is possible, perhaps even likely, that *weather* is related to TBE. To substantiate this linkage, all the other tick behavior factors must be ruled out. Given the tick's short life span (months to a couple of years at most), any climate impacts will not influence an individual tick but the general tick population. If warmer and wetter conditions do result in a larger, more virulent tick population (also possible), then we next need to establish that warmer and wetter conditions are arising from human-induced climate change in the particular environs frequented by the offending ticks. As an example, let's go back to Austria, a country replete with disease-bearing ticks and woods-loving trekkers. Sure, Austria may be getting warmer and wetter based on observations from the official weather station—out in the open, 4.5 feet above ground, and probably near a town—but are the woods and the wet leaves where the ticks hang out actually a better habitat today than it was 30 years ago? Possibly, but the fact is, we'll never know. Short of capturing thousands of ticks, attaching temperature and moisture sensors to them, and following them around for a few decades, we'll never know. In fact, for all we know, the ticks could burrow as deep as they need to find an optimum temperature in the duff, regardless of what the weather station in town says.

So even if the weather changes are generally consistent with creating a tick-friendly environment that is consistent with model projections of how weather will change as climate changes from increasing greenhouse gases, we are stuck with the problem that the tick only cares about the conditions in the few millimeters that surrounds its little arachnid body.

This same approach can be extrapolated to your human health impact of choice. Humans are affected by weather, not climate. Just because weather changes might seem to be consistent with climate change predictions does not make them real climate change impacts. Weather has always exhibited natural variability, even before humans invented "climate change," when these events were simply attributed to the whims of nature. But just like there has to be a reason for every minor fluctuation in the stock market ("the Dow fell six points yesterday on rumors of unrest in Haiti"), so must each weather event have some underlying "cause." Hurricane Katrina could have been exactly the same, or even worse, had it occurred in 1705 as opposed to 2005. It was a Category 3, but a very large storm in geographic extent. Hurricane Carla, which hit Texas in 1961, was a Category 4 and may have been even larger. Without "global warming," would Katrina have been a Category 2 storm? Carla a Category 5? (Hurricanes are classified by forecasters from Category 1 (minimal) to Category 5 (catastrophic). Categories 3 through 5 are considered "major".)

We'll never know. Katrina was a weather event that affected the lives of millions of people. To try to establish whether Katrina-like storms are more common in today's carbon dioxide–rich atmosphere, we need to examine the probability of storms today compared with storms in the past when the atmosphere had markedly less carbon dioxide. A comparison of these differences, or trends over time, with theory about how the atmosphere works, perhaps coupled with models, gives us an idea of what to expect now and in the future. Hurricanes are being used here as an example because there is a vigorous ongoing debate in the tropical climatology community about how and if hurricanes will be affected by higher carbon dioxide levels, or whether any changes will be detectable beyond the substantial interannual and interdecadal variation in hurricane strength and frequency.

If we are ever going to understand how health is related to weather and climate, scientists need to work across disciplines. This statement is pablum to environmental sciences and environmental health researchers who hear this on a weekly basis. But in practice, it rarely happens. Here's a recent, typical example culled from the *New England Journal of Medicine* in its "Perspective" section (basically an opinion piece), this one called "Global Climate Change and Infectious Disease," by Emily K. Shuman, M.D.:

> Climate change is occurring as a result of an imbalance between incoming and outgoing radiation in the atmosphere. As solar radiation enters the atmosphere, some of it is absorbed by the earth's surface and reemitted as infrared radiation, which is then absorbed by greenhouse gases— primarily carbon dioxide, methane, and nitrous oxide— which result from the combustion of fossil fuels and which cannot be effectively removed from the atmosphere because of deforestation. This process generates heat. As the concentrations of greenhouse gases in the atmosphere have reached record levels, global temperatures have risen at a faster rate than at any time since records began to be kept in the 1850s, and temperatures are expected to increase by another 1.8 to 5.8°C by the end of this century. The hydrologic cycle will be altered, since warmer air can retain more moisture than cooler air. Some geographic areas will have more rainfall, and some more drought, and severe weather events—including heat waves and storms—are expected to become more common. For these reasons, the term "climate change" is now preferred over the term "global warming." Because of rising temperatures and changing rainfall patterns, climate change is expected to have a substantial effect on the burden of infectious diseases that are transmitted by insect vectors and through contaminated water.[3]

That may seem harmless enough, but in fact, each statement contains at least one inaccuracy that could have been avoided had a real climatologist been consulted. For example:

> Climate change is occurring as a result of an imbalance between incoming and outgoing radiation in the atmosphere.

Actually, they are almost always out of balance at any given location or time. Winds, ocean currents, storms, and so forth are nature's way of trying to maintain balance.

> As solar radiation enters the atmosphere, some of it is
> absorbed by the earth's surface and reemitted as infrared
> radiation, which is then absorbed by greenhouse gases—
> primarily carbon dioxide, methane, and nitrous oxide—
> which result from the combustion of fossil fuels and which
> cannot be effectively removed from the atmosphere because
> of deforestation.

Infrared radiation is not "reemitted" by the surface; the primary
greenhouse gas is water vapor; and forests remove little methane
or nitrous oxide—try the hydroxl radical and atmospheric oxidation,
respectively. The statement implies that greenhouse gases would
not be increasing if there were no deforestation—also incorrect.
Moving on . . .

> The hydrologic cycle will be altered, since warmer air can
> retain more moisture than cooler air.

Air doesn't "retain moisture" based on temperature—warm air
has a higher vapor pressure at saturation. Just because air is warmer
does not mean it is more humid. Think Sahara desert.

> Some geographic areas will have more rainfall, and some
> more drought, and severe weather events—including heat
> waves and storms—are expected to become more common.
> For these reasons, the term "climate change" is now preferred
> over the term "global warming."

I'm not sure how the first sentence leads to the second. So we just
read that the air is supposed to "retain more moisture." How does
that lead to more drought, exactly? Sounds scary, but the scariest
scenarios are always the least likely. (Just to help out the editorial
writer here, that *may* happen because of changes in the atmospheric
circulation, but this is more of a model result than an observed
change.)

Later in her article, Shuman writes:

> In an attempt to halt climate change, international efforts to
> reduce emissions have already been put in place. The Kyoto
> Protocol has now been ratified by 187 nations (but most
> notably not by the United States) and went into effect in 2005.

This statement leaves the reader with the ludicrous impression that
climate change is only happening because of the human contribution

195

to greenhouse gases, and that it could be "halted" if we simply passed the appropriate legislation. Any reasonably well-taught introductory college course in earth science would demonstrate that climate *change* is the nature of climate, but that's probably not part of the standard premedical curriculum.

Now comes the kicker, which is the standard, boilerplate ending to nearly every opinion piece on the danger of global warming:

> Although governments must take the lead in tackling climate change, I believe that it is also our responsibility as members of the health care community to do our part. Recommendations for ways in which individuals and businesses can reduce their greenhouse gas emissions are available from the Environmental Protection Agency. In addition, though reducing emissions is of the utmost importance, we must remember that the best-case scenario would be a global temperature increase of about 2°C. Therefore, we must also focus our efforts on mitigating the effects of climate change, including its potential impact on the global burden of infectious diseases.

So an article that started out as a review of how global climate change will (allegedly) affect infectious disease has morphed into the need for the U.S. Congress to pass specific legislation and the personal responsibility that each of us has to buy into a collective mindset of group behaviors that will somehow stop the spread of disease across the planet. The writer of this opinion piece specializes in infectious disease, but clearly not climatology. But there is a tremendous double standard inherent in this kind of writing. If I, for example, wrote an article about my suggestions for new techniques in spinal surgery, my work wouldn't see the light of day. Nor should it. My training is in atmospheric science with an emphasis in climatology and its impact on health and mortality, so I know nothing about spinal surgery. But the presumption that the nuances of my profession can be well understood by people with no training in it results in the publication of misinformed, and/or incorrect random musings masquerading as applied science. The literature of many professions—economics, biology, public policy—is overrun with hundreds of comparable examples with virtually analogous language.

An ironic aspect of the climate change and health topic is that for many decades, very few health experts felt that weather had any impact whatsoever on human health. The International Society of Biometeorology was founded in 1956 to bring together disparate researchers interested in the broad area of biometeorology, or how plants, animals, and humans influence and are influenced by the surrounding atmosphere. According to the ISB website: "Over fifty years ago, when the Society was founded, scientists who were interested in environmental and ecological problems were rather isolated. The ISB provided a framework for the exchange of information that was essential to the survival of the discipline." Indeed, the ISB's flagship journal, the *International Journal of Biometeorology*, has a long history of publications focused on climate interactions with plants and animals and relatively little on humans. Part of this resistance could have resulted from intellectual backlash against "climatic determinism" in the first half of the 20th century and its links to Marxism. Certainly, some researchers believed that weather changes influenced human health and well-being, but these ideas were certainly well outside the mainstream of scientific thinking at the time.

Nowadays, we seem to be facing the opposite problem. Weather and climate changes are somehow linked to changes in just about everything, including human health. As it usually does, the real truth lies somewhere in the middle. There is no doubt that the human body responds to changes in its physical surroundings—sweating and sunburn are two obvious examples. But the fundamental question here is, how do long-term changes in climate affect large numbers of people over time and space? Is the human population being adversely affected by the human-induced climate changes that have been observed?

Human individuals and societies, even primitive ones, adapt to weather changes. Traditional housing types and clothing are largely driven by adapting available local raw materials to make life possible (or more comfortable). Technological advances have obviously made dealing with one's local climate an afterthought—for example, the Persian Gulf is completely inhospitable to human life, and London isn't all that keen, either. All of this should be obvious. What is unclear is the implicit assumption made by some climate change experts that we have not or will not adapt to the comparatively small climate *changes* that have occurred over our lifetime. In fact, there is abundant evidence that active adaptations have taken place and that we are actually less at risk now despite the ongoing warming trend.

197

Like the earlier TBE example, malaria is a vector-borne disease transmitted by mosquitoes. Because higher temperatures tend to increase the number and expand the range of mosquitoes and the mosquito-biting frequency, a long-standing climate change/health nostrum is that malaria will become worse with increasing temperatures. Some papers have been published that purportedly link observed climate changes to malaria's spread.

There is little doubt about the basic premises (more mosquitoes and expanded range)—the problem is the outcome (more malaria), because the outcome depends on the age-old EEBE assumption (Everything Else Being Equal). In the climate/health world, EEBE is one assumption that is rarely realistic. The following example is a case study of malaria that is a beautiful demonstration of this problem, but it also serves as an example that cuts across many aspects of the climate/human health arena. Here, I expand on a malaria study discussed in the previous chapter by Indur Goklany.

Peter Gething and his colleagues[4] developed a global map of the occurrence of *Plasmodium falciparum* malaria (the parasite responsible for most of the global malaria burden) for the year 2007. For each location on a 5-kilometer grid, they classified the malaria endemicity into six distinct classes from "risk free" to "holoendemic" (defined here to mean that more than three-fourths of the mosquitoes have *P. falciparum* in their blood). They compared this with a map using the same six groups from the (approximate) year 1900, a time when malaria was believed to pose a major global problem and before the development of malaria intervention programs. The appropriate figures are given in Figure 7.2 (see color insert). As Goklany noted, *nowhere* is malaria endemicity getting worse. But most of these malaria-riddled locales have experienced warming over the last century, so EEBE, there should be more malaria, not less. Just to demonstrate that this warming assumption is correct, Figure 7.2 shows the land surface temperature change from a recent 10-year period minus the temperature for the decade around 1900. Temperature increases are evident over most of the globe, as well as most of the locations where malaria has occurred.

According to Gething and colleagues:

> Comparison of the historical and contemporary maps revealed that endemic/stable malaria is likely to have covered 58% of the world's land surface around 1900 but only

30% by 2007 when *P. falciparum* malaria has become restricted largely to the tropics. Even more marked has been the decrease in prevalence within this greatly reduced range, with endemicity falling by one or more classes in over two-thirds (67%) of the current range of stable transmission. The contemporary map indicates that holoendemic *P. falciparum* malaria is now rare and limited to patches in West Africa totalling around 140,000 km². The Americas are entirely hypoendemic (10% or fewer individuals have malaria parasites, Ed.) for *P. falciparum*, as are very large sections of central and southeast Asia and substantial swathes of Africa.[5]

The authors propose that nonclimatic factors must be swamping the climatic effects, especially direct disease control measures, as well as "indirect effects of a century of urbanization and economic development." In other words, as the standard of living improves, malaria becomes less of an issue.

A logical follow-up question would be to compare the likely size of the climate change impacts relative to the other factors that reduce disease transmission. To address this, Gething and his colleagues examined order-of-magnitude changes in the "reproductive number," which is a measure of how readily an infectious disease will spread within a nonimmune population. Some studies have predicted a doubling or tripling of the reproductive number from climate change by the mid- to late 21st century.[6] Gething and his coauthors summarized their exploration of the size of the climate effect on malaria as follows:

Despite warming global temperatures, the combined natural and anthropogenic forces acting on the disease throughout the twentieth century have resulted in the great majority of locations undergoing a net *reduction* in transmission between *one and three orders of magnitude* (emphasis added, Ed.) larger than the maximum future increases proposed under temperature-based climate change scenarios. . . . When compared to the substantially smaller proposed magnitude of climate-induced effects, an important and simple inference is that [climate change impacts] can be offset by moderate increases in coverage levels of currently available interventions.[7]

In other words, the net impact of climate change on malaria transmission is only from one-tenth to one–one-thousandth the impact of human adaptation. This low net impact does not mean that climate change has not and will not affect global malaria (EEBE), but that, given a broader perspective, global warming is not that important. This point was basically put forth in their remarkably forthright closing statement:

> In an era when the international community has been emboldened to provide guidelines for malaria elimination it is necessary to maintain the correct perspective on the future impact of climate change on malaria epidemiology and by implication its malaria public health importance. The quantification of a global recession in the range and intensity of malaria over the twentieth century has allowed us to review the rationale underpinning high-profile predictions of a current and future worsening of the disease in a warming climate. It suggests that the success or failure of our efforts against the parasite in the coming century are likely to be determined by factors other than climate change.

In a related interview, the lead author observed: "Malaria is still a huge problem, but climate change per se is not something that should be central to the discussion. The risks have been overstated." Paul Reiter, a noted malaria expert who for some time has opined that the linkages between temperature and malaria transmission are exaggerated, commented: "The complexity of malaria and the other vector-borne diseases is astonishing. To bring it down to just one factor—climate change—is totally unjustifiable." Cornell's Laura Harrington agreed, saying, "In the context of vector-borne diseases, climate change is probably going to have a minimal role in comparison to other factors."

So is this the end of the global-warming-equals-spreading-malaria orthodoxy? Of course not. A likely tactic of the believers will be to focus on local climate changes that are by definition greater than large-scale, global changes. For example, there has been an ongoing debate regarding whether it has been warming in Africa's Eastern Highlands, a region where malaria is spreading into higher altitudes. In reviewing this kind of debate, you should always ask two questions: (a) What kinds of local changes might have taken place that could affect transmission? and (b) Is the effect a true climate change signal or simply weather variability, i.e., can the local changes in climate reasonably be linked to human greenhouse gas increases?

These issues must be considered in tandem, as human-induced warming is a global problem. We're much more worried about malaria in equatorial Africa than we are in, say, Naples, Florida, despite the fact that both regions seem to be getting warmer. With greater emphasis on local climate changes, it becomes much harder to make the case that they are related to "global" warming rather than natural, localized variability. Recall our tick discussion.

Science in prospect is often dramatically different from science in retrospect. In prospect, imagine it's the year 1901 and you are holding a map of malaria for the year 1900. Also imagine that you had advance information that global land temperatures would increase by 0.74 degree Celsius (on average). What future malaria forecast would you make? Probably that malaria would be found just about everywhere on the planet, except maybe Antarctica. Of course this forecast would be profoundly incorrect because you would not have anticipated the intervening medical and economic advances.

We are basically in the identical position today. Despite the fact that malaria has been declining nearly everywhere for many decades, we are being asked to ignore all that and believe that small changes in climate are going to overwhelm this long-term trend toward less disease.

The results of the malaria study by Gething and his colleagues (including the editor of this volume) are similar in many ways to research I conducted with my colleagues on U.S. mortality and heat events. I think the similarities tell us something about the inherent nature of the problem of examining the impact of climate change on human systems.

Figure 7.3 shows the number of daily deaths for 29 nonconsecutive years, from 1964 to 1998, versus the 7:00 a.m. temperature. This example is from Kansas City. It is not what anyone would call a highly predictive relationship. In other words, if you know the 7:00 a.m. temperature, you would have virtually no chance of predicting the mortality on that day. This statement is not surprising, of course, because only rarely do people die because of the weather conditions.

But there are several other ways to examine these kinds of data. One is to look at the overall relationship, which is dictated by what's happening at low and high temperatures. When a statistical best-fit line is plotted (solid line in Figure 7.3), we see higher mortality when it is cold and lower mortality when it is warm. This line is picking up the inherent seasonality in mortality data. For a variety of reasons,

Figure 7.3
DAILY MORTALITY IN KANSAS CITY VS. 7:00 A.M. AIR
TEMPERATURE (°C) OVER 29 NONCONSECUTIVE YEARS, 1964–98

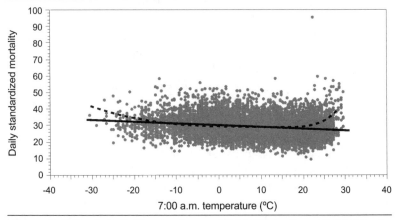

SOURCE: R. E. Davis, P. C. Knappenberger, W. M. Novicoff, and P. J. Michaels, "Seasonality of Climate–Human Mortality Relationships in US Cities and Impacts of Climate Change," *Climate Research* 26 (2004): 61–76.

NOTE: A linear and curved fit to the data represent two different approaches to understanding the weather/mortality relationship.

more people die in winter than in summer, and that applies across all the major causes of death, except cancer.

Another approach is to plot the average mortality value for each temperature (dashed line in Figure 7.3). Now we can see evidence of a subtle U-shaped or J-shaped curve, with more concavity at high temperatures than at low. A very similar curve has been observed for many cities worldwide that have seasonal climates. The key to understanding weather/mortality relationships is to understand this curve. At the cold end, there is a slight and very subtle increase in mortality. It is difficult to visually determine where the increase begins because it is not very marked. This portion of the plot arises because mortality is higher in winter. At the warm end, however, note the much more abrupt increase with higher temperatures. This allows for the estimation of a "threshold temperature" beyond which mortality, on average, increases. This increase is related to hot, humid days or heat waves. When the temperature exceeds this threshold (somewhere around 22 degrees Celsius (72 degrees Fahrenheit) at 7:00 a.m. in Kansas City), more people die on that day or the following day. But it's critical to note that overall, many more people die in winter than in summer. These summer deaths are occurring on unusually warm (and often humid) days.

Based on the same data, different groups of researchers have reached fundamentally different conclusions about the impact of climate change on mortality. The simplest argument (which in this case is wrong) suggests that as the planet warms, fewer people will die because winters will get milder and more people die when it's cold. This result implies a much stronger relationship between mortality and low temperatures than exists in the cold season. Just look at the cold end of the plot—there is very little variability and no obvious upward trend in mortality compared with the rest of plot. In fact, when you compare the data across years, just as many people die in warm winters as in cold winters. In other words, mortality is high not because it is cold but because it is winter. In summer, however, more people die during hot spells—there is a much stronger predictive relationship between warm, humid *days* and high mortality. This relationship is particularly true in northern cities (e.g., New York, Philadelphia, Chicago).

This right-hand side of the U- or J-curve, coupled with the obvious projection that global warming will produce more hot, humid days and longer and/or more severe heat waves, has led other researchers to predict more heat-related deaths, EEBE. Sound familiar? Here yet again, technology stands in the way of a good story. We examined this relationship for a number of large U.S. cities by looking at the trend in heat mortality over time by counting the excess deaths for days that exceeded the "threshold temperature." It's then a simple matter to plot the mortality trend versus the temperature trend (here using an index called the "apparent temperature" or heat index, which combines both temperature and humidity).

Figure 7.4 plots this relationship for each of the 28 cities in our study. If the typical global warming projections are correct, then we should see most of the points in the upper-right quadrant—warming should produce more deaths. But most of the cities are found in the bottom right—warming is associated with fewer deaths. A better way to phrase this is that despite warming, fewer people are dying in heat waves.

Figure 7.4
MORTALITY TREND VS. APPARENT TEMPERATURE TREND FOR EACH OF 28 LARGE U.S. CITIES, 1964–98

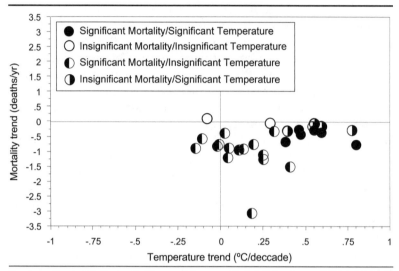

SOURCE: Davis, R. E., P. C. Knappenberger, P. J. Michaels, and W. M. Novicoff, 2005.[8]

NOTE: Statistical significance of the trend is indicated by coloring a portion of the circle (see key). Most cities demonstrate lower mortality despite increasing heat and humidity (the lower, right quadrant of the graph).

The reasons fewer people are dying are fairly obvious—as individuals and as a society, we take measures to isolate ourselves from harmful conditions. The best way to avoid dying in a heat wave is to stay cool, and so we invented air conditioning. The EEBE hypothesis does not take this into account. People still die more often on hot summer days than on moderate or cool summer days for a variety of reasons, poverty being one of them. For this reason, local governments in many cities have heat mitigation plans that target the poor, inner-city areas that are most sensitive to summer heat waves.

I would summarize the salient points on the human mortality issue as follows:

- There is little overall relationship between temperature and deaths on most days;

204

- Despite higher mortality in winter, warmer winters will not reduce deaths because there is little relationship between cold days and excess mortality; and
- Despite longer and hotter heat waves, heat wave mortality has declined because of a variety of human adaptations.

The bottom line is that we have effectively isolated our lives from the effects of extreme heat and cold. The human response to heat is remarkably similar to the human response to malaria.

The next time you hear a report about how U.S. deaths will increase because of increasing carbon dioxide levels, think back to Figure 7.3. The relationship is very weak across most of the temperature range. What effect will a very small increase in temperature have on mortality? None, for all practical purposes, and certainly no effect that is readily detectable given the noise in the data.

This fact provides context for a recent study of the mortality impact of urban carbon dioxide domes by Jacobson.[9] Carbon dioxide is generally believed to be well mixed in the atmosphere. In other words, the levels of carbon dioxide in your backyard should be about the same as those in the backyard of someone on the other side of the planet. This is the reason the famous Keeling carbon dioxide curve from the observatory at Mauna Loa, Hawaii, is used to represent the global trend. The Mauna Loa concentration is around 390 parts per million (ppm), versus a preindustrial background of about 280 ppm. But based on some extensive measurements, Idso, Idso, and Balling and Balling, Cerveny, and Idso estimated that carbon dioxide levels in Phoenix, Arizona, were 550–600 ppm.[10] Compared with the background levels in nonurbanized settings, this estimate could be up to 200 ppm higher given the right weather conditions. Using a model, you can then calculate the impact this increase would have on urban temperatures. It's got to be huge, right? Well, no; it comes out to about one-tenth of a degree Celsius. There is actually a huge impact on temperature, but it arises from the structures built in cities and changes to the natural surface landscape. This urban heat island varies from city to city, but it can raise temperatures on the order of 5 degrees Celsius (and often more), making any impact of the urban carbon dioxide dome (or for that matter, increases from background greenhouse warming) very minor by comparison.

But this scale problem, in which the effect is several orders of magnitude smaller than the observed changes, did not deter Jacobson from making predictions. He noted that 50–100 premature deaths would occur annually in California from carbon dioxide dome impacts. The train of logic here is that higher temperatures increase the reaction rates of certain atmospheric pollutants that have been linked to human health—namely, ozone and particulate matter—and that higher pollutant levels will kill more people, EEBE.

To conduct this study properly, you need to establish the chain of causality. Each step of the relationship has some inherent error. If the net effect is greater than the cumulative error, then you may be on to something. Let's assume that the carbon dioxide dome raises local temperatures by 0.1 degree Celsius and that this is an accurate projection, for the sake of argument. How much will it raise, say, ozone levels? On average, by about 0.1 to 0.2 ppbv (parts per billion volume). Riverside, California (a city with a big ozone pollution problem), has an average daily maximum ozone level of over 100 ppb. Jerrett and others[11] estimate that the risk of respiratory mortality increases by 4 percent for every 10 ppb increase in ozone, on average. So we can see, for example, that the carbon dioxide dome effect would increase the maximum ozone in Riverside by about one one-thousandth, and this would raise mortality by a fraction of a percent, EEBE.

The problem with this kind of analysis is that the effect is completely undetectable given the noise in the data. It is impossible to show this effect by examining long-term data because there are so many confounding factors. In this situation, a model is an ideal weapon—you can say, as Jacobson does, that there must be an effect, but there is no possible way to verify the model because the effect is so small. Unfortunately, the paper entitled "Urban CO2 Domes Have No Impact on Human Health" isn't very sexy. As a result, we get:

> Although modeled pollution changes and their health impacts are uncertain, results here suggests that reducing local CO^2 may reduce 300–1,000 premature air pollution mortalities/yr in the U.S. and 50–100/yr in California, even if CO^2 in adjacent regions is not controlled. Thus, CO^2 emission controls may be justified on the same grounds that NOx [nitrogen oxide], HC [hydrocarbon], CO [carbon monoxide],

206

and PM [particulate matter] emission regulations are justified.

This sure sounds like a good idea until you put it in perspective. About 2.5 million Americans die each year. Let's pick Jacobson's middle projection (650 deaths). Efforts by the Environmental Protection Agency to tax carbon dioxide to reduce local pollution levels would reduce U.S. mortality by 0.026 percent. But if we were to properly attach error bars to these estimates, the numbers are so small that they certainly include zero. In other words, it is a quite reasonable statistical possibility that complete elimination of all urban carbon dioxide domes would have no demonstrable effect. How much would you be willing to pay for that?

It's hard to argue that poor air quality is good for anyone's health. Clearly it's not. Pollution probably mitigates warming by reducing the amount of radiation that reaches the earth's surface (via "global dimming"), but given a choice between slightly higher temperatures and clean air, most people would pick the latter.

Since the passage of the first Clean Air Act during the Nixon administration, EPA has been aggressively pursuing regulation to improve air quality—not a surprise given that EPA is a regulatory body. And it has been successful. Figure 7.5 shows the trends in air quality (from EPA's Air Trends website) since 1980 (or over the available period of record) for some common pollutants: sulfur dioxide (SO_2), nitrogen dioxide (NO_2), ozone, and small and large diameter particulate matter ($PM_{2.5}$ and PM_{10}, respectively). Note that they are all declining. Over the available periods, SO_2 has declined by 71 percent, NO_2 by 46 percent, ozone by 25 percent, and $PM_{2.5}$ and PM_{10} by 19 percent and 31 percent, respectively. Clearly EPA has been successful.

Overall U.S. life expectancy has also improved over time (Figure 7.6). Medical care has improved. The environment is cleaner. Nutrition is better. Prenatal care is almost universally available. Some diseases have been eradicated and others have been mitigated by vaccines. Sanitation is a society ahead of the 19th century. And so on. Add your own favorite reasons not identified here ... the list goes on.

And yet U.S. temperatures have risen, certainly since about 1980 (Figure 7.7). Most pollutants are supposed to worsen in a warmer

Figure 7.5

LONG-TERM TRENDS IN VARIOUS AIR POLLUTANTS IN THE UNITED
STATES OVER THE AVAILABLE PERIODS OF RECORD

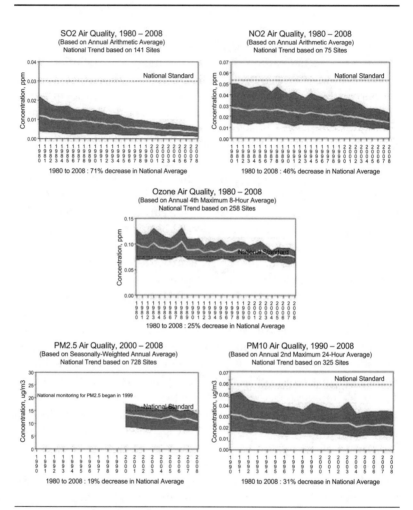

SOURCE: U.S. Environmental Protection Agency, Air Trends website, http://
www.epa.gov/airtrends/index.

environment, and yet they haven't. If in 1970, you were given an
accurate prediction of future temperatures for the next 40 years, you
would probably have predicted higher mortality because of higher

Figure 7.6
U.S. LIFE EXPECTANCY SINCE 1950 AND PROJECTED THROUGH 2050

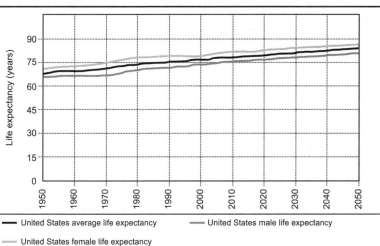

— United States average life expectancy   — United States male life expectancy

— United States female life expectancy

SOURCE: Data360, http://www.data360.org/dsg.aspx?Data_Set_Group_Id = 195.

air pollution concentrations. And you would have been totally incorrect. Sure, EEBE, air quality *should* be much worse now given the warming trend. But mortality is down and air quality has never been better, *despite* "global warming." Yet each year, more and more papers are published about how global warming is going to worsen air quality and generate more premature deaths. EEBE.

While we're looking at mortality trends, let's take a moment to quickly examine tornadoes, the severest of severe weather, the most intense weather vortices on Earth. While they aren't the major cause of weather-related deaths in the United States (heat waves and floods produce more), strong ones can and do level entire small towns, and provide the most action-packed weather news footage, thus receiving the most media attention.

The number of tornadoes observed in the United States has skyrocketed since the 1950s. This increase isn't because of global warming. Instead, we are much better at detecting tornadoes now than we were 60 years ago, owing to technological improvements like Doppler radar. So the identification of nontechnological trends in tornadoes is a thorny problem. Regardless, the number of tornado

Figure 7.7
AVERAGE ANNUAL SURFACE AIR TEMPERATURES FOR THE
CONTIGUOUS UNITED STATES, 1901–2008

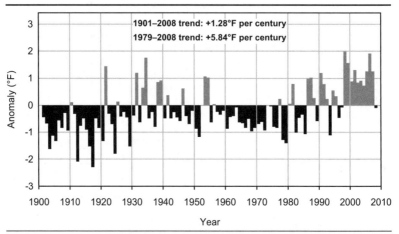

SOURCE: National Climatic Data Center website, http://www.ncdc. noaa.gov.

NOTE: Temperatures are shown as departures from the 1971–2000 mean.

fatalities has declined substantially (Figure 7.8). Tornado forecasting is extremely difficult—forecasters may know a day in advance whether the environment is suitable to support severe thunderstorms, but pinpointing where and when they will occur is very hard to do even a few hours in advance. Therefore, people have little lead-time. Despite these issues, our ability to mitigate against tornado-related mortality has improved dramatically.

The debate about whether hurricanes have or will become more numerous or have or will become more severe from global warming could easily fill a book. Both sides of the argument seem to have legitimate facts in their corner. As with many issues, the truth probably lies somewhere in the middle. So let's look at U.S. mortality arising from tropical cyclones.

The number of annual tropical cyclone deaths is highly variable. Major hurricanes can make landfall in unpopulated areas. Some years with frequent storms don't necessarily have many landfalling storms. Weaker tropical storms can produce major, widespread flooding that raises mortality. So the record has many years with

210

Figure 7.8
U.S. ANNUAL TORNADO-RELATED MORTALITY RATE, 1875–2008
(DEATHS PER MILLION PEOPLE)

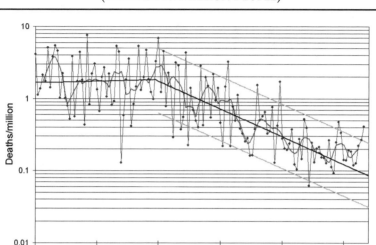

SOURCE: Harold Brooks, "U.S. Annual Tornado Death Tolls," *U.S. Severe Weather Blog*, March 1, 2009, http://www.norman.noaa.gov/2009/03/us-annual-tornado-death-tolls-1875-present/.

very low mortality punctuated with years like 1972 (weak, flood-producing Agnes) or 2005 (the very large Katrina) with massive mortality. This variation makes the calculation of trends difficult.

Arguez and Elsner[12] examined hurricane mortality from 1900 to 1995 by counting deaths over distinct 16-year periods. Within each 16-year block, they calculated the number of years with storms that produced at least 1 death, at least 22 deaths, and at least 60 deaths (Figure 7.9). From 1980 to 1995, no year had 60 or more tropical storm–related deaths, but from 1900 to 1963, all 16-year periods had 4 such years.[13] So this result is consistent with the previous plots for mortality, air quality, and so forth showing long-term improvements. Hurricane warnings have substantially improved over the last 40 years or more since the widespread use of satellite monitoring. Track forecasting has also improved with more advanced integration of tropical cyclones into weather-forecasting models. False alarms

Figure 7.9
NUMBER OF YEARS (PER 16-YEAR PERIOD) WITH AT LEAST *k* DEATHS
IN THE UNITED STATES ARISING FROM TROPICAL CYCLONES

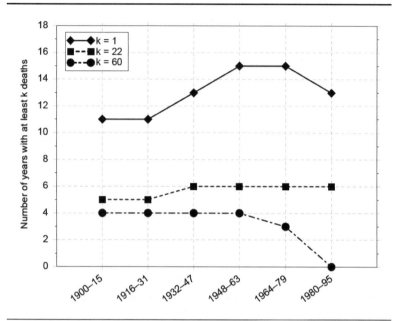

SOURCE: Anthony Arguez and James B. Elsner, "Trends in U.S. Tropical Cyclone Mortality during the Past Century," April 11, 2001, http://myweb.fsu.edu/jelsner/HTML/Research/papers/mortality/mortal.html.

NOTE: For example, from 1900 to 1915, four years had 60 or more tropical cyclone deaths.

(i.e., needless evacuations) are less common, so people in hurricane-prone coastal areas should have more confidence in the forecasts. But note that Figure 7.9 also shows an increase in the number of years with storms that produce at least one death. As more and more people buy coastal property and as coastal development increases, more people are willingly living in hurricane danger zones. Thus, a given landfalling hurricane in 2010 has a much greater likelihood of hitting a populated coastline than it did in 1910. Yes, hurricanes are demonstrating the same trends once again—despite more people living in harm's way (and perhaps with more or stronger hurricanes, though that jury is still out), fewer people are dying from these storms.

One final health example that is a hot new topic: the 2008–10 "novel flu" (aka "swine flu") pandemic has raised influenza in the public consciousness. A long-standing question among biometeorologists is whether the severity of influenza in a given year is related to the climate. Despite a few exceptions, most studies have been unable to identify any connection. Influenza is a disease with a clear seasonality; in fact, respiratory diseases are much more confined to winter than any other disease category, and influenza—and resulting pneumonia—are major contributors to respiratory mortality. But is this seasonal pattern like overall winter mortality, which is high for reasons largely unrelated to weather in a given winter, or does the winter weather affect the severity of the virus or the likelihood of transmission?

In a 2007 laboratory experiment using guinea pigs, Anice Lowen and others[14] placed influenza-infected guinea pigs in cages upwind of healthy guinea pigs and then altered the temperature and humidity conditions. They found that cold, dry air increased the infection rate. But because they used relative humidity as their moisture variable, and because relative humidity depends on temperature, it was impossible to determine whether temperature or moisture was the key factor (again, a reminder to health researchers: please seek the advice of atmospheric professionals!). But Shaman and Kohn[15] reexamined those results in 2009 and found that absolute humidity (a measure of the actual amount of water vapor in the air) was the key factor. In a follow-up study in 2010, Shaman and his colleagues[16] found that the timing of the onset of the influenza season in a given year depended on the absolute humidity, such that less humid years had an earlier onset of the flu season.

The global warming angle here is the linkage to absolute humidity. There is evidence that the humidity is increasing as would be expected with an intensification of the hydrological cycle (in short, higher temperatures lead to more evaporation of surface water (EEBE), making the atmosphere more humid). Shaman and colleagues[17] therefore state: "Absolute humidity is predicted to increase in a warming world. The findings presented here indicate that such changes would decrease IVS [influenza virus survival] and IVT [influenza virus transmission] rates." As much as we'd all like to buy into the notion that global warming will at least relegate flu to the medical history books, this remains pretty unlikely. Influenza transmission and severity depend on many different factors, several of which are not well understood. Research over the past few years may have identified some potential weather linkages, but if weather is really the key driving factor, we would have discovered that long before 2010.

So with flu as with all the other topics covered here, we see that, yes, weather changes probably play a role in the disease. Climate, which, like weather, is always changing and has always changed, can be considered the sum total of weather events over time at a given location. Increased greenhouse gases are almost certainly affecting the global climate (and perhaps even your local climate, where the case is, however, much harder to prove). And some of the weather changes may be related to these greenhouse gas changes, but that is now, and always will be, impossible to prove.

The health of the Earth's citizens will not be dictated by how much the planet warms or doesn't warm—it will be dictated by the quality of life, which depends on technological advances. Some people are better positioned to take advantage of these technologies than others. The more impoverished a nation, the more susceptible its people are to disease and death.

On the other hand, the affluent United States is unaffected by malaria; it is a nation with improving air quality, with increasingly longer life expectancy, with declining heat-related mortality, and it is one becoming increasingly immune from the ravages of severe storms. It is also a place where temperatures have increased significantly over the past century, particularly over the past 30 years. It's little wonder that so many Americans remain unconvinced by global warming alarmism.

8. Learning Fear: Climate Change and Public Education

Neal McCluskey

As Neal McCluskey demonstrates, the federalization of education has led to the institutionalization of scare tactics and exaggeration in the teaching of global warming. As noted in the introduction to this volume, the State of California has clearly cherry-picked state temperature data to paint a picture of rapid warming that does not comport with historical trends. State educational materials also threaten students with death from global warming, intoning, "the question is: will we survive the changes of the future?"

Use of such tactics may produce short-term policy gains but result in an ultimate loss of respect for science when—as most certainly will happen—students mature and survive. As a result of all of this, McCluskey concludes that "what we will need are rational, well-informed adults, what we will get is either people who know little or nothing about climate change or people who are scared to death about it." Not an encouraging forecast.

In 2007, all that stood between Al Gore's climate change fearmongering and British schoolchildren was a Dover truck driver. In the end, the lorry driver defeated the man once just a heartbeat away from the most powerful office in the world.

Well, sort of.

At issue was an effort by Great Britain's Ministries of Education and the Environment to distribute, and have shown in every state school, Gore's Oscar-winning but highly controversial documentary *An Inconvenient Truth*. The movie was the headliner among five films sent to schools as part of the government's "Sustainable Schools Year of Action."

215

Statements from the nation's education and environment secretaries made clear both what the government wanted British children to learn and why they wanted them to learn it. First, as Environment Secretary David Miliband declared, students were to learn that "the debate over the science of climate change is well and truly over." And why should they learn that? Because, explained Education Secretary Alan Johnson, "children are the key to changing society's long term attitude to the environment."[1]

So where does the truck driver come in? At the time the government started foisting Gore on British children, Stuart Dimmock was the father of two sons attending a state school and was also a school governor—a position akin to a board of trustees member. He was also very much concerned that Gore's film was not primarily an educational tool, but a hyperpoliticized piece of global warming propaganda. Animated by that fear, he took the ministry of education to court.

In a highly visible October 2007 ruling, Justice Michael Burton of the England and Wales High Court identified nine major errors in Gore's film, errors attributable to Gore's "alarmism and exaggeration in support of his political thesis." Perhaps most notable of these deceptions is the film's frightening assertion that were Greenland to melt—something *An Inconvenient Truth* suggests is a distinct possibility—sea levels would quickly rise up to 20 feet and submerge the Netherlands, Manhattan, and numerous other highly populated areas. The problem with that scenario: Even if Greenland were to melt away, the liquefaction and resulting 20-foot sea level rise would take at least a millennium to occur—hardly the sudden devastation Gore described—and it's a pretty safe bet that we will find ways of producing energy other than from fossil fuels sometime in the next 1,000 years.

Another of the nine errors was especially important because of its connection to British government policy. This was Gore's pronouncement that human-induced global warming was melting the snows on Mt. Kilimanjaro. The depiction of this in the film was so powerful to David Miliband that he cited it specifically in his statement accompanying the release of the "Year of Action" film pack. The problem with the assertion, Burton wrote, is that there is no scientific consensus that the receding snow on Kilimanjaro is mainly attributable to human-induced climate change.

216

Because of these major errors—and the likely political rather than scientific intention behind their inclusion in Gore's film—Justice Burton ruled that the British government's dissemination of the movie without accompanying guidance for teachers pointing out the errors was illegal promotion of political views. And with that, Dimmock both won his legal case and, perhaps more importantly, succeeded in bringing widespread attention to numerous exaggerations in Gore's global warming propaganda masterpiece.

Despite this victory, neither Dimmock, British families, nor British taxpayers ultimately won completely. While Burton ruled that clarifying information must accompany showings of *An Inconvenient Truth* in state schools, the film can still be shown, with all of its frightening—and misleading—components intact. In other words, British schoolchildren are still legitimate targets in the very political battle over what should, and should not, be taught about climate change.

Ain't This America?

In service of a stated government goal of changing students'—and ultimately society's—attitudes toward climate change, kids in England can be subjected to Al Gore's heavy-handed ways. Now, that's terrible, you say, but ain't this America, with local control of schools, not top-down, European-style statism? What kind of warning does this offer to the good ol' US of A?

A big one.

For one thing, as we shall see, local control of public schools can protect children and taxpayers only so much. If a district chooses to teach about climate change, there is a good chance it will do so in a way that peddles fear and propagates distortions. For the residents of such a district, such a loaded presentation will be just as real a problem as was the British government's decision for the people of England. There is a flip side to this, though: because public schooling is government schooling, it's also possible that climate change will be avoided altogether.

More troubling than what can happen at the level of individual districts is that in the United States local control is fast becoming a thing of the past. Today, state governments dominate the setting of curricula, and if states impose climate change–education requirements, then their entire populations, all at once, become potentially captive audiences to fearmongering and social engineering under the guise of education. And the threat of going the way of England is very real, because Washington right now is on the verge of dictating curricula to every public school in the nation.

Quite simply, no public school child is safe from being exposed to potentially biased, sensationalized climate change education. The dangers start at the district level, grow as one gets to state policy, and are clear and present at the federal level.

Let's examine the climate change–education realities—and dangers—one level at a time.

The District

While today many decisions about what public schools teach and how they teach it are made at government levels above the district, school districts can still have considerable say in what is taught in their classrooms. Unfortunately, the result can be the imposition of controversial—and sensationalized—climate change material on district children. It can also, though, lead to complete avoidance of the topic.

A brouhaha in Federal Way, Washington, illustrates both concerns well. In January 2007—right before an inconvenient controversy erupted in Great Britain—the district was embroiled in its own Gore war, with the inflammatory spark provided by teacher Kay Walls's plan to show *An Inconvenient Truth* to her seventh-grade science class. It was a move opposed by parent Frosty Hardison, whose daughter was in Walls's class, as well as other parents, who sent angry e-mails opposing the screening to the Federal Way School Board.

The complaints resulted in a "moratorium" on showing the film and a disciplinary letter against Walls for failing to seek written permission to show "controversial" material in class. The moratorium was eventually lifted, with screenings allowed if teachers received the written permission of a principal and presented an alternative view approved by both a principal and the superintendent of schools.

The outcome of the Federal Way dispute was much like the resolution in England: students can be subjected to Gore's film, despite its political bent and sensationalism, but some balancing material must be provided. For parents worried about environmentalist indoctrination, who would likely have little say in what constitutes balance, this no doubt provided only limited comfort.

There was another aspect of the Federal Way episode, however, at least as it concerned students still potentially being subjected to Gore's film: the virulent response directed at the school board for halting viewings of the film. When news got out about the moratorium, members of the school board reported receiving thousands of angry e-mails and telephone calls, many obscene. At a school board meeting, board member David Larson was cornered by an attendee who demanded to know if Larson would require a "balanced" presentation of the Holocaust. And to top it all off, the teacher who started the conflict quipped in response to the balancing requirement that she could find only one article with which to do that: a *Newsweek* piece titled "The Cooling World," published in 1975. Board members were under political siege for making what they thought was a wise decision.

The controversy in Federal Way suggests that there are probably teachers, schools, and districts around the country that provide one-sided treatments of climate change that just don't make big news. No doubt in many liberal-skewing districts dissenters just keep silent, lest they end up being attacked.

Aggressive climate change alarmists, however, are likely not the only reason districts might supply heavy-handed treatments of climate change. Many districts, schools, and teachers could be peddling overhyped climate change fear without even realizing it. Most teachers and other school district employees are far from being professional scientists—especially at the elementary and middle school levels—much less climatologists. Few would have the wherewithal to skillfully analyze this very complex subject.

Because of a dearth of expertise in climate science—and numerous other subjects—teachers tend to rely on textbooks to shape their courses and supply much of the information they relate to students. Of course, there are numerous textbooks from which to choose, making it impossible to make a blanket statement applicable to each and every book. That said, textbooks often contain inaccurate information, and sometimes offer very shallow treatments of their subject matter. And in the case of climate change and other environmental issues, they can be given to fear peddling and simplistic good-guy/bad-guy narratives. Of course, environmentalists and government regulators often wear the white hats, while businesspeople are just plain old car-driving, electricity-using folks.

As Michael Sanera and Jane Shaw explain in their 1999 review of textbooks and environmental education titled *Facts Not Fear*: "Unfortunately, many of the materials in schools, including textbooks published by the leading national publishers, are unreliable. They echo the views expressed by the media or politicians or by an uninformed public. It is difficult for parents and teachers to sort the fact from the fiction."[2]

In their review, Sanera and Shaw examine the coverage of numerous environmental issues and furnish what are no doubt especially egregious—but probably not all that atypical—examples of textbook environmental doomsaying. The following example is from their climate change chapter. Note that it comes from a book published in 1992—Prentice Hall's *General Science: A Voyage of Exploration*—when projections of future global warming were less severe than more recent estimates:

> It is the year 2040, and it is very hot. Tourists are visiting an unnamed city—by boat. The entire city, except for the tops of the highest skyscrapers, is under water. "Up ahead is Ruth Stadium," says the guide, "where our local baseball team won the World Series of 2018. You could play water polo in it today, if you wanted to."
>
> One of the tourists mops sweat from his brow. Yes, it is always warm these days, even in January. The continual heat melted the Arctic ice caps and sea levels rose by twenty-five feet. "Is this scene only fantasy?" ask the authors of the science text in which it appears. "Perhaps. But it may someday be fact. Your great-grandchild might be the man riding on the sightseeing boat."[3]

It has not been done since the publication of *Facts Not Fear*, but one suspects a broad examination of not just science textbooks but, as Sanera and Shaw point out, social studies and other texts as well, would reveal that similar material is in use today.

Clearly, it is not unreasonable to think that the biggest threat from mixing climate change and public schooling is that children will be forced to imbibe trumped-up, apocalyptic fearmongering. There is, however, a dangerous flip side: While alarmism appears to be the predominant problem, there is nonetheless strong evidence that the earth is warming and at least some of that is driven by humanity. But with public schooling, there is a good chance that many students won't be taught anything about climate change. Because the topic is highly contentious, as was illustrated in Federal Way, and because government schools are supported by taxpayers on all sides of the issue, many districts might feel compelled to simply avoid discussing climate change. Just as Al Gore acolytes can make things very uncomfortable for their enemies, so can climate change deniers.

Hollowing curricula to avoid conflict is a well-documented public-schooling phenomenon. Noted education historian Diane Ravitch, for instance, explored it in her 2003 book titled *The Language Police: How Pressure Groups Restrict What Students Learn*. She explained:

> Almost by accident, I stumbled upon an elaborate, well-established protocol of beneficent censorship, quietly endorsed and broadly implemented by textbook publishers, testing agencies, professional associations, states, and the federal government. . . . Like others who are involved in education, be they parents or teachers or administrators or journalists or scholars, I had always assumed that textbooks were written on careful research and designed to help children learn something valuable. I thought the tests were designed to assess whether they had learned it. What I did not realize was that educational materials are now governed by an intricate set of rules to screen out language and topics that might be considered controversial or offensive.[4]

Perhaps the clearest warning of the fate that could befall instruction about climate change in many districts is what occurs with evolution, the most volatile science education topic in the nation's history. Warfare over the teaching of human origins can be traced at least as far back as 1925's famous "Monkey Trial," in which the Criminal Court of Tennessee ruled that John Scopes's teaching evolution in a public school violated state law banning such instruction.

Since the Scopes trial, evolution has been defended as a staple of biology curricula, and courts have repeatedly ruled against school districts' efforts to curb or qualify its teaching.[5] But just because evolution appears in curricula does not mean it gets taught. As the *New York Times* reported in 2005: "Even when evolution is in the curriculum it may not be in the classroom, according to researchers who follow the issue. Teaching guides and textbooks may meet the approval of biologists, but superintendents or principals discourage teachers from discussing it. Or teachers themselves avoid the topic, fearing protests from fundamentalists in their communities."[6]

The reality is that evolution in many districts is too heated a topic for many teachers and schools to take up. They don't want to have to fight parents and local officials who disagree with evolution. The same holds true for discussing climate change, which has only recently become a major issue. Indeed, according to a 2010 *New York Times* report, there are already efforts by opponents of teaching evolution in public schools to couple their efforts with opposition to instruction on global warming.[7]

Ultimately, climate change is not an either–or problem, and it needs to be approached as a phenomenon with lots of unknowns and unanswered questions. In many public school districts, however, it appears likely that climate change will be treated as either an existential threat, or not at all. Neither is a very productive approach to tackling this important topic.

The State

While the district level is where curricula have traditionally been set, beginning in the early 1990s, states began to assume responsibility for establishing subject standards and, hence, curricula. This was a response to increasingly urgent warnings that the nation's schools just weren't cutting the mustard.

Seminal in this movement was *A Nation at Risk*, a federal report that in 1983 decried declining academic achievement and a focus on minimal standards. It famously intoned that "if an unfriendly foreign power had attempted to impose on America the mediocre educational performance that exists today, we might well have viewed it as an act of war."[8]

Spurred by this clarion call, states started to take over standards setting and by 2000, 46 states and the District of Columbia had state-level science standards. Five years later, all states but Iowa had established statewide science standards, and by the 2007–08 school year, the No Child Left Behind Act required all states to start assessing science performance (though there were no consequences for poor performance).[9]

Despite almost all states' having science standards and tests, it is difficult to track what each state requires be taught about climate change.[10] There are tallies, however, of which states have set earth science requirements, and it is that subject that is most likely to cover climate issues. According to a 2007 report from the Technical Education Research Centers, every state except Iowa has statewide earth science requirements, and among those, 42 either directly or indirectly address atmosphere, weather, and climate concepts, including the greenhouse effect and "human influence on weather and climate."[11]

It would be an undertaking beyond the scope of this chapter to review all state climate change standards to determine whether they tend to be alarmist, conflict avoiding, or something in between. The state of California, however, is very important both in terms of sheer size—were it an independent nation, its economy would be among the tenth largest in the world—and being out front in environmental regulation.[12] It is then worth examining where the Golden State stands on climate change education.

In 2003, the state enacted a law establishing the California Education and Environment Initiative, which called for the development of environmental principles and concepts that would be compatible with the state's science standards. Interestingly, the law required that seven topics be covered—including integrated waste management, energy conservation, and toxic materials—but did not include climate change among them. That omission did not mean the state could not create material to cover climate change—the California Department of Education and the State Board of Education could write frameworks for other areas—but it is notable that establishing standards for arguably the highest-profile environmental issue was not mandated.[13] In 2005, the list of required topics was expanded to 14, but none specifically mentioned climate change.[14]

The most likely reason for this omission is that, as discussed, public schooling is inherently political, and global warming was considered too contentious a topic to broach. Fear that climate change wouldn't be addressed eventually led State Senator Joe Simitian (D-Palo Alto) to introduce legislation that would mandate its inclusion among the topics for which the state would have to develop educational principles and concepts. Simitian's bill was eventually approved by both houses of California's legislature but vetoed by

Governor Arnold Schwarzenegger, who said Sacramento shouldn't be "overly prescriptive" in specifying school curricula.[15] Apparently, that did not apply to "waste management" and "toxics."

So California appears susceptible to the problem of avoiding climate change education altogether because of the topic's contentiousness. Ultimately, though, the state did undertake production of a climate change curriculum guide, and climate change questions can appear on the state's earth science examination. Unfortunately, the draft state climate change curriculum's "Teacher's Edition" available at the time this chapter was written—a draft assembled by several state agencies, including the state's environmental protection agency and education department—displays the opposite extreme of ignoring climate change: teaching that climate change is coming, and it spells doom.

The final draft of the teacher's guide puts the alarmism front and center. It starts with the cover, which features a photo of seemingly endless, floating chunks of ice, which one can't help but conclude is supposed to evoke thoughts of a melted North Pole. Moving inside, one is treated to a virtual photo album of doom: flame-spewing pipes backed by a desolate, *Mad Max* landscape; a close-up of burning tree trunks in what looks to be a forest fire; the front edge of a huge dust storm about to envelope military and civilian vehicles; and what looks like a World War I landscape of crushed and otherwise devastated foliage.[16]

The verbiage in the introductory pages of the teacher's guide is no less fixated on the worst-case scenario than are the pictures. Key to this is the repeated use of terms and phrases such as "could be" and "as much as," which suggest that the guide is repeatedly giving teachers the upper bounds of potential negative effects of climate change. Unfortunately, it is difficult to confirm that this was what guide writers were doing because the publication has precious few citations, leaving teachers to trust that they are getting good information.

Here are just a few examples of the guide's doom-and-gloom:

- The guide informs teachers that "scientists predict that if the [50-year] warming trend continues, the state's temperatures will rise as much as 10.5° F (5.8° C) by 2100."[17] According to data from the U.S. National Climatic Data Center, the 50-year trend in California temperatures is 0.43 degrees Fahrenheit per decade, or 4.3 degrees per century.[18]This discounts the very real possibility that California warming estimates from the past 50 years have been overestimated due to growing urbanization.[19]

- The guide intones that should climate change continue unabated, the snowpack in the Sierra Nevada Mountains, which furnishes much of the water for Southern California, "could decrease by 70–90 percent by the year 2100." This, it says, would lead to such potential calamities as insufficient drinking water, huge reductions in dam-generated electric power, and too little snow to sustain winter tourism.[20] The problem is that there is much evidence that droughts have long occurred in Southern California, and there's no powerful connection between man-made warming and such droughts.[21]

- One final example: The potential effect of warming on the Golden State's coasts, which the guide suggests could be devastated because "as the Earth continues to warm, sea levels could rise as much as 35 inches by the year 2100."[22] This despite the United Nations' Intergovernmental Panel on Climate Change's midrange rise estimates only clocking in at between 8.5 and 18.5 inches.[23]

To top off all the extreme-end projections that dominate the draft teacher's guide, there is no mention of potential positive effects of global warming, including longer growing seasons and reductions in cold-related injuries and illnesses. In contrast is the following, final note of death and destruction, which reads more like California is facing the planet-devouring supervillain Galactus (of *Fantastic Four* infamy) than potentially modest increases in global temperatures:

> The question is: will we survive the changes of the future? The better we understand the causes and effects of climate change, the better we can predict how Earth will be affected. This understanding is key to our planetary and personal survival as the global climate continues to change.[24]

"Kids," teachers are encouraged by this guide to suggest, "if you don't get a handle on climate change now, both you and the planet could die!"

Fortunately, the teacher's guide is, as mentioned, only a draft and as of this writing, the fearmongering extremism can still be removed. By the time you read this, you should be able to see whether that happened: the final version was to be approved by the fall of 2010.

The Federal Government

So we've gone from decentralized, local control over curricula to greater and greater state control. Today, though, even the states don't constitute the apex of government education involvement. Washington has become increasingly meddlesome since the mid-1960s, when it first leaped in with the Elementary and Secondary Education Act. Under the No Child Left Behind Act—really just the latest reauthorization of the ESEA—it has become the clear driver of education policy nationwide, requiring states to have standards and tests in math and language arts and to get all kids to "proficiency" in those subjects by 2014. And just as Washington has become the driver in education generally, it is arguably becoming the central force behind a growing movement to get environmental education—including climate change—into the schools.

The origin of modern federal involvement in environmental education can be traced to the National Environmental Education Act of 1990, which among several things created the Office of Environmental Education in the Environmental Protection Agency; the Environmental Education and Training Program to "train educational professionals in the development and delivery of environmental education and training programs and studies"; and the National Environmental Education and Training Foundation—now the National Environmental Education Foundation—a "charitable and nonprofit corporation" tasked with advancing environmental training and coordination of environmental education efforts from the local to international levels.[25] NEEF is especially troubling for anyone determined to measure federal versus truly private influence in environmental education because it "is not an agency or establishment of the United States" but it is a U.S. government creation.

While the National Environmental Education Act established ground zero for federal education involvement—EPA's Office of Environmental Education—EPA is hardly the only federal entity involved in environmental education. The National Science Foundation has its Advisory Committee for Environmental Research and

Education and of course funds university-level research on environmental issues. The National Oceanic and Atmospheric Administration runs the National Sea Grant College Program, which "provides
integrated research, outreach, and education programs aimed at
creating tangible benefits for ocean, coastal and Great Lakes environments and communities."[26] The National Aeronautics and Space
Administration—home of the godfather of global warming fear,
James Hansen—of course has its own Global Climate Change Education Office. Indeed, no fewer than 13 federal entities—including
EPA, NASA, and the Departments of Commerce, Defense, State,
and several others—are involved in climate change education as
part of the U.S. Global Change Research Program (USGCRP) Climate
Change Science Program.[27]

As mentioned at the outset of this chapter, there is an especially
concerning aspect of the environmental education movement: Environmental educators often believe that their job is not only to supply
students with information about issues such as climate change but
also to foster changes in students' attitudes toward environmental
issues. That reeks of social engineering and opens very legitimate
fears that environmental education is in fact environmentalist
advocacy.

Many federally connected groups wholeheartedly embrace the
attitude-changing mission. For instance, the National Environmental
Education Advisory Committee—a "citizens' committee" created
by the National Environmental Education Act—lays "the components of environmental education" out thusly:

- **Awareness and sensitivity** to the environment and environmental challenges.
- **Knowledge and understanding** of the environment and environmental challenges.
- **Attitudes** of concern for the environment and motivation to
  improve or maintain environmental quality.
- **Skills** to identify and help resolve environmental challenges.
- **Participation** in activities that lead to the resolution of environmental challenges.[28]

Similarly, EPA is very clear that its environmental education work
is not simply about getting accurate information to students, but

changing attitudes and behavior. As it emphasizes in its 2009 environmental education "highlights" publication:

> One of the single most important drivers of environmental change in the future will be the environmental awareness and attitudes of people in this country and abroad. Environmental awareness influences individual behavior, and individual behavior is a fundamental factor affecting environmental conditions.[29]

Clearly, making a change in attitudes and behavior the ultimate federal environmental education goal is troubling, raising the specter of a green-hued Big Brother. That said, it is also no doubt a widely shared goal among the American people to improve the environment, though they balance that with lots of other goals, including improving housing, growing sufficient food, improving technology that betters the quality of life, and so forth.

Unfortunately, as seems often to be the case at the district and state levels, instilling fear appears to be a primary tactic of people making climate change education material at the federal level. Moreover, rarely if ever is it driven home that concern for the environment needs to be balanced against countless other goods.

Case in point: material from the USGCRP, which has produced the most specific guides about what the federal government thinks Americans should know about climate change. The first is *Climate Literacy: The Essential Principles of Climate Science*, a booklet touted as "a guide for individuals and communities" and "a climate-oriented approach for learners of all ages."[30] The second is a 12-minute video titled *Climate Change Wildlife and Wetlands*, which is intended "to be used in classrooms as an introduction to the topic or in Visitor Centers and in interpreter talks in informal educational settings."[31]

While not as saturated with apocalyptic imagery as California's draft teacher's guide, the USGCRP's booklet still has plenty of scary things to look at, including a dry streambed that appears not to have seen water for decades; imposing smokestacks belching thick gray plumes of soot; and Iowa National Guardsmen rushing to get sandbags in place to prevent river flooding. It also, though, has some chipper pictures, including big windmills in a verdant green field under clear blue skies and what appears to be a grandfather walking with his granddaughters down a leafy forest path.

228

In its prose, *Climate Literacy* is also not as blatantly alarmist as the California teacher's guide, not citing only worst-case estimates and predictions. Still, it is given to fear-inspiring exaggeration.

On its introductory page, for example, *Climate Literacy* says human activities "had a profound influence on Earth's climate," with the term "profound" implying very substantial effects. But this is buttressed only by a quote from the Intergovernmental Panel on Climate Change's Fourth Assessment, which simply states that "the global average net effect of human activities since 1750 has been one of warming."[32] This implies no huge magnitude—no "profound"— changes.

Next there's the last item on an otherwise tame list of "complex interactions" that affect climate. It brings up the "tipping point" threat, warning that "complex interactions may result in climate change that is more rapid and on a larger scale than projected by current climate models."[33] This statement immediately evokes mental images of Dennis Quaid—not to mention the Statue of Liberty— up to his eyeballs in snow from weather gone berserk in the climate change fright fest *The Day After Tomorrow*. But there is very little reason to believe that any climate change will be nearly so quick or dramatic—there will be plenty of time for human beings to adjust.[34]

Finally, while *Climate Literacy* does acknowledge that there could be benefits to global warming—including decreases in cold-related deaths—it makes a point to say that if "warming exceeds 2 to 3° C (3.6 to 5.4°F) over the next century, the consequences of the negative effects are likely to be much greater than the consequences of the positive effects"[35] It does this without noting that at our current rate of warming, the increase by 2100 would fall short of the low-end 2 degrees Celsius threshold.[36] Moreover, the subsequent page rehashes the litany of potentially—but hardly undisputed—bad things that could accompany warming, including dramatically rising sea levels, drought, more extreme bouts of heat and cold, and wider spread of infectious diseases.[37]

The USGCRP's film titled *Climate Change Wildlife and Wetlands* is also largely alarmist, as well as a bit contradictory. Its opening scenes are the film's problem in microcosm, with the narrator imploring kids to "step into the outside" and "take a look around." The narrator continues: "Have you noticed? Nature is different than it used to be. And not just in your yard, but around the world. Drier summers, fiercer storms, milder winters, the weather seems to be all over the map and it's been that way for a while now. The earth's climate is changing."

Why is this alarmist? Aside from the clearly negative "fiercer storms" part, the implication is that things are becoming dangerously unpredictable very fast—heck, we might even be at that apocryphal tipping point!

The contradiction is what comes right after the introduction in which viewers were told to contemplate very short-term changes in the weather to grasp that the earth's climate is changing. Right after the intro comes an EPA "weather expert" explaining that "climate is the long-term average of weather conditions. . . . Climate change is when weather patterns vary outside of the average over time." So which is it: can we see climate change in short-term weather changes or only long-term trends?

Unfortunately, the film's problems don't end there. For one thing, the video has a habit of referring to "scientists" and "experts" as concluding negative implications for climate change, as if all scientists and experts agree about all things global warming. It also wafts in foreboding music while discussing warming and warns of doom for lots of plants and animals. In its defense, though, it notes that climate change is "very complicated," even if it doesn't actually treat it that way.

The good news is that while Washington can spend money on climate education, it allocates a tiny amount relative to overall education and federal spending. In fiscal year 2010, for instance, the EPA's Office of Environmental Education was appropriated just slightly over $9 million—less than Washington spends in a blink of an eye. In addition, while the feds have become increasingly controlling in K–12 education, they have not yet dictated specific curricula. That, however, is changing with recent efforts to create national curriculum standards, something that could drive Washington's environmental education efforts much deeper into the nation's public school classrooms.

Spurred by rampant gaming of No Child Left Behind—especially states defining "proficiency" at low levels, or writing very weak standards—there has been a concerted effort to create "common" standards in language arts and mathematics. The idea is that if all states have the same standards, it will be much harder for a state to claim widespread proficiency when its kids actually can't read.

The problem is that states prone to setting low standards—which according to the standards-ranking Thomas B. Fordham Institute is most of them—will not just voluntarily adopt tough standards.[38] Recognizing this, the Obama administration essentially made signing onto an effort to create national standards by the Council of Chief State School Officers and the National Governors Association—what's known as the Common Core State Standards Initiative—a requirement to compete for part of a $4.35 billion kitty of federal money called the "Race to the Top" fund. Moreover, after the final draft of the standards was completed, states were given until August 2, 2010, to adopt the CCSSI standards as their own to be competitive for Race to the Top cash.

This federal national standards push doesn't appear likely to be a one-shot deal: While the Elementary and Secondary Education Act—the legislative and financial heart of federal education policy—didn't seem destined for quick reauthorization as of the time of this writing, in the administration's reauthorization proposal states' adopting national "college- and career-ready standards" was central to their being able to access tens of billions of dollars in federal ESEA funds.

So Washington is on the verge of funding—and hence ultimately dictating—language arts and mathematics standards for every public school, an unprecedented escalation of federal control and one that constitutes the ultimate centralization of American education. Of course, from the perspective of climate change education, it is important that the immediate subject areas targeted are mathematics and reading, not science. But don't expect it to remain that way.

For one thing, the Common Core State Standards include "standards for English language arts and literacy in history/social studies, science, and technical subjects," meaning that—though the current standards do not prescribe specific scientific subject areas that schools must teach or knowledge that students must have—science is in the minds of national standardizers. And nascent plans are already being made for adding science content standards to the mix. The Fordham Foundation has argued for adding science and then history to the collection of national standards,[39] and Dane Linn, the National Governors Association's national standards point man, has said that his group will look at producing national science standards if there's "success in the first two subjects we're focused on."[40]

Of course, even if science is added to the brotherhood of nationally standardized subjects, that does not necessarily mean that federal climate–change scare curricula will be used. However, there will no doubt be great political pressure from the environmental education community to do so, with the ultimate goal of changing students' attitudes and behaviors to the climate change alarmist view.

Conclusion

When lorry driver Stuart Dimmock took on Al Gore and the showing of *An Inconvenient Truth* at his sons' school, the ultimate victory was in revealing that Gore had played fast and loose with the truth, not, it seems, to faithfully inform viewers but to frighten them. Thankfully for Dimmock, Gore's film was both well known and not intended specifically for schoolchildren. That made it easier for him to draw attention both to the film's numerous exaggerations and to the great dangers of foisting the highly politicized movie on schoolchildren.

Of course, many people consider it important for children to know about climate change and want kids to be well informed. Educating children about climate change in public schools, however, becomes very difficult because there is widespread disagreement—and much that is uncertain—about the causes, potential severity, and possible consequences of climate change, and different groups of parents and taxpayers will want their own perspective to be what is taught. This complexity typically leads either to the crushing of all other viewpoints by whichever group can muster the most political power or to a milquetoast—or nonexistent—treatment of the problem in order to avoid controversy.

The avoidance problem, importantly, must ultimately be dealt with by changing the public education system from one in which government controls the schools and one size must fit all to one in which parents choose among autonomous institutions able to teach different climate change perspectives. Within the current system, however, it certainly does not help that much of the instructional material falls squarely along the overhyped, fearmongering lines of *An Inconvenient Truth*, substantiating the concerns of those who would prefer that climate change not be taught in the public schools at all lest their children be subjected to emotionally charged, environmentalist propaganda masquerading as education.

science

Perhaps most concerning is that there really is strong reason to believe that much climate change education material from government sources is intended, like environmental education generally, not ultimately to inform children but to shape their attitudes and behaviors in "pro-environment" ways. In other words, there is strong evidence that all the fearmongering might not be accidental but part of a conscious effort by state actors to shape the attitudes and behaviors of the nation's children.

None of this bodes well for dealing with climate change and its potential effects. When what we will need are rational, well-informed adults, what we will get is either people who know little or nothing about climate change or people who are scared to death about it.

Notes

Introduction

1. White House, *National Security Strategy* (Washington: Government Printing Office, May 2010), p. 47.

2. Peter Schwartz and Doug Randall, "An Abrupt Scenario and Its Implications for United States National Security," U.S. Department of Defense, October 2003, p. 18.

3. R. A. Kerr, "Galloping Glaciers of Greenland Have Reined Themselves In," *Science* 323 (January 23, 2009): 458.

4. Ryan M. Maue, "Global Tropical Cyclone Climatology," 2010, http://www.coaps.fsu.edu/~maue/tropical/.

5. R. K. Pachauri, "How Would Climate Change Influence Society in the 21st Century?" Presentation at the MIT Energy Initiative's Alliance for Global Sustainability Conference, January 29, 2008, http://mitworld.mit.edu/video/550/.

6. For example, M. L. Clarke and H. M. Rendell, "The Impact of North Atlantic Storminess on Western European Coasts: A Review," *Quaternary International* 195 (2009): 31–41.

7. Patrick J. Michaels, "Evidence for 'Publication Bias' Concerning Global Warming in *Science* and *Nature*," *Energy & Environment* 19 (2008): 287–301.

8. White House, *National Security Strategy*, p. 47.

9. White House, *A National Security for a New Century* (Washington: Government Printing Office, 1997), p. 24.

10. Kurt M. Campbell and others, *The Age of Consequences: The Foreign Policy and National Security Implications of Climate Change* (Washington: Center for New American Security and Center for Strategic and International Studies, November 2007).

11. Quoted in Sam Kornell, "U.S. Military Measures Climate Change: Intelligence Establishment Calling It a Major Security Problem," *Santa Barbara Independent*, May 8, 2008, http://www.independent.com/news/2008/may/08/us-military-measures-climate-change/?print.

12. Ronnie Lipschutz and John Holdren, "Crossing Borders: Resource Flows, the Global Environment and International Stability," *Bulletin of Peace Proposals* 21 (1990): 121–33.

13. John Podesta and Peter Ogden, "The Security Implications of Climate Change," *Washington Quarterly* (Winter 2007–08): 116.

14. International Centre for Trade and Sustainable Development, "India Threatens WTO Case against Proposed 'Carbon Border Taxes,'" *Bridges Weekly Trade New Digest*, March 31, 2010, http://ictsd.org/i/news/bridgesweekly/73378/.

15. Goklany 2009, *The Improving State of the World: Why We're Living Longer, Healthier, More Comfortable Lives on a Cleaner Planet*: 70.

16. Emily K. Shuman, "Global Climate Change and Infectious Disease," *New England Journal of Medicine* 362 (March 25, 2010): 1061–63.

17. Patrick J. Michaels and Robert C. Balling Jr., *Climate of Extremes: Global Warming Science They Don't Want You to Know* (Washington: Cato Institute, 2009).

18. Michael Sanera and Jane S. Shaw, *Facts Not Fear: Teaching Children about the Environment* (Washington: Regnery, 1999), p. 308.

19. National Climatic Data Center, "Climate at a Glance," http://www.ncdc.noaa.gov/oa/climate/research/cag3/ca.html.

20. California Education and Environment Initiative, *The Greenhouse Effect on Natural Systems: Final Draft* (Sacramento: California EEI, 2009), p. 8, http://www.calepa.ca.gov/education/eei/curriculum/EarthScience/E4c/Teachers.pdf.

Chapter 1

1. Kevin Bundy, Brendan Cummings, Vera Pardee, and Kassie Siegel, "*Yes, He Can*: President Obama's Power to Make an International Climate Commitment without Waiting for Congress," Climate Law Institute Working Paper no. 2, http://www.biologicaldiversity.org/programs/climate_law_institute/pdfs/Yes_He_Can_120809.pdf.

2. "The powers not delegated to the United States by the Constitution, nor prohibited by it to the States, are reserved to the States respectively, or to the people."

3. *Barron v. Mayor of Baltimore*, 32 U.S. (7 Pet.) 243 (1833).

4. Robert J. Reinstein, "Completing the Constitution: The Declaration of Independence, Bill of Rights, and Fourteenth Amendment," *Temple Law Review* 66 (1993): 361.

5. See, for example, John Louis Recchiuti, *Civic Engagement: Social Science and Progressive-Era Reform in New York City* (Philadelphia: University of Pennsylvania Press, 2007); and Steven J. Diner, *A Very Different Age: Americans of the Progressive Era* (New York: Farrar, Strauss & Giroux, 1998).

6. See William E. Leuchtenburg, *The Supreme Court Reborn: The Constitutional Revolution in the Age of Roosevelt* (New York: Oxford University Press, 1995).

7. See Richard A. Epstein, *How Progressives Rewrote the Constitution* (Washington: Cato Institute, 2006).

8. *Helvering v. Davis*, 301 U.S. 619 (1937).

9. *NLRB v. Jones & Laughlin Steel Corp.*, 301 U.S. 1 (1937).

10. *United States v. Carolene Products*, 304 U.S. 144 (1938).

11. For an expanded discussion of this issue, see Robert A. Levy and William Mellor, *The Dirty Dozen* (New York: Sentinel, 2008), ch. 4.

12. *Wayman v. Southard*, 23 U.S. 1 (1825).

13. Ibid.

14. *J. W. Hampton, Jr. & Co. v. United States*, 276 U.S. 394 (1928).

15. *Panama Refining Co. v. Ryan*, 293 U.S. 388 (1935); *A.L.A. Schechter Poultry Corp. v. United States*, 295 U.S. 495 (1935).

16. Levy and Mellor, *The Dirty Dozen*, p. 72, citing Kermit L. Hall, ed., *The Oxford Guide to United States Supreme Court Decisions* (New York: Oxford University Press, 1999), p. 232.

17. *Chevron U.S.A., Inc. v. Natural Resources Defense Council*, 467 U.S 837 (1984).

18. Ibid., pp. 842–44.

19. John Locke, Second Treatise of Government, in *Two Treatises of Government*, ed. Peter Laslett (New York: Mentor, 1965): "Lives, Liberties and Estates, which I call by the general Name, *Property*." para. 123.

20. See Roger Pilon, "Property Rights, Takings, and a Free Society," *Harvard Journal of Law and Public Policy* 6 (1983): 165.

21. See Edward H. Corwin, *The "Higher Law" Background of American Constitutional Law* (Ithaca, NY: Cornell University Press, 1955), p. 26: "The notion that the common law embodied right reason furnished from the fourteenth century its chief claim to be regarded as higher law."

22. Art. I, Sec. 8, Cl. 18: "Congress shall have Power. . . . To make all Laws which shall be necessary and proper for carrying into Execution the foregoing Powers. . . . "

23. Art. I, Sec. 8, Cl. 3: "Congress shall have Power. . . To regulate Commerce with foreign Nations, and among the several States, and with the Indian tribes."

24. Witness the debate at this writing, and the suits by 21 states and others, over the putative power of Congress, under the recently enacted Patient Protection and Affordable Care Act, to order individuals to buy health insurance or pay a fine (or tax) for failing to do so, raising the question, is there anything Congress cannot regulate under the commerce clause?

25. In fact, the first great commerce clause case involved a conflict between a federal coasting statute and a state statute that granted a monopoly restricting interstate commerce in the ferrying business. *Gibbons v. Ogden*, 22 U.S. (9 Wheat.) 1 (1824).

26. See Randy E. Barnett, "The Original Meaning of the Commerce Clause," *University of Chicago Law Review* 68 (2001): 101.

27. Administrative Procedure Act (APA), ch. 324, 60 Stat. 237 (1946).

28. 5 U.S.C. § 706(2)(A) (2009).

29. Harold H. Bruff, "Legislative Formality, Administrative Rationality," *Texas Law Review* 63 (1984): 207, 210.

30. Thomas W. Merrill, "Capture Theory and the Courts: 1967–1983," *Chicago-Kent Law Review* 72 (1997): 1039, 1075–76.

31. Patrick M. Garry, "The Unannounced Revolution: How the Court Has Indirectly Effected a Shift in the Separation of Powers," *Alabama Law Review* 57 (2006): 689, 699.

32. Ibid., p. 710; and Alfred C. Aman Jr., "Administrative Law in a Global Era: Progress, Deregulatory Change, and the Rise of the Administrative Presidency," *Cornell Law Review* 73 (1988): 1101, 1152.

33. 449 F.2d 1109, 1111 (D.C. Cir. 1971).

34. 401 U.S. 402 (1971).

35. Ibid., p. 413.

36. Ibid., p. 416. See also Garry, "The Unannounced Revolution," p. 710 (discussing this shift).

37. 463 U.S. 29 (1983).

38. Ibid., p. 57. See also Garry, "The Unannounced Revolution," pp. 710–11, quoting William F. Fox, *Understanding Administrative Law*, 4th ed. (New York: LEXIS Publishing, 2000), p. 325: "When the Court wishes to invoke [the Hard-Look Doctrine], it will; when it wishes to be much more lenient with regard to an agency's action, the doctrine will be disregarded."

39. 549 U.S. 497 (2007).

40. Exec. Order no. 12,291, 3 C.F.R. 127 (1981), reprinted as amended in 5 U.S.C. 601 (2000).

41. Bruff, "Legislative Formality, Administrative Rationality," p. 234.

42. Exec. Order no. 12,866, 3 C.F.R. 638 (1993), reprinted as amended in 5 U.S.C. 601 (2000).

43. Office of Management and Budget, "Proposed Bulletin on Peer Review and Information Quality," *Federal Register*, September 15, 2003, p. 54023-02.

44. Jody Freeman and Adrian Vermeule, "Massachusetts v EPA: From Politics to Expertise," in *The Supreme Court Review 2007*, ed. Dennis J. Hutchinson, David A. Strauss, and Geoffrey R. Stone (Chicago: University of Chicago Press, 2007), pp. 57–58.

45. See, for example, David S. Caudill, "Images of Expertise: Converging Discourses on the Use and Abuse of Science in Massachusetts v. EPA," *Villanova Environmental Law Journal* 18 (2007): 185, 195; Jeffrey Brainard, "How Sound Is Bush's 'Sound Science'?" *Chronicle of Higher Education*, March 5, 2004, p. A18; and OMB Watch, "OMB Bulletin on Peer Review: Making Science Vulnerable to Political Manipulation," August 29, 2003, http://www.ombwatch.org/node/1562.

46. 42 U.S.C. § 7521(a)(1).

47. National Research Council, *Climate Change: An Analysis of Some Key Questions* (Washington: National Academy Press, 2001).

48. "Control of Emissions from New Highway Vehicles and Engines, Notice of Denial of Petition for Rulemaking," *Federal Register*, September 8, 2003, p. 52922.

49. *Massachusetts v. EPA*, 549 U.S. 497 (2007).

50. *Lujan v. Defenders of Wildlife*, 504 U.S. 555, 560–61 (1992).

51. Andrew P. Morriss, "Litigating to Regulating: *Massachusetts v. Environmental Protection Agency*," in *Cato Supreme Court Review, 2006–2007* (Washington: Cato Institute, 2007), pp. 193, 200; and Brief of the Cato Institute and Law Professors Jonathan H. Adler, James L. Huffman, and Andrew P. Morriss as Amici Curiae in Support of Respondents, 2006 WL 3043962 (2006).

52. Endangerment and Cause or Contribute Findings for Greenhouse Gases under Section 202 of the Clean Air Act, at 17 (December 7, 2009).

53. Bundy and others, *"Yes He Can,"* p. 13.

54. 42 U.S.C. § 7401.

55. The Supreme Court has previously upheld the Clean Air Act as constitutional under the commerce clause. *United States v. Ho*, 311 F.3d 589, 601–4 (5th Cir. 2002), rejecting commerce clause challenge to work practice standards for asbestos under the Clean Air Act; and *Allied Local & Reg'l Mfrs. Caucus v. EPA*, 215 F.3d 61, 81–83 (D.C. Cir. 2000), rejecting commerce clause challenge to the Clean Air Act.

56. Michael Sugar, "Massachusetts v. Environmental Protection Agency," *Harvard Environmental Law Review* 31 (2007): 531, 532–33.

57. Clean Air Act § 302(g), 42 U.S.C. 7602(g) (2000).

58. Id. § 108, 42 U.S.C. § 7408 (2000).

59. "National Ambient Air Quality Standards for Particulate Matter," *Federal Register*, July 18, 1997, p. 38,652 (codified at 40 C.F.R. 50.6 [2003]).

60. Section 110 of the Clean Air Act requires states to submit state implementation plans to ensure that all metropolitan areas will meet NAAQS requirements. 42 U.S.C. § 7410. Jonathan H. Adler, *"Massachusetts v. EPA* Heats Up Climate Policy No Less than Administrative Law: A Comment on Professors Watts and Wildermuth," *Northwestern University Law Review Colloquy* 102 (2007): 32, 39–40.

61. 42 U.S.C. § 7410 (2000).

62. 42 U.S.C. § 7509(b)(1) (2000): "The Administrator may impose a prohibition, applicable to a nonattainment area, on approval by the Secretary of Transportation of any projects or the awarding by the Secretary of any grants... effective upon the selection by the Administrator of this sanction."

63. *Whitman v. Am. Trucking Ass'ns*, 531 U.S. 457, 475–76 (2001).

NOTES FOR PAGES 29–32

64. Ibid., p. 471. See also Thomas J. Stukane, "EPA's Bubble Concept after *Chevron v. NRDC*: Who Is to Guard the Guards Themselves?" *Natural Resources Lawyer* 17 (1985): 647, 669: "The 1970 Amendments imposed Draconian mandates for the abatement of pollution, regardless of cost."

65. 42 U.S.C. § 7410(a)(2)(A).

66. § 111(a)(1), 42 U.S.C. 7411(a)(1) (2006).

67. Before constructing a new "major stationary [emissions] source," or modifying an existing source to increase emissions significantly, a company must first obtain a PSD permit. See 40 C.F.R. § 52.21 (2009); see also 42 U.S.C. § 7475 (2006). A source is "major" if it may emit 100 tpy (tons per year) of a pollutant and it falls within one of 28 categories, or if it is any other type of facility and has the potential to emit 250 tpy of an air pollutant. 40 C.F.R. § 52.21(b)(1)(i).

68. Bundy and others, *"Yes He Can,"* p. 16.

69. Roughly 1.2 million buildings and facilities—the vast majority of which are not currently subject to PSD regulation—emit at least 250 tpy of carbon dioxide. George F. Allen and Marlo Lewis, "Finding the Proper Forum for Regulation of U.S. Greenhouse Gas Emissions: The Legal and Economic Implications of *Massachusetts v. EPA*," *University of Richmond Law Review* 44 (2010): 919, 923–24, citing Portia M. E. Mills and Mark P. Mills, "A Regulatory Burden: The Compliance Dimension of Regulating CO_2 as a Pollutant," U.S. Chamber of Commerce, September 2008, pp. 7–10, http://secure.uschamber.com/assets/env/regulatory_burden0809.pdf.

70. EPA estimates that PSD permit applications could jump from approximately 300 to 41,000 per year, "Prevention of Significant Deterioration and Title V Greenhouse Gas Tailoring Rule; Proposed Rule," *Federal Register*, October 27, 2009, p. 55,301. In addition, Title V permit applications would increase from 15,000 to 6.1 million per year. Ibid., pp. 55,295, 55,304.

71. EPA acknowledges that the "enormous numbers of these permit applications" would "vastly exceed the current administrative resources of the permitting authorities." Ibid., p. 55,294.

72. Ibid., p. 55,292.

73. See *Clinton v. New York*, 524 U.S. 417, 438 (1998); and *INS v. Chadha*, 462 U.S. 919, 954 (1983): "Amendment and repeal of statutes, no less than enactment, must conform with Art. I."

74. *Southeastern Legal Foundation, Inc. v. United States EPA*, D.C. Circuit no. 01-1131.

75. Bundy and others, *"Yes He Can,"* discussing Title II.

76. 42 U.S.C. § 7521(a)(1) (2000).

77. Ibid. §§ 7547, 7571.

78. "Regulating Greenhouse Gas Emissions under the Clean Air Act," *Federal Register*, proposed July 30, 2008, pp. 44,354, 44,432 (to be codified at 40 C.F.R. ch. 1).

79. Alder, *"Massachusetts v. EPA* Heats Up Climate Policy," p. 37.

80. Energy Policy and Conservation Act of 1975, Pub. L. 94-163, 89 Stat. 871 (codified at 49 U.S.C. §§ 32901–19 [2000]).

81. "Proposed Rulemaking to Establish Light-Duty Vehicle Greenhouse Gas Emission Standards and Corporate Average Fuel Economy Standards," *Federal Register*, September 28, 2009, p. 49454.

82. "Notice of Intent to Develop New Greenhouse-Gas and Fuel Economy Standards for Light-Duty Vehicles, Model Years 2017-2025." EPA, September 30, 2010.

83. Clean Water Act of 1977, Pub. L. 95-217, 91 Stat. 1566 (codified in scattered sections of 33 U.S.C.).

84. Bundy and others, *"Yes He Can,"* p. 17, citing Antarctic Climate & Ecosystems Cooperative Research Centre, *Position Analysis, CO₂ Emissions and Climate Change: Ocean Impacts and Adaptation Issues* (Hobart, Tasmania: ACECRC, 2008), p. 3.

85. Ibid., citing Glenn De'ath, Janice M. Lough, and Katharina E. Fabricius, "Declining Coral Calcification on the Great Barrier Reef," *Science* 116 (2009); and A. Whitman Miller, Amanda C. Reynolds, Cristina Sobrino, and Gerhardt F. Riedel, "Shellfish Face Uncertain Future in High CO₂ World: Influence of Acidification on Oyster Larvae Calcification and Growth in Estuaries," *PLoS ONE* 4 (2009): e5661.

86. Thomas J. Crowley and Robert A. Berner, "Enhanced CO₂ and Climate Change," *Science* 292 (May 4, 2001): 870–72.

87. Federal courts have previously upheld the Clean Water Act as constitutional under the commerce clause. *United States v. Deaton*, 332 F.3d 698, 705–8 (4th Cir. 2003), cert. denied, 541 U.S. 972 (2004). But see *Solid Waste Agency of N. Cook County v. U. S. Army Corps of Eng'rs*, 531 U.S. 159, 166–68 (2001), interpreting federal jurisdiction over isolated wetlands narrowly on federalism grounds.

88. 33 U.S.C. § 1251(a).

89. See ibid. § 1313; 40 C.F.R. § 130.3; 40 C.F.R. § 131.11(b).

90. 33 U.S.C. § 1313(d).

91. See ibid., at § 1313(e); and 40 C.F.R. §§ 130.6, 130.7(d)(2).

92. "Ocean Acidification and Marine pH Water Quality Criteria," *Federal Register*, April 15, 2009, p. 17,484.

93. See Aman, "Administrative Law in a Global Era," p. 1136, citing William H. Rodgers, *Environmental Law, Air and Water*, vol. 1 (St. Paul, MN: West Publishing, 1986), sec. 1.3, p. 19: "Among the more salient examples of absolutism in environmental law are the goals in the Clean Water Act calling for fishable/swimming water everywhere by 1983 and no discharges anywhere by January 1, 1985."

94. The Endangered Species Act of 1973, 7 U.S.C. § 136, 16 U.S.C. § 1531 et seq., P.L. 93-205, 87 Stat. 884 (1973).

95. 16 U.S.C. § 1533(a)(1).

96. 1536(a)(1). See Bundy and others, *"Yes He Can."*

97. Bundy and others, *"Yes He Can,"* p. 19, citing 16 U.S.C. §§ 1532(3).

98. Bradford C. Mank, "Protecting Intrastate Threatened Species: Does the Endangered Species Act Encroach on Traditional State Authority and Exceed the Outer Limits of the Commerce Clause?" *Georgia Law Review* 36 (2002): 723, 731–32, citing 16 U.S.C. § 1538(a)(1)(B).

99. 16 U.S.C. § 1532, Pub. L. 97-304, §§ 4(b), 19, October 13, 1982, 96 Stat. 1420.

100. 515 U.S. 687, 698 (1995). But see *Lujan v. National Wildlife Federation* at 883, holding that the harm alleged must fall under the "zone of interests protected by the statute" in order for plaintiffs to have standing to sue under the ESA.

101. *TVA v. Hill*, 437 U.S. 153, 184 (1978).

102. "Endangered and Threatened Wildlife and Plants; Designation of Critical Habitat for the Polar Bear (*Ursus maritimus*) in the United States; Proposed Rule," *Federal Register*, October 29, 2009, p. 56,070: "The underlying causes of climate change are complex global issues that are beyond the scope of the Act."

103. National Environmental Policy Act of 1969, Pub. L. 91-190, 83 Stat. 852 (codified in scattered sections of 42 U.S.C.).

104. 42 U.S.C. § 4321.

105. Ibid. § 4332(C).

106. T. C. McKinney, "Overview of NEPA Review Processes," http://www. efw.bpa.gov/environmental_services/NEPAProcessOverview.pdf. Moreover, the determination of whether federal action is likely to have significant environmental impacts requires the preparation of an environmental assessment—a process that also involves the public and takes 7 to 12 months. Ibid.

107. 42 U.S.C. 4322(2)(F).

108. Bundy and others, *"Yes He Can,"* p. 20.

109. Ibid., citing American Rivers, Center for Biological Diversity, Conservation Law Foundation, Defenders of Wildlife, Earthjustice, International Center for Technology Assessment, Marine Fish Conservation Network, Natural Resources Defense Council, National Wildlife Federation, Ocean Conservancy, Southern Environmental Law Center, the Wilderness Society, Letter to the Hon. Nancy Sutley, Chair, Council on Environmental Quality, November 24, 2009.

110. *Center for Biological Diversity v. Nat'l Highway Traffic Safety Admin.*, 508 F.3d 508 (9th Cir. 2007), holding that the government's revision of CAFE standards requires the preparation of an EIS.

111. U.S. Const. art. II.

112. Ibid., § 2.

113. See Nigel Purvis, "The Case for Climate Protection Authority," *Virginia Journal of International Law* 49 (2009): 1007, 1018, discussing obstacles to treaty ratification.

114. Conference of the Parties to the Framework Convention on Climate Change: Kyoto Protocol, December 10, 1997, 37 I.L.M. 22.

115. Purvis, "The Case for Climate Protection Authority," p. 1019.

116. *Medellín v. Texas*, 552 U.S. 491 (2008).

117. See Jonathan B. Wiener, "Commentary, Think Globally, Act Globally: The Limits of Local Climate Policies," *University of Pennsylvania Law Review* 155 (2007): 1961, 1966–67, urging international action on climate change; and Robert R. Nordhaus, "New Wine into Old Bottles: The Feasibility of Greenhouse Gas Regulation under the Clean Air Act," *New York University Environmental Law Journal* 15 (2007): 53, 54, stating that the Clean Air Act cannot control global carbon dioxide levels.

118. Purvis, "The Case for Climate Protection Authority," p. 1021, noting that since World War II, executive agreements have made up almost 90 percent of all international pacts signed by the United States.

119. S. Exec. Rep. no. 102-55, at 14 (1992).

120. Louis Henkin, *Foreign Affairs and the United States Constitution*, 2d ed. (New York: Oxford University Press, 1996).

121. 42 U.S.C. § 7671p(a).

122. Inimai M. Chettiar and Jason A. Schwarz, "The Road Ahead: EPA's Options and Obligations for Regulating Greenhouse Gases," New York University School of Law, Institute for Policy Integrity, April 2009, pp. 55–57.

123. 33 U.S.C. § 1251(c).

124. 16 U.S.C. § 1537(b)(2).

125. Pub. L. 100-204, 101 Stat. 1407–09 (1987).

126. Ibid. § 1103(a)(3).

127. Ibid. § 1103(a)(4).

128. Ibid. § 1103c.

129. 22 U.S.C. §§ 2656c(a), 2656d.

130. Hannah Chang, "International Executive Agreements on Climate Change," Columbia Law School Center for Climate Change Law working paper, November

2009, http://www.law.columbia.edu/null/download?&exclusive=filemgr.down load&file_id=163020, quoting 22 U.S.C. §§ 3502–3.

131. 22 U.S.C. §3504.

132. Chang, "International Executive Agreements on Climate Change," p. 17.

133. 22 U.S.C. §§ 2151p(b), p-1(c).

134. Ibid. § 2151d(b)(1).

135. Ibid. § 2151d(b)(2).

136. U.N. Framework Convention on Climate Change, arts. 4, 12, May 9, 1992, 1771 U.N.T.S. 164.

137. Chang, "International Executive Agreements on Climate Change," p. 12.

138. S. Exec. Rep. 102-55, 102d Cong. (1992), p. 14.

139. See John Harwood, "Mixed Bag for Obama on Climate Change Deal amid the Recession," *New York Times*, December 21, 2009: "The agreement the United States reached with Brazil, China, India and South Africa lacked commitments to achieve its stated goals, was nonbinding and was not formally affirmed by participants, in any case."

140. Energy Policy Act, 42 U.S.C. § 13388, establishing the Global Climate Change Response Fund.

141. Chang, "International Executive Agreements on Climate Change," p. 13.

142. Convention for the Unification of Certain Rules for International Carriage by Air, S. Treaty Doc. No. 106-45, May 28, 1999.

143. Convention on International Civil Aviation, December 7, 1944, 61 Stat. 1180, 15 U.N.T.S. 295.

144. Ibid., p. 37.

145. § 231, 42 U.S.C. 7571(a)(2)(A).

146. Chang, "International Executive Agreements on Climate Change," p. 14, citing Control of Air Pollution from Aircraft and Aircraft Engines; Emission Standards and Test Procedures, *Federal Register*, December 30, 1982, pp. 58462, 58464.

147. *Youngstown Sheet & Tube Co. v. Sawyer*, 343 U.S. 579, 635–37 (1952) (Jackson, J., concurring).

148. U.S. Const. art. II, § 1.

149. Ibid. § 3.

150. Ibid. §§ 1–3. See Bundy and others, "Yes He Can," p. 9, discussing such authority.

151. Vienna Convention on the Law of Treaties, May 23, 1969, art. 2.1(a), 1155 U.N.T.S. 311.

152. Bundy and others, "Yes He Can," p. 10, comparing Michael D. Ramsey, "Executive Agreements and the (Non)Treaty Power," *North Carolina Law Review* 77 (1998): 134, 218–35 (arguing that executive agreements have no domestic effect), with Purvis, "The Case for Climate Protection Authority," p. 1028 (asserting that sole executive agreements carry the same force as a federal statute). See also Congressional Research Service, 106th Cong., *Treaties and Other International Agreements: The Role of the United States Senate*, study prepared for the Committee on Foreign Relations, 106th Cong. 2d sess., 2001, Committee Print 106-71, pp. 93–95, noting inconsistencies in case law regarding whether sole executive agreements override prior, contrary federal statutes.

153. Bundy and others, "Yes He Can," p. 10, citing *Am. Ins. Ass'n v. Garamendi*, 539 U.S. 396 (2003); *Dames & Moore v. Regan*, 453 U.S. 654 (1981); *U.S. v. Pink*, 315 U.S. 203 (1942); and *U.S. v. Belmont*, 301 U.S. 324 (1937); but see *Medellin v. Texas*, 128 S. Ct. at 1371–72 (2008), suggesting that the effect of these cases may be limited to the

international claims settlement context, where presidential power is "supported by a particularly longstanding practice of congressional acquiescence."

154. 552 U.S. 491 (2008).

155. Chang, "International Executive Agreements on Climate Change," p. 2.

156. Henkin, *Foreign Affairs and the United States Constitution*.

157. Chang, "International Executive Agreements on Climate Change," p. 2.

158. *Youngstown Sheet & Tube Co. v. Sawyer*, 343 U.S. 579, 637 (1952) (Jackson, J. concurring).

159. Ibid.

160. Chang, "International Executive Agreements on Climate Change," p. 11, summarizing Office of the Legal Adviser, U.S. Department of State, Int'l Agreements Other than Treaties Reported to Congress under Case Act, http://www.state.gov/s/l/treaty/caseact/.

161. Oona A. Hathaway, "Presidential Power over International Law: Restoring the Balance," *Yale Law Journal* 119 (2009):140, 152.

162. Bundy and others, *"Yes He Can,"* p. 9, citing S. Res. 98, 105th Cong., § 1(2) (1997) (enacted).

163. Ibid.

164. Case-Zablocki Act, Pub. L. 92-403, *U.S. Statutes at Large* 86 (1972): 619 (codified at 1 U.S.C. § 112b [2000]); 22 C.F.R. §§ 181.2, 181.3.

165. Purvis, "The Case for Climate Protection Authority," p. 1027.

Chapter 2

1. Timothy Searchinger and others, "Use of U.S. Croplands for Biofuels Increases Greenhouse Gases through Emissions from Land-Use Change," *Science* 319 (February 29, 2008): 1238–40.

2. Gabriel Calzada Álvarez, "Study of the Effects on Employment of Public Aid to Renewable Energy Sources," Rey Juan Carlos University, Madrid, http://www.juandemariana.org/pdf/090327-employment-public-aid-renewable.pdf.

3. Patrick J. Michaels and Robert C. Balling Jr., *Climate of Extremes: Global Warming Science They Don't Want You to Know* (Washington: Cato Institute, 2009); and Patrick J. Michaels, *Meltdown: The Predictable Distortion of Global Warming by Scientists, Politicians, and the Media* (Washington: Cato Institute, 2004).

4. Michael E. Mann, Raymond S. Bradley, and Malcolm K. Hughes, "Global-Scale Temperature Patterns and Climate Forcing over the Past Six Centuries," *Nature* 392 (April 23, 1998): 779–87.

5. Stephen McIntyre and Ross McKitrick, "Hockey Sticks, Principal Components, and Spurious Significance," *Geophysical Research Letters* 32 (2005): L03710.

6. Patrick J. Michaels at http://www.cato.org/pub_display.php?pub_id = 10578.

7. N. A. Pivivarova, "How Warming Is Made: The Case of Russia," Institute for Economic Analyses, Moscow, December 2009.

8. U.S. Energy Information Administration, http://tonto.eia.doe.gov/cfapps/ipdb project/IEDIndex3.cfm?tid = 90&pid = 44&aid = 8.

9. V. K. Riana, "Himalayan Glaciers: A State-of-Art Review of Glacial Studies, Glacial Retreat and Climate Change," Ministry of Environment and Forests, Government of India, 2009, http://scienceandpublicpolicy.org/images/stories/papers/reprint/Raina-Himalayan%20Glaciers%20Reprint.pdf.

10. David Rose, "Glacier Scientist: I Knew Data Hadn't Been Verified," *Daily Mail* (UK), January 24, 2010, http://www.dailymail.co.uk/news/article-1245636/Glacier-scientists-says-knew-data-verified.html.

11. The document "Global Review of Forest Fires" published by the World Wildlife Foundation and the International Union for Conservation of Nature can be found at http://data.iucn.org/dbtw-wpd/edocs/2000-047.pdf.

12. Scott R. Saleska, Kamel Didan, Alfredo R. Huete, and Humberto R. da Rocha, "Amazon Forests Green-Up during 2004 Drought," *Science* 318 (October 26, 2007): 612.

13. Intergovernmental Panel on Climate Change, "Climate Change 2007: Synthesis Report," Geneva, 2007, p. 52.

14. M. Parry, C. Rosenzweig, and M. Livermore, "Climate Change, Global Food Supply and Risk of Hunger, *Phil. Trans. Royal Society B* 360 (2005): 2125-2138.

15. R. K. Pauchari, opening address at UN Summit on Climate Change, New York, September 22, 2009, http://www.ipcc.ch/pdf/presentations/rkp-statement-unccs-09.pdf.

16. Intergovernmental Panel on Climate Change, *Climate Change 2007: Impacts, Adaptation, and Vulnerability* (Cambridge: Cambridge University Press, 2007), p. 547.

17. C. Matulla, W. Schöner, H. Alexandersson, H. von Storch, and X. L. Wang, "European Storminess: Late Nineteenth Century to Present," *Climate Dynamics* 31 (2008): 125–30.

18. L. Barring and H. von Storch, "Scandinavian Storminess since About 1800," *Geophysical Research Letters* 31 (2004): L20202.

19. Susan Solomon and others, eds., *Climate Change 2007: The Physical Science Basis* (Cambridge: Cambridge University Press, 2007), p. 351.

20. Ibid., Chapter 4 Executive Summary, pp. 339–40.

21. Ibid., "Summary for Policymakers," pp. 2–18.

22. See *Cryosphere Today* website, http://arctic.atmos.uiuc.edu/cryosphere/.

23. Donald J. Cavalieri, Per Gloersen, Claire L. Parkinson, Josefino C. Comiso, and H. Jay Zwally, "Observed Hemispheric Asymmetry in Global Sea Ice Changes," *Science* 278 (November 7, 1997): 1104–6.

24. Claire L. Parkinson, Donald J. Cavalieri, Per Gloersen, H. Jay Zwally, and Josefino C. Comiso, "Arctic Sea Ice Extents, Areas, and Trends, 1978–1996," *Journal of Geophysical Research* 104 (1999): 20837–56.

25. H. Jay Zwally, Josefino C. Comiso, Claire L. Parkinson, Donald J. Cavalieri, and Per Gloerson, "Variability of Antarctic Sea Ice, 1979–1998," *Journal of Geophysical Research* 107(C5) (2002): 3041 (emphasis added).

26. Josefino C. Comiso and Fumihiko Nishio, "Trends in the Sea Ice Cover Using Enhanced and Compatible AMSR-E, SSM/I, and SMMR Data," *Journal of Geophysical Research* 113 (2008): C02S07.

27. John Turner and others, "Non-Annular Atmospheric Circulation Change Induced by Stratospheric Ozone Depletion and Its Role in the Recent Increase of Antarctic Sea Ice Extent," *Geophysical Research Letters* 36 (2009): L08502.

28. U.S. Global Change Research Program, *Global Climate Change Impacts in the United States* (New York: Cambridge University Press, 2009), http://downloads.globalchange.gov/usimpacts/pdfs/climate-impacts-report.pdf.

29. David W. J. Thompson, John J. Kennedy, John M. Wallace, and Phil D. Jones, "A Large Discontinuity in the Mid-Twentieth Century in Observed Global-Mean Surface Temperature," *Nature* 453 (May 29, 2008): 646–49.

30. Ross R. McKitrick and Patrick J. Michaels, "Quantifying the Influence of Anthropogenic Surface Processes and Inhomogeneities on Gridded Global Climate Data," *Journal of Geophysical Research* 112 (2007): D24S09.

31. Susan Solomon and others, "Contributions of Stratospheric Water Vapor to Decadal Changes in the Rate of Global Warming," *Science* 327 (March 5, 2010): 1219–23.

32. V. Ramanathan and G. Carmichael, "Global and Regional Climate Changes Due to Black Carbon," *Nature Geoscience* 1 (2008): 221–27.

Chapter 3

1. Thomas S. Kuhn, *The Structure of Scientific Revolutions* (Chicago: University of Chicago Press, 1962).

2. Susan Solomon and others, eds., *Climate Change 2007: The Physical Science Basis* (Cambridge: Cambridge University Press, 2007).

3. Ibid., "Summary for Policymakers," pp. 2–18.

4. Ibid., p. 693.

5. Mikyoung Jun, Reto Knutti, and Douglas W. Nychka, "Spatial Analysis to Quantify Numerical Model Bias and Dependence: How Many Climate Models Are There?" *Journal of the American Statistical Association* 108, no. 483 (2008): 934–47.

6. Ibid., p. 935.

7. Ibid.

8. Tim Mitchell, "CRU TS 1.2," http://www.cru.uea.ac.uk/cru/data/hrg/timm/grid/CRU_TS_1_2.html.

9. See "CRU TS 2.0 and Time-Series Analysis: Advice for Users," http://www.cru.uea.ac.uk/cru/data/hrg/timm/grid/ts-advice.html.

10. P. D. Jones, M. New, D. E. Parker, S. Martin, and I. G. Rigor, "Surface Air Temperature and Its Changes over the Past 150 Years," *Reviews of Geophysics* 37 (1999): 173–99.

11. David E. Parker, "Climate: Large-Scale Warming Is Not Urban," *Nature* 432 (November 18, 2004): 290.

12. Roger A. Pielke and Toshihisa Matsui, "Should Light Wind and Windy Nights Have the Same Temperature Trends at Individual Levels Even if the Boundary Layer Averaged Heat Content Change Is the Same?" *Geophysical Research Letters* 32 (2005): 21813.

13. A. T. J. de Laat and A. N. Maurellis, "Industrial CO_2 Emissions as a Proxy for Anthropogenic Influence on Lower Tropospheric Temperature Trends," *Geophysical Research Letters* 31 (2004): L05204.

14. Ross R. McKitrick and Patrick J. Michaels, "Quantifying the Influence of Anthropogenic Surface Processes and Inhomogeneities on Gridded Global Climate Data," *Journal of Geophysical Research* 112 (2007): D24S09; and A. T. J. de Laat and A. N. Maurellis, "Evidence for Influence of Anthropogenic Surface Processes on Lower Tropospheric and Surface Temperature Trends," *International Journal of Climatology,* 26 (June 2006): 897–913.

15. Ross R. McKitrick and Patrick J. Michaels, "A Test of Corrections for Extraneous Signals in Gridded Surface Temperature Data," *Climate Research* 26 (2004): 159–73.

16. Ross R. McKitrick and Patrick J. Michaels, "Erratum: A Test of Corrections for Extraneous Signals in Gridded Surface Temperature Data," *Climate Research* 27 (2004): 265–68.

17. R. E. Benestad, "Are Temperature Trends Affected by Economic Activity? Comment on McKitrick & Michaels (2004)," *Climate Research* 27 (2004): 171–73.

18. Ross R. McKitrick and Patrick J. Michaels, "Are Temperature Trends Affected by Economic Activity? Reply to Benestad (2004)," *Climate Research* 27 (2004): 175–76.

19. De Laat and Maurellis, "Evidence for Influence of Anthropogenic Surface Processes."

20. McKitrick and Michaels, "Quantifying the Influence of Anthropogenic Surface Processes."

21. See East Anglia Confirmed Emails from the Climate Research Unit website. http://www.eastangliaemails.com.

22. Michaels recently informed me that he has had a similar problem with no less than *five* manuscripts in the last two years.

23. Shortly after a draft of this paper circulated on the Internet, the editor of the *Bulletin of the American Meteorological Society*, Jeffrey Rosenfeld, called me to say that *BAMS* had no record of receiving my e-mails. I sent him copies of all the e-mails, and at his suggestion resubmitted the article proposal as a test. All these e-mails were received without difficulty. He sincerely apologized for *BAMS*'s failure to respond to my submission and said there simply was no record of the journal's having received them.

Chapter 4

1. White House, *National Security Strategy* (Washington: Government Printing Office, May 2010), p. 47.

2. Jon Barnett, "Security and Climate Change," *Global Environmental Change* 13 (2003): 8.

3. Daniel Deudney, "The Case against Linking Environmental Degradation and National Security," *Millennium: Journal of International Studies* 19, no. 3 (1990): 461–62.

4. Geoffrey Dabelko and P. J. Simmons, "Environment and Security: Core Ideas and US Government Initiatives," *SAIS Review* 17.1 (1997): 135.

5. Ibid., pp. 127, 136.

6. Jon Barnett, "Security and Climate Change,"p. 9.

7. White House, *A National Security for a New Century* (Washington: Government Printing Office, 1997), p. 24.

8. Dabelko and Simmons, "Environment and Security," pp. 131–32.

9. CNA Corporation, *National Security and the Threat of Climate Change* (Alexandria, VA: CNA Corporation, 2007), p. 41.

10. Ibid.

11. Gordon R. Sullivan quoted in CNA Corporation, *National Security and the Threat of Climate Change*, p. 10.

12. Kurt M. Campbell and others, *The Age of Consequences: The Foreign Policy and National Security Implications of Climate Change* (Washington: Center for New American Security and Center for Strategic and International Studies, November 2007).

13. Kurt M. Campbell, ed., *Climatic Cataclysm: The Foreign Policy and National Security Implications of Climate Change* (Washington: Brookings Institution, 2008), pp. 220, 221–22.

14. Kurt M. Campbell and Richard Weitz, "Conclusion: The Clear Implications of Global Climate Change," in Campbell, *Climatic Cataclysm*, pp. 213–14.

15. R. James Woolsey, "A Partnership Deal: Malevolent and Malignant Threats," in Campbell, *Climatic Cataclysm*, pp. 175–77.

16. Barnett, "Security and Climate Change," p. 13.

17. John Podesta and Peter Ogden, "The Security Implications of Climate Change," *Washington Quarterly* 31 (Winter 2007–08): 116.

18. Dabelko and Simmons, "Environment and Security," pp. 131.

19. Quoted in Sam Kornell, "U.S. Military Measures Climate Change: Intelligence Establishment Calling It a Major Security Problem," *Santa Barbara Independent*, May 8, 2008, http://www.independent.com/news/2008/may/08/us-military-measures-climate-change/?print.

20. Barnett, "Security and Climate Change," p. 14.

21. Ivan Eland, *The Empire Has No Clothes: U.S. Foreign Policy Exposed* (Oakland, CA: Independent Institute, 2008), pp. 12, 56.

22. Deudney, "Case against Linking Environmental Degradation and National Security," pp. 461–62.

23. Jon Barnett, "Destabilizing the Environment—Conflict Thesis," *Review of International Studies* 26 (2000): 274.

24. Podesta and Ogden, "Security Implications of Climate Change," p. 116.

25. Peter Schwartz and Doug Randall, "An Abrupt Scenario and Its Implications for United States National Security," U.S. Department of Defense, October 2003, p. 18.

26. Deudney, "Case against Linking Environmental Degradation and National Security," p. 470.

27. Barnett, "Security and Climate Change," p. 10.

28. CNA Corporation, *National Security and the Threat of Climate Change*, p. 15; and Chattahbox, "Military Admits Global Warming a Threat to National Security," August 9, 2009, http://chattahbox.com/us/2009/08/09/military-admits-global-warming-a-threat-to-national-security/.

29. Julian Simon, *The Ultimate Resource* (Princeton, NJ: Princeton University Press, 1981).

30. Ronnie Lipschutz and John Holdren, "Crossing Borders: Resource Flows, the Global Environment and International Stability," *Bulletin of Peace Proposals* 21 (1990): 121–33.

31. Deudney, "Case against Linking Environmental Degradation and National Security," pp. 470–73, 474.

32. Ibid.

33. General Charles F. "Chuck" Wald, former deputy of the European Command, quoted in Associated Press, "Military: Global Warming May Cause War," April 17, 2007, http://www.military.com/NewsContent/0,13319,132519,00.html.

34. Ronnie Lipschutz, "What Resource Will Matter? Environmental Degradation as a Security Issue," in *Environmental Dimensions of Security: Proceedings from a AAAS Annual Meeting Symposium*, ed. Elizabeth Kirk (Washington: American Association for the Advancement of Science, 1992), pp. 1–8.

35. CNA Corporation, *National Security and the Threat of Climate Change*, p. 18. See also Aaron T. Wolf, Annika Kramer, Alexander Carius, and Geoffrey Dabelko, "Water Can Be a Pathway to Peace, Not War,"*Navigating Peace*, no. 1, July 2006, http://www.wilsoncenter.org/topics/pubs/NavigatingPeaceIssue1.pdf, which was cited for the argument that attempts to resolve control over scarce water resources create peace, not war.

36. Daniel Deudney, "Environmental Security: Muddled Thinking," *Bulletin of Atomic Scientists*, April 1991, pp. 23–28; and Stephan Libiszewski, "Integrating Political and Technical Approaches: Lessons from the Israeli-Jordanian Water Negotiations," in *Conflict and the Environment*, ed. Nils Petter Gleditsch (Dordrecht, Netherlands: Kluwer Academic Publishers, 1997), pp. 385–402.

37. Barnett, "Destabilizing the Environment," p. 278.

38. Ibid., pp. 276–77, 284.

39. Ibid., pp.278–79.

40. Studies summarized in Barnett, "Security and Climate Change," p. 11.

41. CNA Corporation, *National Security and the Threat of Climate Change*, p. 44.

42. Dabelko and Simmons, "Environment and Security," p. 134.

43. U.S. Department of Defense Quadrennial Defense Review, quoted in "US Military: Climate Change Is a Key Security Issue," Greenbang website, February 2, 2010; and Suzanne Goldenberg, "Pentagon to Rank Global Warming as Destabilising Force," *Guardian* (UK), January 31, 2010, http://www.guardian.co.uk/world/2010/jan/31/pentagon-ranks-global-warming-destabilising-force/print.

44. Quoted in Jean Williams, "U.S. Military and Intelligence: Global Warming Increasing National Security Risks," *Seattle Policy Examiner*, August 16, 2009, http://www.examiner.com/environmental-policy-in-seattle/u-s-military-and-intelligence-global-warming-increasing-national-security-risks.

45. Barnett, "Security and Climate Change," p. 11.

46. Thomas Homer-Dixon and Valerie Percival, *Environmental Scarcity and Violent Conflict: Briefing Book* (Toronto: American Association for the Advancement of Science, 1996), pp. 7–9, quoted in Barnett, "Destabilizing the Environment," p. 282.

47. Barnett, "Security and Climate Change," p. 10.

48. Ronnie Lipschut and John Holdren, "Crossing Borders: Resource Flows, the Global Environment, and International Stability," *Bulletin of Peace Proposals*, 21 (1990), pp. 121–133.

49. Barnett, "Destabilizing the Environment," p. 274.

50. Joshua W. Busby, "Climate Change and National Security: An Agenda for Action," CSR no. 32, Council on Foreign Relations, November 2004.

51. CNA Corporation, *National Security and the Threat of Climate Change*, p. 16.

52. Podesta and Ogden, "Security Implications of Climate Change," p. 116.

53. Barnett, "Security and Climate Change," pp. 11–12.

54. Deudney, "Case against Linking Environmental Degradation and National Security," p. 473.

55. Campbell and Weitz, "Conclusion," p. 219.

56. CNA Corporation, *National Security and the Threat of Climate Change*, p. 6.

57. Ibid., p. 13.

58. Ibid., p. 17.

59. Ibid., p. 6.

60. Ibid., p. 37.

61. Ibid., p. 24.

62. Podesta and Ogden, "Security Implications of Climate Change," p. 118.

63. Ibid.

64. CNA Corporation, *National Security and the Threat of Climate Change*, p. 15.

65. Ibid., pp. 20, 21.

66. Ibid., p. 30. Comments of General Anthony (Tony) Zinni were cited in "Climate Change Worries Military Advisers," National Public Radio, April 16, 2007, http://www.npr.org/templates/story/story.php?storyId = 9580815.

67. CNA Corporation, *National Security and the Threat of Climate Change*, p. 30.

68. Podesta and Ogden, "Security Implications of Climate Change," p. 121.

69. CNA Corporation, *National Security and the Threat of Climate Change*, p. 31.

70. Ibid., p. 30.

71. Jay Gulledge, "Three Plausible Scenarios of Future Climate Change," in Campbell, *Climatic Cataclysm*, p. 53.

72. Peter Schwartz and Doug Randall, "An Abrupt Scenario," p. 4.

73. Ibid., p. 19.

74. Woolsey, "A Partnership Deal," pp. 176–77.

75. An extensive discussion of this is given in "Climate of Extremes: Global Warming Science They Don't Want You to Know," by Patrick J. Michaels and Robert C. Balling Jr.

76. For example, Lester Brown made this argument in Lester R. Brown, "Redefining National Security," Worldwatch Paper no. 14, October 1977; and so did Wilson in T. Wilson, "Global Climate, World Politics and National Security," in *World Climate Change: The Role of International Law and Institutions*, ed. V. Nanda (Boulder, CO: Westview Press, 1983), pp. 71–77.

77. CNA Corporation, *National Security and the Threat of Climate Change*, p. 6.

78. Quoted in Mark Townsend and Paul Harris, "Now the Pentagon Tells Bush Climate Change Will Destroy Us," *The Observer* (UK), February 22, 2004.

79. Allan W. Shearer, "Whether the Weather: Comments on 'An Abrupt Climate Change Scenario and Its Implications for United States National Security,'" *Futures* 37 (2005): 458.

80. CNA Corporation, *National Security and the Threat of Climate Change*, p. 33.

81. Suzanne Goldenberg, "Pentagon to Rank Global Warming as Destabilising Force."

82. Ty Tagami, "Military Considers Global Warming Threat," *Atlanta Journal-Constitution*, January 19, 2010, http://www.ajc.com/news/nation-world/military-considers-global-warming-278622.html.

83. William H. McMichael, "Report: Climate Change a Major Military Issue," *Army Times*, April 16, 2007.

84. CNA Corporation, *National Security and the Threat of Climate Change*, p. 33.

85. U.S. Navy, Office of Naval Research, Naval Ice Center, "Naval Operations in an Ice-Free Arctic: Symposium, 17–18 April 2001, Washington, D.C.," final report, 2001.

86. Environmental News Service, "Military Panel: Climate Change Threatens National Security," April 16, 2007, http://www.ens-newswire.com/ens/apr2007/2007-04-16-05.asp.

87. "US Military: Climate Change Is a Key Security Issue," Greenbang website, February 2, 2010, http://www.greenbang.com/us-military-climate-change-is-a-key-security-issue_13506.html.

88. CNA Corporation, *National Security and the Threat of Climate Change*, p. 37.

89. "US Military Launches War on Global Warming," Reuters, August 2008, http://www.newscientist.com/article/dn14498?full = true&print = true.

90. CNA Corporation, *National Security and the Threat of Climate Change*, pp. 39–40.

91. Busby, "Climate Change and National Security," pp. 12, 16.

92. Ibid., p. 15.

Chapter 5

1. U.S. Energy Information Administration, "International Energy Annual 2006," release date June-December 2008, Table H1, http://www.eia.doe.gov/pub/international/ielf/tableh1co2.xls.

2. Chip Knappenberger, "Climate Impacts of Waxman-Markey (the IPCC-Based Arithmetic of No Gain)," MasterResource blog, May 6, 2009, http://master resource.org/2009/05/page/3/.

3. Jason Bordoff, "International Trade Law and the Economics of Climate Policy: Evaluating the Legality and Effectiveness of Proposals to Address Competitiveness and Leakage Concerns" (paper presented at a conference on "Climate Change, Trade and Competitiveness: Is a Collision Inevitable?" Brookings Institution, Washington, June 9, 2008).

4. In reality, the president cannot "commit" the United States to any emission reduction without an act of Congress or by direction from the U.S. Environmental Protection Agency, and both these activities are potentially reversible with a change in political leadership.

5. Aaditya Mattoo, Arvind Subramanian, Dominique van der Mensbrugghe, and Jianwu He, "Reconciling Climate Change and Trade Policy," World Bank Policy Research Working Paper no. 5123, November 2009, http://www-wds.worldbank. org/external/default/WDSContentServer/IW3P/IB/2009/11/12/000158349_20091 112173455/Rendered/PDF/WPS5123.pdf.

6. Bordoff, "International Trade Law and the Economics of Climate Policy."

7. Ibid.

8. Senator Sherrod Brown and others, letter to Sens. John Kerry, Lindsey Graham, and Joe Lieberman, April 15, 2010, http://brown.senate.gov/imo/media/doc/ Manufacturing%20Letter%20Final.pdf.

9. Many legal articles and books have been written on the interface between WTO rules and climate change policies. See, for example, chaps. 2 and 3 of Gary Clyde Hufbauer, Steve Charnovitz, and Jisun Kim, *Global Warming and the World Trading System* (Washington: Peterson Institute for International Economics, 2009). Robert Howse and Antonia Eliason, "Domestic and International Strategies to Address Climate Change: An Overview of the WTO Legal Issues," in *International Trade Regulation and the Mitigation of Climate Change*, ed. Thomas Cottier, Olga Nartova, and Sadeq Z. Bigdeli (Cambridge, UK: Cambridge Univeristy Press, 2009). Howse and Eliason; and Cottier and others (forthcoming).

10. If all emission allowances were given freely to all industries, it is less likely that the WTO definition of a subsidy would be met. For one thing, if the government charges no one for emission allowances, it is not clear that any revenue has been forgone. For another, the "subsidy" would not be specific to certain industries— another test of whether a subsidy is actionable. The problem appears to occur when only a subset of allowances is given away, and given on a nonrandom basis. Indeed, giving allowances away randomly would, through Coasean bargaining, reduce emissions without the unseemly lobbying that the proposed policy has created.

11. Robert Howse and Antonia Eliason, "Domestic and International Strategies to Address Climate Change: An Overview of the WTO Legal Issues," in *International Trade Regulation and the Mitigation of Climate Change*, ed. Thomas Cottier, Olga Nartova, and Sadeq Z. Bigdeli (Cambridge, UK: Cambridge Univeristy Press, 2009). Howse and Eliason; and Cottier and others (forthcoming).

12. World Trade Organization, "Agreement on Subsidies and Countervailing Measures," Article 6.3(a).

13. Bordoff, "International Trade Law and the Economics of Climate Policy."

14. Ibid., p. 25.

15. For more on why the initial allocation of carbon allowances may not be "neutral," see the recent paper by economists Robert Hahn and Robert N. Stavins, "Why Cap-and-Trade Should (and Does) Have Appeal to Politicians," April 13, 2010, http://voxeu.org/index.php?q=node/4865.

16. Bordoff, "International Trade Law and the Economics of Climate Policy," p. 26.

17. As Table 5.1 shows, China accounts for less than 15 percent of imports in all "energy-intensive" goods categories except steel. On the basis of current import levels, then, the threshold for avoiding the imposition of the international reserve allowance program could, in theory, be met without China fulfilling any of the conditions that follow.

18. Paul Krugman, "Climate, Trade, Obama," The Conscience of a Liberal (blog), *New York Times*, June 29, 2009, http://krugman.blogs.nytimes.com/2009/06/29/climate-trade-obama/.

19. Ludivine Tamiotti and others, *Trade and Climate Change: A Report by the United Nations Environmental Programme and the World Trade Organization* (Geneva: WTO Secretariat, 2009), http://www.wto.org/english/res_e/booksp_e/trade_climate_change_e.pdf.

20. In a dispute on taxes levied under the U.S. Superfund law, a GATT panel ruled that the United States could apply a domestic tax on certain chemicals to imports as well when those imports used the same chemicals in the process of their production. The panel did not specify that the taxed chemicals had to be physically incorporated into the imported products. "United States—Taxes on Petroleum and Certain Imported Substances: Report of the Panel adopted on 17 June 1987 (L/6175 - 34S/136)," June 5, 1987, http://www.worldtradelaw.net/reports/gattpanels/superfund.pdf.

21. See, for example, the conclusion of a leading trade expert that "for a U.S. competitiveness provision to target only countries with no emission cuts in place would most likely violate MFN (the United States would then be treating 'like' products differently based on their origin)." Joost Pauwelyn, "U.S. Federal Climate Policy and Competitiveness Concerns: The Limits and Options of International Trade Law," Working Paper 07/02, Nicholson Institute for Environmental Policy Solutions, Duke University, April 2007, http://nicholasinstitute.duke.edu/climate/policydesign/u.s.-federal-climate-policy-and-competitiveness-concerns-the-limits-and-options-of-international-trade-law.

22. Javier de Cendra, "Can Emissions Trading Schemes Be Coupled with Border Tax Adjustments? An Analysis vis-à-vis WTO Law," *Review of European Community and International Environmental Law* 15 (2006): 131–45.

23. Summary Testimony of Gary N. Horlick before the United States Senate Committee on Finance, July 8, 2009, pp. 2–3, http://finance.senate.gov/imo/media/doc/Gay%20Horlick1.pdf.

24. World Trade Organization, "European Communities Measures Affecting Asbestos and Asbestos-Containing Products," WT/DS135/AB/R), March 12, 2001, http://www.wto.org/english/tratop_e/dispu_e/135abr_e.pdf.

25. A similar, if less straightforward, case can be made that Waxman-Markey might also violate the "national treatment" requirement of Article III of the GATT. While

Article I forbids discrimination between imports from one country and imports from another country, Article III forbids discrimination between imports and domestically produced goods. Once again, the issue turns on the "like product" question: specifically, whether imports produced in a process that emits more carbon (and for which importers are therefore required to obtain more emission allowances) are "like" domestic products produced in a process that emits less carbon (and for which domestic producers are therefore required to obtain fewer allowances). If the imports and domestic goods are judged to be like products, then the more burdensome requirement imposed on the imports would violate the national treatment requirement of Article III.

26. Also potentially applicable is Article XX(b), which provides an exception for measures "necessary to protect human, animal, or plant life or health." The requirement that the measures be "necessary," however, is a relatively stringent one compared with Article XX(g)'s exception for measures merely "relating to" conserving exhaustible natural resources. Accordingly, the analysis here focuses on the comparatively wider loophole of Article XX(g).

27. World Trade Organization, *United States—Import Prohibition of Certain Shrimp and Shrimp Products*, WT/DS58/AB/R, November 6, 1998, http://www.wto.org/english/tratop_e/dispu_e/58abr.pdf.

28. Ibid., para. 180.

29. Ibid., para. 165 (emphasis added).

30. Indeed, many developing countries have more stringent carbon-emission standards, particularly for transport, than the United States does. So it is not unequivocally true to say that developing countries have more lenient climate change policies.

31. Robert Howse and Antonia Eliason, "Domestic and International Strategies to Address Climate Change: An Overview of the WTO Legal Issues," in *International Trade Regulation and the Mitigation of Climate Change*, ed. Thomas Cottier, Olga Nartova, and Sadeq Z. Bigdeli (Cambridge, UK: Cambridge Univeristy Press, 2009). Howse and Eliason; and Cottier and others (forthcoming).

32. A related question pertains to the amount of the tariff/fee/adjustment measure. Should it be based on the emissions of the country of origin or based on the emissions when making an equivalent good domestically? These questions are legally and economically significant.

33. Sheldon Alberts, "U.S. Climate Bill Would Be 'Disaster': Prentice Urges DC to Drop Proposed Sanction," Canwest News Service, May 14, 2009, http://www.canada.com/components/print.aspx?id = 1593753.

34. International Centre for Trade and Sustainable Development, "India Threatens WTO Case against Proposed 'Carbon Border Taxes,'" *Bridges Weekly Trade New Digest*, March 31, 2010, http://ictsd.org/i/news/bridgesweekly/73378/.

35. Matthew Yglesias, "Making China Part of the Solution," Think Progress (blog), May 16, 2009, http://yglesias.thinkprogress.org/archives/2009/05/making-china-part-of-the-solution.php.

36. Susan Schwab, letter to Honorable Joe Barton, March 4, 2008, http://commontragedies.files.wordpress.com/2008/03/document_daily_01.pdf.

37. Brian Ellsworth, "Brazil Wants CO2 Cuts Based on Historic Emissions," Reuters, July 2, 2009, http://www.reuters.com/article/idUSTRE5615EF20090702.

38. "Interview with President Obama on Climate Bill," *New York Times*, June 28, 2009, http://www.nytimes.com/2009/06/29/us/politics/29climate-text.html?_r = 2.

39. Darren Samulesohn, "Obama Open to Trade Protections in Senate Climate Bill, Adviser Says," Greenwire (blog), *New York Times*, April 20, 2010, http://www.ny times.com/gwire/2010/04/20/20greenwire-obama-open-to-trade-protections-in-senate-clim-18632.html.

40. "Industry Plots Climate Change Senate Strategy, Seeks Tougher Tariffs," *Inside U.S. Trade*, July 3, 2009.

41. Horlick, Summary Testimony, p. 2.

42. James Bacchus, "Combating Climate Change," *Forbes*, April 26, 2010.

Chapter 6

1. United Nations Environment Programme, *Climate Change and North-South Relations*, Climate Change Fact Sheet 109, May 1, 1993, http://massacre.otago.ac.nz/static/Mirrors/Climatechange-Factsheets_Mirror/fs109.html; and Indur M. Goklany, "Strategies to Enhance Adaptability: Technological Change, Economic Growth and Free Trade, *Climatic Change* 30 (1995): 435.

2. Indur M. Goklany, "Potential Consequences of Increasing Atmospheric CO_2 Concentration Compared to Other Environmental Problems," *Technology* 7S (2000): 189–213; and Anthony Costello and others, "Managing the Health Effects of Climate Change," *Lancet* 373 (2009): 1693–1733.

3. Intergovernmental Panel on Climate Change, *Climate Change 2007: Impacts, Adaptation, and Vulnerability* (Cambridge: Cambridge University Press, 2007), pp. 13, 20.

4. Jody Freeman and Andrew T. Guzman, "Seawalls Are Not Enough: Climate Change & U.S. Interests" (Version 3.1), *Columbia Law Review* 100, no. 2 (2009): 134–37.

5. Ibid.

6. Mary Robinson in *Global Humanitarian Forum* (2009). "Key Points on Climate Justice," Working Paper (Geneva: GHF, 2009, p. 1).

7. United Nations Framework Convention on Climate Change, *Climate Change: Impacts, Vulnerabilities and Adaptation in Developing Countries* (Bonn: UNFCCC, 2007), pp. 20–22.

8. Ibid., p. 20.

9. Indur M. Goklany, "A Climate Policy for the Short and Medium Term: Stabilization or Adaptation?" *Energy & Environment* 16 (2005): 667–80.

10. Indur M. Goklany, "Integrated Strategies to Reduce Vulnerability and Advance Adaptation, Mitigation, and Sustainable Development," *Mitigation and Adaptation Strategies for Global Change* 12 (2007): 755–86.

11. Freeman and Guzman, "Climate Change and U.S. Interests," p. 116, fn 62.

12. Indur M. Goklany, "Saving Habitat and Conserving Biodiversity on a Crowded Planet," *BioScience* 48 (1998): 941–53; and Indur M. Goklany, *The Improving State of the World* (Washington: Cato Institute, 2007), p. 25.

13. UN Food and Agricultural Organization, *State of Food Insecurity 2009* (Rome: FAO, 2009), p. 11.

14. Ibid. and FAO, "The State of Food Insecurity in the World," policy brief, 2009, http://www.fao.org/economic/es-policybriefs/multimedia0/presentation-the-state-of-food-insecurity/en/.

15. Freeman and Guzman, "Climate Change and U.S. Interests," p. 157.

16. Goklany, *The Improving State of the World*; and World Bank, *World Development Indicators*, 2010, http://databank.worldbank.org.

17. Indur M. Goklany, "Have Increases in Population, Affluence and Technology Worsened Human and Environmental Well-Being?" *Electronic Journal of Sustainable Development* 1 (2009), http://www.ejsd.org/docs/HAVE_INCREASES_IN_POPULATION_AFFLUENCE_AND_TECHNOLOGY_WORSENED_HUMAN_AND_ENVIRONMENTAL_WELL-BEING.pdf.

18. Goklany, *The Improving State of the World*, p. 40.

19. Intergovernmental Panel on Climate Change, *Climate Change 2001: Impacts, Adaptation, and Vulnerability* (Cambridge: Cambridge University Press, 2001), p. 463.

20. Peter W. Gething and others, "Climate Change and the Global Malaria Recession," *Nature* 465 (2010): 342–45.

21. Ibid., p. 344

22. Indur M. Goklany, "Is a Richer-but-Warmer World Better than Poorer-but-Cooler Worlds?" *Energy & Environment* 18 (2007): 178–81.

23. Living Proof Project (2009). Progress against Malaria: Winning the Fight against a Deadly Disease, p. 3. http://www.gatesfoundation.org/livingproofproject/Documents/progress-against-malaria.pdf.

24. World Bank, PovCalNet, http://iresearch.worldbank.org/PovcalNet/povDuplic.html.

25. UNFCCC, *Climate Change*, p. 20.

26. Indur M. Goklany, "Deaths and Death Rates from Extreme Weather Events: 1900–2008," *Journal of American Physicians and Surgeons* 14 (2009): 104.

27. Ibid.

28. Ibid.

29. World Health Organization, Global Burden of Disease and Risk Factors: 2004 Update (Geneva: WHO, 2008)

30. Ibid.

31. Ibid., p. 102.

32. Freeman and Guzman, "Climate Change and U.S. Interests," p. 139.

33. United Nations, *Millennium Development Goals Report 2008* (New York: United Nations, 2008), p. 42.

34. World Bank, *World Bank Data Search*, 2010, http://search.worldbank.org/data?qterm=mdgs+safe+water&language=EN&format=html.

35. UNFCCC, *Climate Change*.

36. Goklany, *The Improving State of the World*.

37. "A much less recognized connection between water and energy are the vast amounts of energy used to treat, distribute, and use water. Water is heavy (1 liter weighs one kilogram), so moving it requires a lot of energy. Energy needs are particularly high for places where water is pumped from very deep wells, or where it is piped over long distances and steep terrain. Additionally, heating water is energy-intensive. In California, for example, 19% of the electricity use, 33% of the non-electricity natural gas, and 33 million gallons of diesel consumption is water-related." UN Global Compact, "Climate Change and the Global Water Crisis: What Businesses Need to Know and Do," May 2009, p. 4.

38. Goklany, *The Improving State of the World*.

39. IPCC, *Climate Change 2001*, pp. 254–57, 285.

40. Goklany, "Strategies to Enhance Adaptability"; and Goklany, "Saving Habitat."

41. Goklany, "Saving Habitat"; and Goklany, *The Improving State of the World*.

42. Millennium Ecosystem Assessment, "Millennium Ecosystem Assessment Synthesis Report," prepublication final draft, approved by MA Board on March 23, 2005 (on file with author).

43. Goklany, *The Improving State of the World*, p. 162.

44. World Health Organization, *Global Health Risks: Mortality and Burden of Disease Attributable to Selected Major Risks* (Geneva: WHO, 2009), http://www.who.int/health info/global_burden_disease/global_health_risks/en/index.html.

45. Goklany, *The Improving State of the World*.

46. Ibid.

47. Ibid.

48. World Bank, *World Development Indicators 2009* (Washington: World Bank, 2009).

49. William Easterly, "Easterly on Growth, Poverty, and Aid," Library of Economics and Liberty podcast, February 11, 2008, http://www.econtalk.org/archives/2008/02/easterly_on_gro.html.

50. Dilip Ratha, Sanket Mohapatra, and Ani Silwal, "Migration and Remittance Trends 2009: A Better-than-Expected Outcome So Far, but Significant Risks Ahead," Migration and Development Brief 11, World Bank, November 3, 2009, http://site resources.worldbank.org/INTPROSPECTS/Resources/334934-1110315015165/MigrationAndDevelopmentBrief11.pdf.

51. World Bank, *World Development Indicators 2009*, pp. xii, 12.

52. Indur M. Goklany, "Meeting Global Food Needs: The Environmental Trade-Offs between Increasing Land Conversion and Land Productivity," *Technology* 6 (1999): 125.

53. Goklany, "Integrated Strategies"; and Goklany, *The Improving State of the World*.

54. Intergovernmental Panel on Climate Change, *Special Report on Emissions Scenarios* (New York: Cambridge University Press, 2000).

55. Goklany, "Integrated Strategies."

56. Nicholas Stern, *The Economics of Climate Change: The Stern Review* (London: Her Majesty's Treasury, 2006).

57. Freeman and Guzman, "Climate Change and U.S. Interests," p. 127.

58. Richard S. J. Tol, "The Social Cost of Carbon: Trends, Outliers and Catastrophes," *Economics: The Open-Access, Open-Assessment E-Journal* 2 (2008): 9, http://www.economics-ejournal.org/economics/journalarticles/2008-25.

59. Indur M. Goklany, "Discounting the Future," *Regulation* 32 (Spring 2009): 36–40.

60. Richard S. J. Tol and Hadi Dowlatabadi, "Vector-Borne Diseases, Development & Climate Change," *Integrated Assessment* 2 (2001): 173–81.

61. Goklany, "Have Increases Worsened Human and Environmental Well-Being?"

62. Goklany, *The Improving State of the World*, chap. 9; and Goklany, "Discounting the Future," pp. 36–40.

63. Goklany, "Integrated Strategies"; and Goklany, "Is a Richer-but-Warmer World Better?"

64. Martin Parry and others, "Effects of Climate Change on Global Food Production under SRES Emissions and Socio-Economic Scenarios," *Global Environmental Change* 14 (2004): 53–67.

65. Intergovernmental Panel on Climate Change, *Climate Change 2001: Impacts, Adaptation, and Vulnerability* (Cambridge: Cambridge University Press, 2001); Intergovernmental Panel on Climate Change, *Climate Change 2007: Impacts, Adaptation, and Vulnerability* (Cambridge: Cambridge University Press, 2007).

66. Ibid.; and Martin Parry and others, "Climate Change and World Food Security: A New Assessment," *Global Environmental Change* 9 (1999): S51–S67.

67. N. W. Arnell, "Climate Change and Global Water Resources: SRES Emissions and Socio-Economic Scenarios," *Global Environmental Change* 14 (2004): 31–52.

68. Goklany, "Is a Richer-but-Warmer World Better?" pp. 1034–35.

69. Parry and others, "Effects of Climate Change on Global Food Production," p. 57; and Goklany "Is a Richer-but-Warmer World Better?" pp. 1032–33.

70. Goklany, *The Improving State of the World*); and Goklany, "Is a Richer-but-Warmer World Better?"

71. Robert J. Nicholls, "Coastal Flooding and Wetland Loss in the 21st Century: Changes under the SRES Climate and Socio-Economic Scenarios," *Global Environmental Change* 14 (2004): 69–86.

72. Goklany, *The Improving State of the World*, pp. 1036–37.

73. M. van Lieshout, R. S. Kovats, M. T. J. Livermore, and P. Marten, "Climate Change and Malaria: Analysis of the SRES Climate and Socio-Economic Scenarios," *Global Environmental Change* 14 (2004): 87–99.

74. Martin Parry, ed., "Special Issue: An Assessment of the Global Effects of Climate Change under SRES Emissions and Socio-Economic Scenarios," *Global Environmental Change* 14 (2004): 1–99.

75. Goklany, *The Improving State of the World*; and Goklany, "Have Increases Worsened Human and Environmental Well-Being?"

76. Goklany, "Have Increases Worsened Human and Environmental Well-Being?"

77. Goklany, "Deaths and Death Rates."

78. Gary W. Yohe and others, "A Synthetic Assessment of the Global Distribution of Vulnerability to Climate Change from the IPCC Perspective that Reflects Exposure and Adaptive Capacity," Center for International Earth Science Information Network, Columbia University, 2006: 4, http://sedac.ciesin.columbia.edu/mva/ccv/.

79. Richard S. J. Tol, Kristie L. Ebi, and Gary W. Yohe, "Infectious Disease, Development, and Climate Change: A Scenario Analysis," *Environment and Development Economics* 12 (2007): 687–706.

80. Goklany, "Have Increases Worsened Human and Environmental Well-Being?"

81. IPCC, *Climate Change 2007*, p. 20.

82. For example, Freeman and Guzman, "Climate Change and U.S. Interests."

83. Parry and others, "Effects of Climate Change on Global Food Production; Arnell, "Climate Change and Global Water Resources," pp. 31–52; and Nigel W. Arnell and others, "The Consequences of CO_2 Stabilization for the Impacts of Climate Change," *Climatic Change* 53 (2002): 413–46.

84. See Indur M. Goklany, "Global Public Health: Global Warming in Perspective," *Journal of American Physicians and Surgeons* 14 (2009): 69–75; and Goklany, "Discounting the Future."

85. As noted, malaria accounts for a disproportionately large share of the global burden of vector-borne disease.

86. Goklany, "Global Public Health," pp. 69–75.

87. This information is not readily apparent from the abstract in Arnell, "Climate Change and Global Water Resources"; but see Goklany, "Global Public Health,", pp. 72–74; and Taikan Oki and Shinjiro Kanae, "Global Hydrological Cycles and World Water Resources," *Science* 313 (2006): 1068–72.

88. IPCC, "Summary for Policymakers," in *Climate Change 2007: Impacts, Adaptation and Vulnerability*, ed. M. L. Parry and others (Cambridge: Cambridge University Press, 2007).

89. Goklany, "Is a Richer-but-Warmer World Better?"; Goklany, "Global Public Health."

90. Oki and Kanae, "Global Hydrological Cycles."

91. Arnell, "Climate Change and Global Water Resources."

92. Goklany, *The Improving State of the World.*

93. Goklany, "Saving Habitat"; MEA, "Millennium Ecosystem Assessment Synthesis Report."

94. Goklany, "Saving Habitat"; and Goklany, "Climate Policy for the Short and Medium Term."

95. Goklany, "Is a Richer-but-Warmer World Better?"

96. Goklany, Is Climate Change the 'Defining Challenge of Our Age'?" *Energy & Environment* 20, no. 3 (2009): 279–302; Goklany, "Climate Policy for the Short and Medium Term"; and Goklany, "Discounting the Future."

97. Tol, Ebi, and Yohe, "Infectious Disease, Development, and Climate Change."

98. Goklany, "Climate Policy for the Short and Medium Term"; and Goklany, *The Improving State of the World.*

99. FAO, *State of Food Insecurity 2009.*

100. World Bank, *World Development Indicators 2009.*

101. Rafael E. De Hoyos and Denis Medvedev, "Poverty Effects of Higher Food Prices: A Global Perspective," World Bank Policy Research Working Paper 4887, 2009, p. 32.

102. World Health Organization, *Global Health Risks.*

103. A. J. McMichael and others, "Global Climate Change," in *Comparative Quantification of Health Risks: Global and Regional Burden of Disease due to Selected Major Risk Factors*, ed. M. Ezzati, A. Lopez, A. Rodgers, and C. Murray (Geneva: World Health Organization, 2004), p. 1546; see also Goklany, "Global Public Health," p. 70.

104. Goklany, "Climate Policy for the Short and Medium Term."

105. Goklany, "Strategies to Enhance Adaptability"; Goklany, "Climate Policy for the Short and Medium Term"; and Indur M. Goklany, "Is Climate Change the 'Defining Challenge of Our Age'?" *Energy & Environment* 20 (2009): 279–302.

106. Goklany, "Defining Challenge."

Chapter 7

1. J. Süss, "Tick-Borne Encephalitis in Europe and Beyond: The Epidemiological Situation as of 2007," *Eurosurveillance* 13 (2008): 1–8.

2. Austria, Croatia, Czech Reublic, Denmark, Estonia, Finland, France, Germany, Hungary, Italy, Latvia, Lithunia, Norway, Poland, Russia, Slovakia, Slovenia, Sweden, Switzerland.

3. Emily K. Shuman, "Global Climate Change and Infectious Disease," *New England Journal of Medicine* 362 (March 25, 2010): 1061.

4. Peter W. Gething and others, "Climate Change and the Global Malaria Recession," *Nature* 465 (2010): 342–45.

5. Ibid.

6. See Willem J. M. Martens, Theo H. Jetten, and Dana A. Focks, "Sensitivity of Malaria, Schistosomiasis and Dengue to Global Warming," *Climatic Change* 35 (1997): 145–56; S. W. Lindsay and Willem J. M. Martens, "Malaria in the African Highlands: Past, Present and Future," *Bulletin of the World Health Organization* 76 (1998): 33–45; and P. Martens and others, "Climate Change and Future Populations at Risk of Malaria," *Global Environmental Change* 9 (1999): S89–S107.

7. Gething and others, "Climate Change and the Global Malaria Recession."

8. R. E. Davis, P. C. Knappenberger, P. J. Michaels and W. M. Novicoff, "Evidence of Adaptation to Increasing Heat Wave Intensity and Duration in U.S. Cities (2005)," *Proceedings of the 17th International Congress of Biometeorology of the International Society of Biometeorology*, Garmisch-Partenkirchen, Germany, 341–44.

9. M. Z. Jacobsen, "Enhancement of Local Air Pollution by Urban CO_2 Domes," *Environmental Science and Technollogy*, 44 (2010), 2597–2600.

10. Craig D. Idso, Sherwood B. Idso, and Robert C. Balling Jr., "An Intensive Two-Week Study of an Urban CO_2 Dome in Phoenix, Arizona, USA," *Atmospheric Environment* 35 (2001): 995–1000; and Robert C. Balling Jr., Randall S. Cerveny, and Craig D. Idso, "Does the CO_2 Dome of Phoenix, Arizona, Contribute to Its Heat Island?" *Geophysical Research Letters* 28 (2001): 4599–4601.

11. Michael Jerrett and others, "Long-Term Ozone Exposure and Mortality," *New England Journal of Medicine* 360 (2010): 1085–95.

12. Anthony Arguez and James B. Elsner, "Trends in U.S. Tropical Cyclone Mortality during the Past Century," April 11, 2001, http://myweb.fsu.edu/jelsner/HTML/Research/papers/mortality/mortal.html#tthFtNtAAB.

13. An update of these data for 1996–2009 would at least include Hurricane Katrina in 2005, so that trend was broken.

14. Anice C. Lowen, Samira Mubareka, John Steel, and Peter Palese, "Influenza Virus Transmission Is Dependent on Relative Humidity and Temperature," *PLoS Pathogens* 3 (2007): e151.

15. Jeffrey Shaman and Melvin Kohn, "Absolute Humidity Modulates Influenza Survival, Transmission, and Seasonality," *Proceedings of the National Academy of Sciences* 106 (2009): 3645–46.

16. Jeffrey Shaman, Virginia E. Pitzer, Cécile Viboud, Bryan T. Grenfell, and Marc Lipsitch, "Absolute Humidity and the Seasonal Onset of Influenza in the Continental United States," *PLoS Biology* 8 (2010): e1000316.

17. Reference 25, p. 3650.

Chapter 8

1. Quotes taken from *Dimmock v. Secretary of State for Education and Skills* (now Secretary of State for Children, Schools and Families), EWHC 2288 (Admin), 2007.

2. Michael Sanera and Jane S. Shaw, *Facts Not Fear: Teaching Children about the Environment* (Washington: Regnery, 1999), p. 2.

3. Ibid., p. 123.

4. Diane Ravitch, *The Language Police: How Pressure Groups Restrict What Students Learn* (New York: Knopf, 2003), p. 3.

5. Most recently, a move by the Dover, Pennsylvania, school district to affix stickers stating that evolution is a theory, not a fact, and pointing students to the intelligent design book *Of Pandas and People* was ruled unconstitutional in a U.S. district court.

6. Cornelia Dean, "Evolution Takes a Back Seat in U.S. Classes," *New York Times*, February 1, 2005.

7. Leslie Kaufman, "Darwin Foes Add Warming to Targets," *New York Times*, March 3, 2010.

8. U.S. Department of Education, *A Nation at Risk*, archived information, April 1983, http://www.ed.gov/pubs/NatAtRisk/risk.html.

9. Paul R. Gross, *The State of State Science Standards: 2005* (Washington: Thomas B. Fordham Institute, 2005).

10. It is possible that some entity tracks this—you can't prove a negative—but groups such as the North American Association for Environmental Education, the National Science Teachers Association, and the Campaign for Environmental Education reported to the author that they were unaware of any comprehensive tally of state climate change education requirements.

11. Martos Hoffman and Daniel Barstow, *Revolutionizing Earth System Science Education for the 21st Century* (Cambridge, MA: TERC, 2007), p. 34.

12. For instance, in 2002 California became the first state to pass legislation that would regulate greenhouse gas emissions from cars and light trucks, and in 2006 it became the first state to enact legislation capping industrial expulsion of greenhouse gases.

13. Assembly Bill No. 1548 (Pavley, Chapter 665, Statutes of 2003), p. 92.

14. Assembly Bill No. 1721 (Pavley, Chapter 581, Statutes of 2005), pp. 93–94.

15. John Boudreau, "Governor Vetoes Climate Change Curriculum," *San Jose Mercury News*, July 26, 2008.

16. California Education and the Environment Initiative, *The Greenhouse Effect on Natural Systems: Final Draft* (Sacramento: California EEI, 2009), http://www.calepa.ca.gov/Education/EEI/Curriculum/EarthScience/E4c/E4cTE.pdf.

17. Ibid., p. 6.

18. National Climatic Data Center, "Climate at a Glance," http:/www.ncdc.noaa.gov/oa/climate/onlineprod/drought/xmgr.html.

19. Patrick J. Michaels and Robert C. Balling Jr., *Climate of Extremes: Global Warming Science They Don't Want You to Know* (Washington: Cato Institute, 2009), p. 168.

20. California Education and the Environment Initiative, *Greenhouse Effect on Natural Systems*, p. 7.

21. Michaels and Balling, *Climate of Extremes*, pp. 167–69.

22. California Education and the Environment Initiative, *Greenhouse Effect on Natural Systems*, p. 8.

23. Michaels and Balling, *Climate of Extremes*, p. 100.

24. California Education and the Environment Initiative, *Greenhouse Effect on Natural Systems*, p. 8.

25. U.S. Public Law 101-619. 101st Cong., 2d Sess., November 16, 1990.

26. National Sea Grant College Program, *Strategic Plan 2009–2013: Meeting the Challenge*, http://www.seagrant.umn.edu/downloads/national_strategic_plan_final.pdf.

27. All are listed in U.S. Global Change Research Program/Climate Change Science Program, *Climate Literacy: The Essential Principles of Climate Science*, March 2009, http://downloads.climatescience.gov/Literacy/Climate%20Literacy%20Booklet%20Low-Res.pdf.

28. National Environmental Education Advisory Committee, *Setting the Standards, Measuring Results, Celebrating Successes: A Report to Congress on the Status of Environmental Education in the United States*, March 2005, http://www.epa.gov/enviroed/pdf/reporttocongress2005.pdf.

29. U.S. Environmental Protection Agency, *Environmental Education Highlights: 2009*, inside cover, http://www.epa.gov/enviroed/pdf/2009_EEHighlights.pdf.

30. USGCRP, *Climate Literacy*.

31. U.S. Global Change Research Program/Climate Change Science Program, "Climate Change Wildlife and Wetlands: A Toolkit for Formal and Informal Educators,"

http://www.globalchange.gov/resources/educators/toolkit/video (accessed April 23, 2010).

32. USGCRP, *"Climate Literacy."*

33. Ibid.: "Climate is regulated by complex interactions among components of the Earth system."

34. Indur M. Goklany, *The Improving State of the World: Why We're Living Longer, Healthier, More Comfortable Lives on a Cleaner Planet* (Washington: Cato Institute, 2007), pp. 304–7.

35. .USGCRP, *"Climate Literacy".*

36. Michaels and Balling, *Climate of Extremes,* Figure 1.5.

37. USGCRP, *"Climate Literacy".*

38. For a full ranking, see Chester E. Finn Jr., Liam Julian, and Michael J. Petrilli, *The State of State Standards, 2006* (Washington: Thomas B. Fordham Institute, 2006).

39. William H. Schmidt, Richard Houang, and Sharif Shakrani, *International Lessons about National Standards* (Washington: Thomas B. Fordham Institute, 2009), p. 6.

40. Sean Cavanagh, "Coming Next for Common Standards: Science and Social Studies?" *Curriculum Matters* (blog), *Education Week,* October 16, 2009, http://blogs.ed week.org/edweek/curriculum/2009/10/common_standards_in_science_an.html.

Index

active adaptations, 197
adaptive capacity
  of developing world, 158, 171–78, 183
  technological changes and, 160
  underestimation of, 176–78
Administrative Procedures Act, 26
agricultural production. *see* crop productivity
air pollution. *see* pollution
air quality, 207, 208f
Amazon forest, 61
American Clean Energy and Security Act (ACES)
  electricity generation and, 47
  EPA's findings and, 66–68
  ethanol production and, 47
  mandates adopted by, 45–46
  passing of, 44
Amman, Caspar, 58
An Inconvenient Truth (movie)
  errors in, 216
  legal case against, 216–17
  showing of, 216, 232
Antarctic sea ice, 63, 64, 65
anti-submarine equipment, 125
AR4 paper. *see* Fourth Assessment Report
Arctic Oscillation, 82, 83, 85
atmospheric circulation, 79, 83, 85
aviation, treaties governing, 39

Babbit v. Sweet Home Chapter of Communities for a Great Oregon, 34
Bacchus, James, 155
Barnett, Jon, 102, 104, 105
Benestad, Rasmus, 80, 88, 89
Bill of Rights, 17, 21
biofuel mandates
  chronic hunger and, 162
  food prices and, 170
  malnutrition and, 8
black carbon (soot), 68
border measures
  carbon leakage and, 134

climate change and, 154–55
  Waxman-Markey bill and, 130, 152
border-tax adjustments, 143, 144
Bordoff, Jason, 132
Bowman, Admiral Frank "Skip," 99
Boxer, Senator Barbara, 50
Bradley, Ray, 51, 52
Briffa, Keith, 58
Brodie, Bernard, 108, 115
Brookings Institution, 5
Browner, Carol, 152
Burton, Justice Michael, 216
Busby, Joshua W., 126
Bush, George H. W., 98
Bush, George W., 47, 66, 101, 127

CAFE standards, 32
California
  environmental education in, 222–25
  temperature trends in, 11f, 12f
Calvert Cliff's Coordinating Committee v. Atomic Energy Commission, 26
Campbell, Kurt, 5, 100
cap-and-trade bill
  description of, 45
  emission reductions and, 45
  energy-intensive goods and, 130
  introduction to, 2, 3
  leakage concept of, 130–35
  obstacles in way of, 130
  passing of, 129
  unpopularity of, 50–51, 53–55, 68
  see also Waxman-Markey bill
carbon capture and storage, 47, 68
carbon dioxide dome impacts, 206
carbon dioxide emissions
  ACES and, 45
  Clean Air Act and, 29–32
  Clean Water Act and, 32–33
  introduction to, 1, 2
  projections, 153t
  WTO and, 6
  see also greenhouse gas emissions; international trade
carbon dioxide levels, 193

261

269

Contributors

Roger Pilon is vice president for legal affairs at the Cato Institute where he holds the B. Kenneth Simon Chair in Constitutional Studies. He is the founder and director of Cato's Center for Constitutional Studies and the publisher of the *Cato Supreme Court Review*. He is also an adjunct professor of government at Georgetown University through The Fund for American Studies. Pilon's writings have appeared in the nation's major media and he is a frequent guest on radio and TV. He lectures and debates at universities and law schools across the country and often testifies before Congress. Prior to joining Cato he held five senior posts in the Reagan administration, including at the departments of State and Justice. He has taught philosophy and law and was a national fellow at Stanford's Hoover Institution. Pilon holds a BA from Columbia University, an MA and a PhD from the University of Chicago, and a JD from the George Washington University School of Law. In 1989 the Bicentennial Commission presented him with the Benjamin Franklin Award for excellence in writing on the U.S. Constitution. In 2001 Columbia University's School of General Studies awarded him its Alumni Medal of Distinction.

Evan Turgeon is a legal associate at the Cato Institute's Center for Constitutional Studies. At Cato, he files *amicus curiae* briefs with the U.S. Supreme Court and revises articles for publication in the *Cato Supreme Court Review*. He holds a J.D. from the University of Virginia School of Law and a B.A. in International Relations and German from Tufts University. He has published on energy policy, national security, and economic philosophy.

Patrick J. Michaels is senior fellow in environmental studies at the Cato Institute and distinguished senior fellow in the School of Public Policy at George Mason University. He is a past president of the American Association of State Climatologists and was program chair for the Committee on Applied Climatology of the American Meteorological Society. Michaels was also a research professor of environmental sciences at the University of Virginia for 30 years. Michaels is a contributing author and reviewer of the United Nations Intergovernmental Panel on Climate Change, which was awarded the Nobel Peace Prize in 2007. His writing has been published in the major scientific journals, and he was an author of the climate paper of the year awarded by the Association of American Geographers in 2004. He has appeared on most of the worldwide major media. Michaels holds AB and SM degrees in biological sciences and plant ecology from the University of Chicago, and he received a PhD in ecological climatology from the University of Wisconsin at Madison in 1979.

Ross McKitrick is a professor of economics at the University of Guelph and specializes in environmental economics. He has published many studies on the economic analysis of pollution policy, economic growth and air pollution trends, climate policy options, the measurement of global warming, and statistical methods in paleoclimatology. His latest book is *Economic Analysis of Environmental Policy*, published by the University of Toronto Press (Fall 2010). He has also published numerous invited book chapters, newspaper and magazine essays, and think-tank reports. In 2003 his (coauthored) book *Taken By Storm: The Troubled Science, Policy and Politics of Global Warming* won the Donner Prize for the best book on Canadian Public Policy. Professor McKitrick has been cited in media around the world as an expert on the science and policy of global warming. He has made invited academic presentations in Canada, the United States, and Europe, and has testified before the U.S. Congress and the Canadian Parliamentary Finance and Environment Committees. In 2006 he was one of 12 experts from around the world asked to brief a panel of the U.S. National Academy of Sciences on paleoclimate reconstruction methodology.

Ivan Eland is senior fellow and director of the Center on Peace & Liberty at The Independent Institute. Dr. Eland is a graduate of Iowa State University and received an MBA in applied economics and a PhD in public policy from George Washington University. He has been director of defense policy studies at the Cato Institute, and he spent 15 years working for Congress on national security issues, including stints as an investigator for the House Foreign Affairs Committee and Principal Defense Analyst at the Congressional Budget Office. He also has served as Evaluator-in-Charge (national security and intelligence) for the U.S. General Accounting Office (now the Government Accountability Office), and has testified on the military and financial aspects of NATO expansion before the Senate Foreign Relations Committee, on CIA oversight before the House Government Reform Committee, and on the creation of the Department of Homeland Security before the Senate Judiciary Committee. Dr. Eland is the author of *Partitioning for Peace: An Exit Strategy for Iraq; Recarving Rushmore: Ranking the Presidents on Peace, Prosperity, and Liberty; The Empire Has No Clothes: U.S. Foreign Policy Exposed; Putting "Defense" Back into U.S. Defense Policy;* and *The Efficacy of Economic Sanctions as a Foreign Policy Tool.*

Sallie James is a policy analyst with the Cato Institute's Center for Trade Policy Studies. Before joining Cato in 2006, James was an executive officer in the Office of Trade Negotiations in the Australian Government's Department of Foreign Affairs and Trade, where she worked on industrials market access negotiations. James previously served as a senior adviser at the Australian Department of Agriculture, Fisheries and Forestry. She received her bachelor of economics and master of economics degrees from the University of Adelaide, and her PhD in agricultural economics from the University of Western Australia.

Dr. Indur M. Goklany is an independent scholar who has worked with federal and state governments, think tanks, and the private sector for over 35 years. He has written extensively on the interactions between globalization, economic development, environmental quality, technological change, climate change, and human well-being. He has been involved with the Intergovernmental Panel on Climate Change as an author, U.S. delegate, and reviewer. He was part of the U.S. team that negotiated the UN Framework Convention on Climate Change, and was later a delegate to that organization. Goklany managed the emissions trading program in the Environmental Protection Agency. He was the first Julian Simon Fellow at the Property and Environment Research Center, a visiting fellow at the American Enterprise Institute, and the winner of the Julian Simon Prize and Award in 2007. A long-time proponent of the notion that economic and technological progress assisted by globalization are critical to human and environmental progress, he is the author of *Clearing the Air: The Real Story of the War on Air Pollution; The Precautionary Principle: A Critical Appraisal of Environmental Risk Assessment;* and *The Improving State of the World: Why We're Living Longer, Healthier, More Comfortable Lives on a Cleaner Planet,* all published by the Cato Institute in Washington, D.C.

Robert E. Davis is professor of climatology in the Environmental Sciences Department at the University of Virginia, where he began teaching in 1988. His research emphases include large-scale climatology and climate change, biometeorology, air quality, and coastal storms. Davis' research has twice garnered him Climate Paper of the Year awards from the Association of American Geographers, including his research on heat-related mortality trends in the United States. He has served as chair of the Association of American Geographers Climate Specialty Group, chair of the American Meteorological Society's Committee on Biometeorology and Aerobiology, editor of the journal *Climate Research,* and was an invited expert in the 2009 workshop on climate and human health sponsored by the National Oceanic and Atmospheric Administration and the Centers for Disease Control.

Neal McCluskey is the associate director of Cato's Center for Educational Freedom. Prior to arriving at Cato, McCluskey served in the U.S. Army, taught high-school English, and was a freelance reporter covering municipal government and education in suburban New Jersey. More recently, he was a policy analyst at the Center for Education Reform. McCluskey is the author of the book, *Feds in the Classroom: How Big Government Corrupts, Cripples, and Compromises American Education,* and his writings have appeared in such publications as the *Wall Street Journal, Baltimore Sun,* and *Forbes.* McCluskey holds a master's degree in political science from Rutgers University.

Cato Institute

Founded in 1977, the Cato Institute is a public policy research foundation dedicated to broadening the parameters of policy debate to allow consideration of more options that are consistent with the traditional American principles of limited government, individual liberty, and peace. To that end, the Institute strives to achieve greater involvement of the intelligent, concerned lay public in questions of policy and the proper role of government.

The Institute is named for *Cato's Letters*, libertarian pamphlets that were widely read in the American Colonies in the early 18th century and played a major role in laying the philosophical foundation for the American Revolution.

Despite the achievement of the nation's Founders, today virtually no aspect of life is free from government encroachment. A pervasive intolerance for individual rights is shown by government's arbitrary intrusions into private economic transactions and its disregard for civil liberties.

To counter that trend, the Cato Institute undertakes an extensive publications program that addresses the complete spectrum of policy issues. Books, monographs, and shorter studies are commissioned to examine the federal budget, Social Security, regulation, military spending, international trade, and myriad other issues. Major policy conferences are held throughout the year, from which papers are published thrice yearly in the *Cato Journal*. The Institute also publishes the quarterly magazine *Regulation*.

In order to maintain its independence, the Cato Institute accepts no government funding. Contributions are received from foundations, corporations, and individuals, and other revenue is generated from the sale of publications. The Institute is a nonprofit, tax-exempt, educational foundation under Section 501(c)3 of the Internal Revenue Code.

CATO INSTITUTE
1000 Massachusetts Ave., N.W.
Washington, D.C. 20001
www.cato.org